GOLDEN GLORY

*A publication of
Leisure Press.
597 Fifth Avenue; New York, N.Y. 10017*

Library of Congress Catalog Card Number: 83-80696

ISBN: 0-88011-198-4

*Cover design: Diana J. Goodin
Book design: Brian Groppe
Layout and production: Rick Binger*

Front cover photo provided by Herb Juliano,
Notre Dame Athletic Department

Notre Dame vs Purdue
GOLDEN GLORY

by
Ned Colletti

LEISURE PRESS

Table Of Contents

GOLDEN GLORY

Foreword

Beneath the splendor of the Notre Dame mystique walked 90-year-old Donald (Chet) Grant. It was a winter afternoon. A day when the sun's rays ricocheted against the Golden Dome to the new fallen snow. On this day Chet Grant came to share the underlying facts of a great college football rivalry.

He came dressed in a three-piece gray pinstripe suit with a white-on-white dress shirt and tie. He removed his cap displaying a thinning white-thatched top. His vice-grip handshake revealed a man who had withstood the test of time. His crystal-clear memory revealed a man who had witnessed decades upon decades of Notre Dame athletic history.

Through nearly a year of research I had built a foundation with bricks aplenty. But now was a chance to have Chet Grant—one month shy of his 91st birthday—add the cement and fill in the blanks.

"The rivalry was always full of rugged competition," he said. "Purdue was more in our class. We respected Purdue as a he-man institution. Another factor was psychological. Purdue always wanted to beat us badly. And we wanted to do nothing but the same to them."

He has surveyed a vast majority of the 54 meetings, beginning in 1920 when he was a back-up quarterback for one of Knute Rockne's great teams.

We spoke of the rivalry, of Rockne.

"The Rock was a very well-rounded man," Grant said. "He was, like the phrase in the theatre, 'A Man For All Seasons'. And I don't mean just football.

"He was an actor. But he was very competitive. Basically, he had the most positive quality of all—true humility. Even an actor has to be sincere.

"He knew how to treat his players. Every player was different and every player needed to be treated different. He wasn't too proud a man to treat every player the right way."

Grant has served the University of Notre Dame as a student, player, fan and sports historian. With a memory as vibrant as a northern stream,

Chet was able to assemble the frayed pieces of a tradition that newspapers and books could not recreate.

Perhaps the undertaking of this project had its roots buried deep in my childhood. In the scrapbook of my mind there is a fall afternoon in 1964 during the days of Notre Dame's great passing/receiving combination of John Huarte and Jack Snow. It is alive in my mind as if it occurred yesterday.

Not quite in my teens, I recall listening to a Notre Dame football broadcast on a transistor radio while I was sitting on the front lawn of my parents' home.

I was holding a football. It was nestled against my chest. I wore a sweatshirt my dad had brought home from work. A friend had given it to him. The sweatshirt had the words Notre Dame stitched in the rainbow arch across the front.

As the game ended and the Notre Dame Victory March poured through the small speaker, I remember thinking Notre Dame was something special.

Love the Irish or hate them, Notre Dame is something special.

It wasn't until later, much later in life that I realized and came to appreciate the fortitude and combativeness inbred in the Purdue athlete.

Mention the name Notre Dame anywhere on this continent and perhaps anywhere in the sporting world and the first association that flashes across everyone's mind is football. To a large degree, it is safe to say that people may know very little about football, but they do know that Notre Dame is famous for it.

But what of Purdue?

Except for those familiar with the university itself, Purdue is just another university—renowned for its engineering program and for having astronaut Neil Armstrong as an alum.

These are simple facts of life. Notre Dame is synonymous with football—worldwide. Purdue is not.

Yet, the Purdue athlete possesses the driving spirit of every successful American underdog. It has never mattered that Purdue's football teams have yet to win a National Championship, have yet to produce a Heisman Trophy winner, have made only one Rose Bowl appearance. While on the other hand, Notre Dame has 10 National Championship titles and six Heisman Trophy winners and a far more impressive bowl appearance list even though Notre Dame refused to play in bowl games for most of its history. What has mattered to the faithful of Purdue and those with an eye for the overall picture is the competitive nature of the athlete.

The old classic line is 'anything can happen' and that is what Purdue truly believes. And that is what makes the rivalry so beautiful.

Consider that in the 95 years of Notre Dame football only the University of Southern California—a football power in its own right—has beaten Notre Dame more times than Purdue.

Purdue has beaten Notre Dame 19 times while Southern Cal has defeated the Irish 23. When you think back to the great teams that should have at least caused Notre Dame trouble—certainly more often than Purdue—you think of Army, Pittsburgh, Michigan and Michigan State. Those four teams have provided Notre Dame with some truly outstanding confrontations. But the facts remain: Michigan State has beaten Notre Dame 16 times, Pittsburgh 13, Michigan 11 and Army eight. Consider that only five teams in college football history have beaten Notre Dame 10 or more times.

It has been such a great rivalry because the Boilermakers have exemplified the gameness and grand tradition of the Fightin' Irish.

Purdue has taken Rockne's slogan, "Don't die gamely, fight to live," and used it against Notre Dame.

A Notre Dame player so aptly spelled out the Notre Dame tradition to a Miami of Florida player in 1982 when with seconds remaining and the Irish appearing to be doomed to defeat a visiting player told the Notre Dame player "It's over."

"It is never over," the Notre Dame player replied. "This is Notre Dame." So be it. Notre Dame won.

The Irish have become famous for winning the games they were not supposed to win. Consider the 1977 game against Purdue when Joe Montana rallied the Irish to victory after coming off the bench late in the game.

But also consider the 1979 game when Purdue's Mark Herrmann rallied Purdue in the second half over Notre Dame. And consider what happened in 1981 when Purdue's junior quarterback Scott Campbell directed Purdue on a last minute touchdown drive and then boldly completed a pass for a two-point conversion upsetting Notre Dame 15-14.

Yes, it has happened both ways in this series.

Perhaps, Purdue has captured my heart because of its spirit. Time and time again Purdue has come up with the effort and heroics that so wholeheartedly represent the greatness of Notre Dame.

It was exhibited when Purdue broke Notre Dame's unbeaten streaks of 39, 13, 13 and 12 games.

It has been that way ever since Alpha Jamison ripped through the Notre Dame line for the first touchdown on the first play of the series in 1896.

"Yes," Chet Grant admitted, "Purdue still causes us trouble from time to time and I doubt if it will ever be any different."

In the fall of 1982, Vagas Ferguson, the former Notre Dame All-America halfback, stood near the tunnel leading to the Notre Dame dressing room. As the final seconds elapsed leaving Notre Dame 28-14 winners over Purdue, Vagas reflected on what the rivalry meant to him.

"It was always a big game for us," he said. "We always knew that Purdue would come after us with everything.

"The Purdue game is always played early in the season. But regardless of when it is played, every game has a bearing on a possible National Championship, on a major bowl bid or on a higher ranking down the line. The Purdue game not only had a bearing on all those factors, but we knew it meant the bragging rights of an entire state."

You can take it from Chet Grant, who has witnessed the last 60-plus years of the rivalry. Or you can take it from a modern day hero, Vagas Ferguson.

The Purdue-Notre Dame rivalry has meant something special to the people of both schools, to the state of Indiana, to the midwest. It has a special meaning to champions trying to stay that way and to underdog challengers looking to capture that one victory to last a lifetime.

The series is something very special.

It always has been. It always will be.

Ned Colletti
April, 1983

*To Gayle for her love
and understanding,*

*To Ned Louis III, may he
grow to enjoy the
nature of sports,*

*To Doug, for his love
and dedication to the game.*

Boilermaker Pete, the Purdue mascot. (Photo courtesy of Purdue University)

Notre Dame Leprechaun Pete Bourjaily, an Irish mascot. (Photo courtesy of Notre Dame University)

Section I
1896-1907

The Seeds Are
Planted During
The Early Years

In the pre-20th Century, college football was more recreational than the reckless rambunctious days that followed.

In those 1890's both schools included football as part of the university's extracurricular programs. The emphasis was not that strong.

It wasn't until the concept of a league began to take shape that university administrators started getting glorious visions. They saw football as a big-time sport that would not only build pride and character among students and athletes alike but also become a source of revenue and pride for the university as a whole.

Before Purdue and Notre Dame met for the first time, Purdue President James Smart called a meeting of seven big midwestern universities. The meeting took place in Chicago in early January, 1895. Smart had an idea. The concept of a conference was appealing to all involved. Included in the meeting were representatives from the University of Chicago, Illinois, Michigan, Minnesota, Northwestern, Wisconsin and, of course, Purdue. Not included was Notre Dame.

The first ill feelings probably began developing at that point. The meetings in Chicago laid the foundation for what became known as the Western Conference and later the Big Ten. It was great for those involved, but it was a blow to Notre Dame's pride.

Michigan withdrew from the conference in 1905 and Notre Dame applied for the vacated position. It was rejected because it was too small and the impression left upon the Notre Dame administrators was that the school and the program had better grow and develop a reputation.

Finally, in 1910 another meeting took place that forever kept Notre Dame out of the conference. The conference board felt the league could live better without the pushy Irish. Notre Dame was locked out forever.

By the time the teams played each other for the first time in 1896, Purdue's program had become recognized as an experienced and talented unit.

Through the first eight meetings from 1896 through 1907, Notre Dame began taking a solid hold on becoming a respected team.

The first hero of the series was Alpha Jamison who scored four touchdowns and four extra points accounting for 20 of Purdue's 28 points in the 28-22 opening victory.

But within four years Notre Dame had improved to a 6-3-1 record with five shutouts. It must be remembered that the Notre Dame schedule still wasn't quite the match of Purdue's at that point in 1899.

The blood began to boil in 1901 when both teams had a chance at winning the State Championship—which consisted more of bragging rights than a silver plated trophy.

What is considered to be the first great game of the series came off in 1902 when both teams battled to a 6-6 deadlock in Lafayette. Both teams were powerful, well coached and well-assembled. They had both been domineering.

Following the tragic great train wreck of 1903 that took a number of Purdue lives, the Boilermakers rebounded. In the next two meetings Purdue simply humiliated Notre Dame, winning by 36-0 and 32-0 scores. In those days scoring 36 points was paramount to scoring 60 today.

Notre Dame's pride had been shattered. In 1906 the Irish took advantage of the game's only break—a high snap over the punter's head that rolled out of the end zone. Notre Dame's 2-0 victory is the lowest point total in the 54-game history of the series.

For the fifth straight time, Notre Dame was forced to travel to Lafeyette in 1907. By then the pendulum had begun swinging away from Purdue. For the second straight game, Notre Dame shutout Purdue, 17-0.

Through the first eight games, both teams had a 3-3-2 record. There has not been a tie in the series in the 80-plus years since 1902. During the eight-game opening stretch, the jury was still out on just which team was superior. Notre Dame, though, had proven to Purdue and the other members of the Western Conference that it was indeed a good school with a more than competitive football team.

Certainly, the founding father of Notre Dame, the Reverend Edward Frederick Sorin, could not have realized what his seed would one day grow into.

The same can be said for John Purdue, the gentleman who raised enough money to change the course of a university when it appeared doomed to lack progression. He provided the cash that changed the Indiana Arts College of Agriculture and Industrial Arts into Purdue—an institution of academic and athletic renown.

1896

And So It Came To Pass...

NOTRE DAME, IND.—"Notre Dame won (earned the right to choose) the kick-off and sent the ball thirty-five yards to (Cloyd) Marshall, who, by help of interference, returned the ball to the centre. (Al) Jamison then stepped through the left tackle, and made straight for the goal without anyone stopping. Purdue kicked goal. Score, 6 to 0."

And so it came to pass that in the beginning, it was Jamison, Purdue's only five-time letterman and captain, who first set off across Cartier Field at Notre Dame and notched the first points for Purdue bringing up the curtain on Indiana's greatest football rivalry and one of the country's great interstate meetings.

It was Jamison who earned his special place in Purdue history on the afternoon of November 14, 1896 by scoring four touchdowns and kicking four extra points accounting for 20 points. As a runner, he was an early-day Leroy Keyes.

Purdue won 28-22, thus casting the first stone as it matched its experience and pride against a Notre Dame squad that was inexperienced by comparison.

The *Notre Dame Scholastic* and *Purdue Exponent* school newspapers provided lengthy coverage of the first encounter. The outcome was important to both institutions; it was essential that both tried to gain the early upper hand. Purdue's program had been growing and had become established. It went on to finish the 1896 season with a 4-2-1 record compared to Notre Dame which finished at 4-3. The records were similar, but Notre Dame's opposition was rather inferior to Purdue's.

BUSINESS REPLY MAIL
FIRST CLASS   PERMIT NO   38   CARMEL, NY

POSTAGE WILL BE PAID BY ADDRESSEE

Guideposts®

PO Box 856
Carmel NY   10512-9970

Three reasons to give Guideposts for Christmas now:

1. IT'S ALMOST CHRISTMAS. Did you forget anyone? Guideposts is the perfect gift for everyone on your list.

2. IT'S FAST AND EASY. Don't send money now. Just mail this postage-free card and we'll start your 12-issue Guideposts Christmas gifts with rush processing on the December 1994 Christmas issue!

3. YOU GET A FREE GIFT. Guideposts 1994 Scenic Wall Calendar featuring 12 full color photos that capture the natural beauty of the season. It's large size offers plenty of room for memos, dates & appointments. Yours free with just one new Guideposts gift order!

Guideposts Christmas Gifts only $10.97 per subscription
($12.97 Outside the U.S.)

☐ Bill me later   ☐ Payment enclosed...send no bill

Your Name _____
(please print)

Address _____ **Apt.** _____

City _____ **State** _____ **ZIP** _____

☐ Start or ☐ Renew my own subscription.   ☐ Regular or ☐ Big Print*

Yes, send a 1-year gift subscription as my Christmas gift to:

Name _____
(please print)

Address _____ **Apt.** _____

City _____ **State** _____ **ZIP** _____

☐ Regular or ☐ Big Print*

Name _____
(please print)

Address _____ **Apt.** _____

City _____ **State** _____ **ZIP** _____

☐ Regular or ☐ Big Print*

*Intended for the visually impaired.
Your gift subscription(s) will start with the December issue.
A gift card will be sent in your name to the person(s) named above.

200290120

Obtaining both respect and a tougher schedule were two reasons why Notre Dame wanted so badly to defeat Purdue in the opener. Notre Dame had just begun to take its football playing seriously.

The coaches for the first game were S.M. Hammond for Purdue and Frank E. Hering for Notre Dame. Hammond only coached Purdue in 1896. Hering, who was also the Notre Dame captain that season, coached for three seasons, becoming the first coach at Notre Dame to last longer than one year.

L.A. Downs, conveniently an 1894 Purdue graduate, served as the official for Purdue while Thorpe of Princeton did the honors for Notre Dame.

The *Purdue Exponent* carried the following analysis: "When Purdue started to meet the team of Notre Dame that eventful day, no one seemed to entertain any ideas that the meeting would be so near defeat. On the other hand, everyone appeared to be surprisingly confident that the score would set up zero on one side and rise up to double numbers on the other."

Alpha Jamison, left, who scored the first touchdown of the series along with "Smilin'" Billy Moore. (Photo courtesy of Notre Dame University)

Yes, surprise, surprise.

"Notre Dame," the *Exponent* continued, "instead of playing a weak and careless game, put up the best kind of game throughout and played to win from first to last.

"Purdue had run into a good large-sized surprise."

Purdue was also one of the first teams to realize that Notre Dame was never to be taken lightly—even at that early stage.

In the end, it was Purdue's experience and offensive power, especially in its backfield and specifically in the running of Jamison, that kept the Irish, who did not have the luxury of a scrub team to practice against, out of reach. But the pattern had been established. Purdue had seen Notre Dame and been respectfully impressed. Notre Dame had seen Purdue and realized that its dream of earning respect and a more competitive schedule was within reach.

The *Notre Dame Scholastic* explained, "They (Notre Dame) did not understand Purdue's interference (blocking); hence, the large end gains. They made up for this deficiency, however, when they were on the offensive. Not once did Purdue down us with a loss, and not once did our backs fumble the ball.

"The anxiously awaited game with Purdue is now a matter of history, and, though it did not make us champions of the State, it demonstrated beyond a doubt that Purdue has not an undisputed title to the honor, and furthermore, it proved that Notre Dame can justly claim recognition from the Western Conference."

Jamison's 45-yard touchdown run to open the game provided the Purdue team with a 6-0 lead following his conversion.

Notre Dame's Bill Kegler was "pushed across for the touchdown" later in the opening half but Notre Dame, which would experience kicking problems all afternoon, missed the two-point conversion. Purdue still led 6-4.

The teams volleyed back and forth. Every time Notre Dame would score and draw within a touchdown, Purdue, led by Jamison, would storm right back and nullify Notre Dame's touchdown with one of its own. Plus Jamison's conversions coupled with Notre Dame's kicking woes continued to inch the Boilers out of reach.

Jamison's second touchdown and conversion gave Purdue a 12-4 lead before Bob Brown scored for Notre Dame and Kegler missed his second consecutive conversion putting Notre Dame behind 12-8.

Jamison scored for the third time and converted, giving Purdue an 18-8 margin. Kegler countered with a touchdown but Fred Schillo's conversion failed setting Notre Dame six points back, 18-12, even though it had matched Jamison's three touchdowns. The difference was the conversions.

Jamison's 30-yard run set up Billy Moore's touchdown late in the game. Notre Dame blocked Jamison's kick but still trailed 22-12 with the sun beginning to fade.

Jamison completed the Purdue scoring with his fourth and final dash and ensuing conversion, putting Purdue in front 28-12.

John Murphy scored the last two Notre Dame touchdowns and Jack Mullen converted one of two conversions leaving the final score 28-22. Notre Dame's record slipped to 2-3 while Purdue improved to 4-2.

"The time was not up," the *Notre Dame Scholastic* reported, "but the game was called on account of darkness."

To commemorate the 40th game of the series in 1968, Donald "Chet" Grant, a former Notre Dame player and coach and later a Notre Dame sports historian, did a *South Bend Tribune* interview with "Smiling" Billy Moore, the Purdue back who scored the fourth Purdue touchdown in the first game.

Billy Moore graduated from Purdue in 1898 with an engineering degree. He came to South Bend at the turn of the century. In the late 1920s, Knute Rockne was planning to promote the building of a football stadium at Notre Dame. He asked Moore to locate, lay out and stake the site that is today Notre Dame Stadium.

Billy Moore died a year after his interview with Chet Grant. He was 94. Here is an excerpt of Grant's Billy Moore interview.

"A thousand spectators pressed against the double wire fence that held them off the field or (they) sat in carriages and with hoarse-voiced enthusiasm encouraged their favorites. The great majority were wearing blue and gold (Notre Dame colors), but Purdue, though among strangers, was not without friends. There was no carriage decorated with black and yellow and filled with strong-lunged rooters for the visitors."

"The thing I remember most," Moore told Grant, "was that the field—if you wanted to call it that—was just south of the gymnasium. They were building it at that time (it opened in 1898) and on the west side of the field must have been the engineering building.

"On the other side was Juniper Road and there were minims (grade school students) standing over there...

"It was a great day for both sides. We each scored five touchdowns, but they missed two extra points (actually four) and we missed one."

Nearly 90 years into the future, Notre Dame and Purdue still have great days at each other's expense.

1899

Notre Dame Ties One On

LAFAYETTE, IND.—For two seasons Notre Dame and Purdue went their separate ways. Purdue continued to play a schedule made up of established teams. Notre Dame added Michigan State to its schedule in 1897 and played Michigan, Michigan State, Illinois and Indiana in 1898. As Notre Dame's respect grew, so did the calibre of its schedule.

Notre Dame was also drawing notice for having players with experience along with a few selected players who, allegedly, did not attend the university.

In 1899, Notre Dame played a 10-game schedule, easily its longest season to date. It finished with a 6-3-1 record including a school record five shutouts. Purdue, meanwhile, dropped to 4-4-1.

The balance had already begun to sway. Notre Dame was building into a competitive football team and the rest of the Western Conference (the forerunner of the Big Ten), whose members would always withhold Notre Dame from its ranks, was beginning to take notice.

On November 18, 1899, Notre Dame took a 6-2 record into its first game at Lafayette and Stuart Field. Its success was well publicized, but it was Purdue that controlled most of the game before the Notre Dame squad could rally in the waning moments for a 40-yard field goal by Angus McDonald. Notre Dame had climbed back for a 10-10 tie.

The major change in scoring instituted in 1898 did not affect the outcome. Both teams scored a touchdown (worth five points in 1899 compared to four points in 1896) and both teams converted a field goal (which was still worth five points).

The *Purdue Exponent* had previewed the contest as a game in which Purdue could win despite its mediocre record and the budding power of Notre Dame.

"We will certainly defeat Notre Dame," the *Exponent* reported, "if our players practice faithfully this week and if the student body encourages them by its presence and yells at them during the practice games."

The State Championship was at stake, according to the somewhat biased *Exponent.* And after Alex A. (Vivo) Smith scored the first touchdown for Purdue, the *Exponent* all but wrote off Notre Dame.

"After various attempts extending somewhat over an hour, in an attempt to wrest from us the State Championship honors, the Notre Dame team wrapped their blankets about them and silently stole away.

"Full of confidence and regarding the comparative scores of the two teams, as evidence of their (Notre Dame) superiority, they expected an easy victory and were even willing to bet that Purdue would not score.

Purdue's Alex 'Vivo' Smith. (Photo courtesy of Purdue University)

"That willingness changed to 'wish I hadn't' when after 10 minutes of play our old reliable "Vivo" Smith pushed the ball over the visitors' goal line for the first touchdown of the game."

Notre Dame claimed Purdue had the advantage of the home grounds and nearly 500 fans, who according to the *Exponent,* were greatly offsetting what should have been a Notre Dame weight and experience advantage. There was also the all-important injury factor.

"Our plucky (J.M. Davidson) Davy who went into the game with four inches of padding over his back where he was kicked in practice last week and both his ankles strengthened by heavy leather straps went up against the giant (John) Eggeman, who tips the scale at 247 pounds.

"Davidson played both halves and did not seem to be troubled in the least by the big man across the line.

"Most of the Notre Dame men were playing their third or fourth year and some were recruits from the famous South Bend Athletic Club. Their experienced men should have played around with our green (inexperienced) men on the line. But anyone who saw the game knew that they found them about as easy to handle as a row of five-ton boulders."

Captain E.C. Robertson turned in a typically great performance for Purdue. He combined great leadership with a combination of traditional and trick plays.

"The men from the north," reported the *Exponent,* "were so completely fooled by the trick plays he worked in rapid succession that they did not know where they were at.

"The fake place kick worked to perfection the first time it was ever tried allowing Captain Robertson to drop down 25 yards and soon after the 'real-thing' (by Robertson) added five points to our score.

"Probably the prettiest run of the day was made by (F.J.) McCoy. On a kickoff, (R.B.) MacKenzie tried for the ball, but it was too high and slipped through his hands, rolling back under the goal posts where McCoy picked it up and dodging around the post darted through the whole team.

"It looked for a moment as though "Mac" would duplicate (H.L.) Byers' run in the Earlham game (of a few weeks earlier) but with only one man between him and the goal and plenty of room to dodge, "Mac" slipped and fell after having dodged the whole Notre Dame team and the ball was on the 30-yard line."

The *Purdue Exponent* explained the day's scoring this way:

"The duplicate scoring was remarkable. Purdue's (Vivo) Smith made a touchdown and Robinson failed an easy goal (extra point). Notre Dame then pushed the pigskin over the line (a touchdown by captain Jack Mullen), and MacDonald missed an easier one, when it would have won the game. Then in rapid succession "Robbie" and McDonald each made a place kick."

Purdue was coached by Alpha Jamison, the first-game hero. Notre Dame was under the leadership of James McWeeney who led it to the best record (6-3-1) in the 11-year existence of the program.

The tie, however, was considered a defeat for Notre Dame. The Purdue fans viewing Notre Dame for the first time in Lafayette and realizing the battle their team had put up against the powerful Notre Dame squad responded in cheers.

"That's what. What's what. That's what they all say. What do they say? Purdue!"

Purdue captain E.C. Robertson. (Photo courtesy of Purdue University)

1901

Notre Dame Streams To First Win Behind Salmon

NOTRE DAME, IND.—For the first time, the series took on more than mere "bragging-rights" significance. After a one-year absence, Purdue and Notre Dame returned to meet each other at Cartier Field. Both teams entered with 4-1-1 records. More importantly, both teams had legitimate chances at the Indiana State Championship.

Notre Dame Coach Pat O'Dea was in his second season as the head coach and had assembled the first truly great Notre Dame team.

The focus of the entire state was on South Bend that November 9th day. A crowd of Purdue fans gathered at Stuart Field in Lafayette to watch the old telegraph machine click the results of the battle.

"This scheme of securing 'special-service' reports is becoming popular in the West," the *Purdue Exponent* reported. "And it is now used at almost all important games. It looks queer to see a crowd around a telegraph booth howling delight one moment and hushed in silence the next, but when reports are carefully prepared the effect is almost as if one were at the scene of the contest. The cost is $20 and a small fee will be charged at the gate."

What the Purdue faithful heard that day was a hard-fought Notre Dame victory. Purdue fell 12-6 in what was described as one of the fiercest battles of the season.

Meanwhile, at Cartier Field the "largest and most enthusiastic crowd to ever see a football contest" was on hand.

Notre Dame scored 14 minutes into the first quarter when Louis "Red" Salmon broke loose for a five-yard run. Salmon also converted the extra point.

Purdue had difficulty with the powerful team from Notre Dame. It wasn't until the opening minutes of the second half that the Boilermakers began causing Notre Dame problems. Purdue went to a realigned offense known as the Princeton tandem involving William Berkshire, J.M. Davidson and H.G. Leslie.

With the "tandem" in full force, Purdue tied the game on a five-yard run by Joe Knapp after the Boilermakers had blocked a punt. J.F. Miller's conversion gave Purdue a 6-6 deadlock.

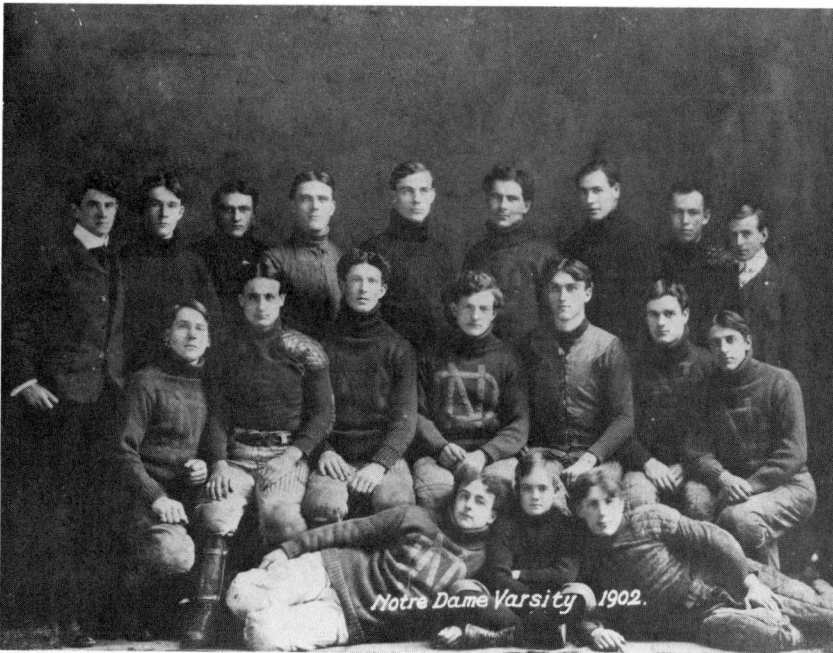

Irish captain Louis "Red" Salmon and 1902 team. Salmon is seated in the center of the middle row. (Photo courtesy of Notre Dame University)

The constant hammering away by the Notre Dame running back combination of Salmon, Jim Doar and Harley Kirby kept pounding Purdue's line. Finally, late in the game, Doar scored the deciding touchdown on an eight-yard run. Salmon again added the conversion.

"The score," the *Notre Dame Scholastic* contended, "was not indicative of how well Notre Dame played."

Notre Dame lost two scoring chances to fumbles—one that Purdue recovered on the one-yard line and another on the 15-yard line.

"Purdue put up a most wonderful game," the *Purdue Exponent* countered. "There was no fumbling (on its part) and not a dispute arose the entire game and no dirty ball was indulged in by either team. Considering the fierceness of play both teams escaped with few injuries.

"Inasmuch as Purdue cannot fly the championship banner, they wish to see it land on the Notre Dame field which it will if Notre Dame can defeat Indiana University next Saturday.

"The defeat lost all chance of Purdue winning the state championship and the boys returned home with the proud record of having made a good fight and only losing through the superior play of Notre Dame."

For the first time, the *Exponent* was forced to admit, "Purdue was outclassed."

And so was Indiana the next weekend as Notre Dame dropped the Hoosiers 18-5 at Cartier Field. O'Dea's team finished with an 8-1-1 record losing only to Northwestern 2-0. One of the wins and the lone tie came against the South Bend Athletic Club, which opened and closed the Notre Dame season.

After its promising 4-1-1 start, Purdue finished with a 4-4-1 record, losing its final three games to Notre Dame, Illinois (28-6) and Northwestern (10-5).

Notre Dame finished in splendid form winning its last seven games of the season including three following the victory over Purdue. The seven-game winning streak was the longest in Notre Dame history. Before it was over, Notre Dame had added two more victories over Michigan State and Lake Forest before losing to Michigan in the third game of the 1902 season.

1902

The First Great Game

LAFAYETTE, IND.—The biggest day in the early stages of college football was the Thanksgiving Day game. The game historically brought out the townspeople for the special occasion.

In 1902, the rivalry between Notre Dame and Purdue had progressed to such a level that in the fourth meeting between the schools, it was decided that Thanksgiving Day would serve as the perfect day to renew the battle.

Both teams had displayed tremendous scoring power against inferior talent. Just two weeks earlier, Notre Dame had crushed American Medical College 92-0 and one week earlier Purdue had pummeled state rival Butler 87-0.

For the first time the series was played in back-to-back years. The crowd that braved frigid temperatures to watch two teams battle, not only each other but also a slippery field, was considered the largest to ever witness a game in the state.

"The crowd," the *Notre Dame Scholastic* reported, "was the largest ever seen on Stuart Field. Had it been a fair day there is no doubt that the attendance would have exceeded 5,000."

As it was, a crowd of 2,600 came out to watch what was described as the greatest game in the history of Indiana. What they saw was a thrilling 6-6 decision. Purdue with a 7-2 record on the line including five straight shutouts came racing back in the waning moments to secure the deadlock.

"At 2:40 p.m. the referee's whistle sounded the opening of the greatest

29

football contest ever held in the State," reported the *Notre Dame Scholastic.* "Experts who watched it declared it to be one of the hardest and fiercest fought contests ever held in the State."

The hero for Notre Dame was once again captain Louis "Red" Salmon. After Notre Dame had fought its way deep inside Purdue territory, Purdue's defense began slamming the door in an attempt to keep its shutout streak intact.

Once within three feet of the goal, Purdue's defense stood tough until Salmon finally negotiated the final yard.

Salmon's conversion gave Notre Dame a 6-0 lead at the 20-minute mark. The lead stood until the final moments mainly due to the playing conditions.

"There was no more scoring in the first half," reported the *Purdue Exponent.* "The evening before (the game) the field was covered with straw to protect it from the snow and volunteer students cleared it (before game time). It was too wet for fast play and caused a lot of fumbling.

"Constant fumbling hurt Purdue, one coming at the Notre Dame 15-yard line. All plays centered around a large mud hole on the east side of the field.

"In the second half, all the play was in Notre Dame territory."

Purdue's C. Zimmerman had apparently brought the Boilers back with a 15-yard run. The touchdown was nullified when Purdue backs were detected running before the snap.

But as the contest continued and additional snow began falling during the second half, both teams tired and it appeared as if Salmon's touchdown would be the ultimate difference.

The advantage at that point belonged to Purdue which had 35 players available compared to a meager total of 12 for the visitors from Notre Dame.

Purdue kept sending in fresh players and Notre Dame tried valiantly to hold on. Salmon not only scored the only Notre Dame touchdown and kicked its only conversion, but he was also doing his best to continually punt Notre Dame out of danger despite a sprained ankle and slippery ball. He averaged 30 yards a punt, giving Notre Dame breathing room.

With only a few minutes remaining, Purdue moved within 20 yards of a touchdown. Finally, the Boilers called on reserve G. Miller who blasted over for the touchdown with seconds remaining. Before time expired H.G. Leslie added the conversion, giving Purdue a tie.

One of the great early battles was history. The townspeople of Lafayette were thrilled with the outcome as well as with the determination with which both teams played. The people invited players from both schools home for Thanksgiving dinner.

The game concluded a 6-2-1 season for James F. Faragher's Notre

Dame team, a team that lost only to Michigan 23-0 in the third game of the season (breaking a nine-game winning streak) and to Knox 12-5.

Purdue Coach C.M. Best's team was exactly that—one of Purdue's best. It finished with a 7-2-1 record achieving all seven victories by shutouts. Its only losses came in back-to-back games against the University of Chicago (33-0) and the University of Illinois (29-5).

The teams that met that blustery Thanksgiving Day were two of the country's finest. Consider it fitting that neither should lose but rather they should settle for the second tie in the brief history of the series.

1904

Purdue "Cutts" Down Notre Dame

LAFAYETTE, IND.—Oliver F. Cutts had a yearning for a more complete life. He was a lawyer in his heart, a college football coach to those of Purdue. It wasn't long after he announced his intention to retire from coaching and practice law out West that the Purdue backers picked up the chant, "We want Cutts! We want Cutts!"

"We want Cutts! is the slogan and let's not rest until the desired result is accomplished," proclaimed the *Purdue Exponent*.

In the end it was Cutts who obtained his desired result and left the coaching profession. He not only left his mark on Purdue but also on Notre Dame. In his last game as Purdue coach, his Boilermakers dismantled Notre Dame 36-0 on a Thanksgiving Day in Lafayette.

While the Stuart Field crowd filled the crisp autumn air with Cutts' name, the Boilers, led by H.L. Thomas and Walt Krull, filled the scoreboard with Boilermaker points.

Thomas, a fullback, and Krull, the kicker, accounted for 21 points in the 36-0 rout. The victory gave Purdue a 9-3 record and the State Championship. The dozen decisions were the most recorded by either team in a given year, excluding bowl appearances.

Notre Dame, behind the coaching of the former great running back Louis "Red" Salmon, the "Red-Topped Terrier," would finish with a 5-3 record.

Purdue had missed the 1903 Notre Dame team, one of the best in the country. The 1903 Irish finished with an 8-0-1 record and amazingly shutout every opponent including Northwestern, which returned the

H.L. Thomas scored three touchdowns for Purdue in the 1904 game. (Photo courtesy of Purdue University)

favor on Notre Dame, accounting for the tie.

Purdue never played Notre Dame in 1903 because of the great train wreck that killed part of the Purdue caravan travelling to Indianapolis to play Indiana in their annual meeting scheduled for October 31.

About 9:45 a.m., October 31, a special 14-car train crashed into a 10-car section of steel-constructed coal cars being backed down the track inside the Indianapolis city limits.

Newspapers reported the first car (of wooden construction) of the Purdue train was cut in half with the floor lying under the tender and the roof resting on the second car of the section of coal cars.

A total of 15 Purdue players or coaches were killed in the crash. The victims were assistant coach Edward Robertson, trainer Patrick McClaire and players Thomas Bailor, Walter Hamilton, Bariel Drollinger, Walter Roush, Russell Powell, Joseph Coastes, Charles Furr, George Shaw, Samuel Truitt, Samuel Squibb, Wilburt Price, Jay Hamilton and Charles Grubb. Lafayette businessman Newton Howard, a guest of the team because of his intense support, was also killed.

Coach Cutts and manager-player Harry G. Leslie, who was later to become the governor of Indiana, were injured. The Purdue band, riding in the second car of the special train, miraculously escaped serious injury when the car left the track and plunged down an embankment.

Memorial Gymnasium on the Purdue campus is named in memory of those fatally injured in the wreck.

The Boilermakers allowed Indiana the right to claim a forfeit victory. But the Hoosiers simply chose to consider the game a no-contest. The rest of the Purdue schedule was cancelled.

By the time the teams met in 1904, nearly two years had passed since the two powerhouses met on Thanksgiving Day in 1902 and played to a 6-6 decision.

Notre Dame's 1904 squad had been battered and beaten by the time it arrived in Lafayette to close out the season. The Boilermakers on the other hand were prepared to extend their winning streak to five games. Purdue had no trouble in accomplishing its mission.

"After 70 minutes of desperate fighting, the likes of which Stuart Field has never seen before, Notre Dame was compelled to relinquish her claim to the State Championship," the *Notre Dame Scholastic* reported.

Purdue's offense was built around the sturdy fullback Thomas who scored three touchdowns including the first barely five minutes into the game.

"It (Purdue's offensive line) battered our linemen until they could barely stand.

"Captain Frank Shaughnessy played his final game of college football. When it was over he was so badly bruised and battered he could barely talk."

The Purdue crowd realized its team's dominance and in acknowledgment of Shaughnessy's spirited play gave the Notre Dame player ovation after ovation.

After Thomas' first touchdown Krull converted the extra point. The *Purdue Exponent* in reporting Krull's success wrote rather boastfully, "Krull made good on the extra point. He always does."

Certainly no one could debate his expertise on this afternoon. He was six-for-six on his point after tries following two more Thomas touchdowns and one TD each by D.M. Allen, Emeis and J.R. Mowrey.

The rout was complete. Purdue, little more than a year after the tragedy of the train wreck, had demolished its biggest rival to claim its first State Championship since 1899 and in the process registered the first shutout of the series.

After five meetings, Purdue held a 2-1-2 advantage over its neighbors from the north.

1, Miller; 2, Robertson; 3, Nufer, Trainer; 4, D. Long; 5, Flemming; 6, Halsted; 7, Meyer; 3, Emeis; 9, Mowrey; 10, Adams; 11, Frushour; 12, Thomas; 13, Cutts, Coach; 14, King; 15, Hewitt; 16, Sprau; 17, Shackelton; 18, Worsham; 19, Johnson; 20, Krull; 21, Allen, Capt.; 22, I. Long; 23, Wellinghoff; 24, McCormick.
PURDUE UNIVERSITY.

Purdue squad of 1904. (Photo courtesy of Purdue University)

35

1905

Boilers Baffle Notre Dame Again

LAFAYETTE, IND.—The Purdue alumni had lost on its attempt to keep Oliver F. Cutts from abandoning their ranks. In Cutts' place was A.E. Hernstein, a Michigan graduate.

There is no way of knowing how the Purdue fans felt about Cutts' departure. By the time six games had been played, Hernstein's team was still undefeated. Counting the five wins Cutts' squad had assembled at the end of the 1904 season, the Boilermakers had run off a string of nine straight wins before tying Indiana and beating Missouri.

The 11-game unbeaten streak was ended when Purdue lost 19-0 to Chicago. Not about to let one loss stand in the way of an outstanding season, Purdue picked up where it left off a year earlier against Notre Dame. For the second straight season, Purdue had handed Notre Dame a shutout, 32-0.

If anyone cared what had become of Oliver F. Cutts, nobody bothered to put it down in print.

The victory meant another state title for Purdue and another solid victory over Notre Dame.

"They (Purdue) have a team to be proud of and one that ranks among the best in the West," the *Notre Dame Scholastic* praised.

Indeed, Purdue's team was one of the best of its day. Whereas H.L. Thomas had ravaged the Notre Dame defense for three touchdowns a year earlier, D.M. Allen matched Thomas' feat in the 1905 game.

Just three minutes had elapsed when Allen scored his first touchdown and quarterback Thomas Johnson had kicked the extra point.

Slowly, methodically, Purdue kept moving downfield against the Irish. J. Hoffmark, E.P. King and Allen, on a 15-yard run, all scored first half touchdowns giving Purdue a 21-0 lead. Johnson missed the last three extra points.

In the second half, Allen finished off yet another Purdue drive with runs of 12 and then eight yards giving Purdue a 26-0 lead. Conville's 15-yard run followed by Allen's first conversion attempt of the afternoon finished off Notre Dame 32-0.

In his only year as a Notre Dame coach, Henry J. McGlew's team finished with a 5-4-0 record while A.E. Hernstein was wiping away the Cutts' Legacy with a 6-1-1 record and a State Championship.

It would be 28 years before Notre Dame was again shut out by Purdue, but the Irish would not have to wait nearly as long to turn the trick on the Boilermakers.

D.M. Allen produced three touchdowns against the Irish. (Photo courtesy of Purdue University)

Notre Dame meets Purdue in 1906 clash at Stuart Field. (Photo courtesy of Purdue University)

1906

Notre Dame's Two Points Are Two Too Many For Purdue

LAFAYETTE, IND.—Gone was the powerful offense of Purdue, gone was the stellar coaching ability reflected by Oliver F. Cutts and A.E. Hernstein, gone was the thrill of victory while the monotony of defeat fell heavily onto Purdue.

After successive shutout victories over Notre Dame the previous two years, Purdue suddenly lost the magic it had managed to capture. After building a respectable 26-8-2 record in its four previous years, Purdue slipped to 0-5, its worst season in the first 20 years of the program. Not only did Purdue finish without a victory, it also finished with a mere five points, all scored during a 29-5 defeat to Wisconsin.

It became so bad at Purdue that the townspeople vowed not to attend games unless they were nearly assured a victory. Why nearly 2,000 watched Notre Dame beat Purdue that season defies the fans ultimatum— only the magnitude of the rivalry could attract the fans.

The rivalry also brought out the best from Purdue. Notre Dame, on its way to a 6-1 record, matched Purdue's ineffective offense and also couldn't score. It was up to the Notre Dame defense to rescue the Irish.

The defense blocked R.W. Fleming's goal line punt, sending the ball bounding out the back of the goal line, giving Notre Dame two points and a safety. The two points held up as Notre Dame finally broke the shutout spell with a 2-0 victory.

The game attracted more than the townspeople. The Wabash team sat on the east side of the field rooting for Purdue. On the west side sat the Indiana squad cheering for Notre Dame.

Indiana got its wish and a week later everyone knew why the Hoosiers were backing Notre Dame—Indiana blanked Notre Dame 12-0 in Indianapolis for the State Championship.

Despite what the score might reflect., Notre Dame did have the game under control from the outset. Notre Dame had no fewer than four touchdowns called back because of various infractions. Clarence Sheehan, Pat Beacom, Oscar Hutzell and Dom Callicrate all made their way into the end zone only to have the touchdowns waved off. Callicrate had scored on a magnificent 60-yard run.

"While the score would indicate a hard fight and a narrow escape," Notre Dame Coach Thomas A. Barry told the *Notre Dame Scholastic,* "in point of fact we outclassed Purdue in every department of the game. And at no time did they ever threaten our goal, whereupon we gained almost at will.

"My team surprised me, it is true, but I knew that they had the stuff in them, if it could only be gotten out.

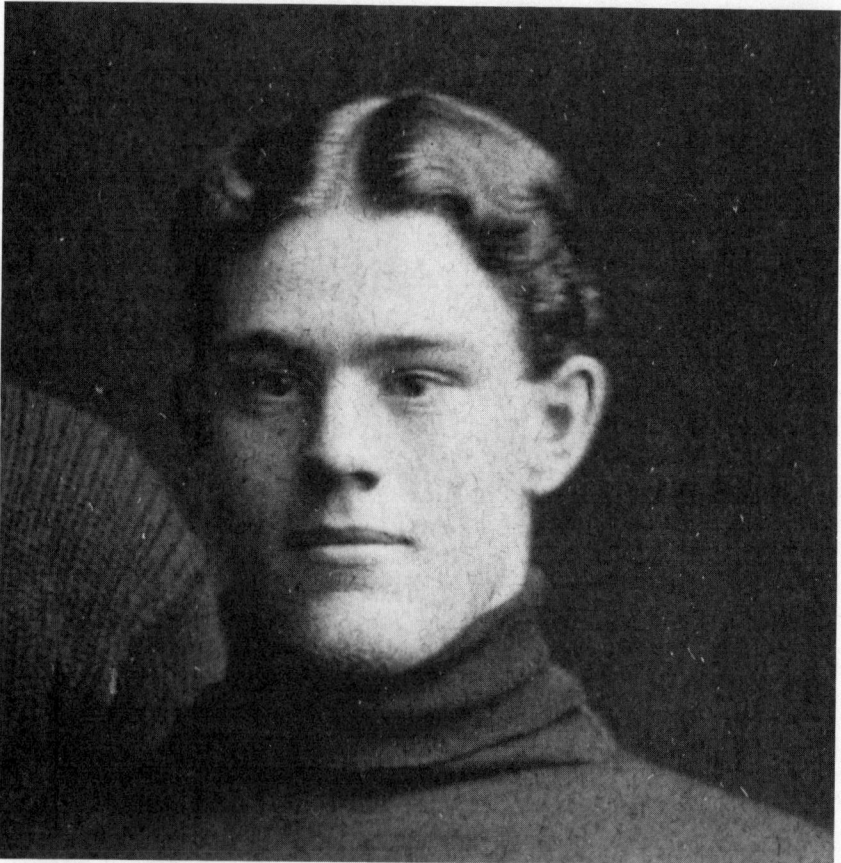

Purdue punter R.W. Fleming. (Photo courtesy of Purdue University)

"They simply tightened up around Saturday, hence their easy victory over Purdue. Which, however, should have been 17 to 0, at least."

It was considered a typical college game by the *Purdue Exponent*. The *Exponent* reported that both teams held each other in high esteem and that "the Purdue rooters are always partial to Catholics."

The *Notre Dame Scholastic* even went as far as to record the insights of the three officials.

From head linesman Kilpatrick of Wisconsin: "Purdue was slow in charging and did not have a diversity of plays ... Notre Dame tried a number of trick plays."

From umpire Kennedy of Chicago: "Notre Dame played the stronger game, and while they were given more than the ordinary number of penalties, they were justly deserved."

From referee Lowenthal of Illinois: "The best team won."

Even Purdue Coach M.E. Witham concurred with the last statement.

"The score, of course, is quite disappointing to me," he said. "The boys put up a good defense at critical stages of the game, but their offensive play was very weak. I think (end Leroy) Wyant was a little discriminated against, as he was fouled repeatedly. Chapman and Gordon having taken ill yesterday after drilling all week, completely broke up the backfield, and thus you see we were unfortunate."

Unfortunate they were—not only in 1906 but also in 1907.

1907

'O' Woe
For Old Purdue

LAFAYETTE, IND.—The tide had definitely turned, leaving Purdue washed ashore, tired, haggard and worse for the wear inflicted on it by the 1907 season.

For the second straight season, Purdue finished with an 0-5 record and for the second straight year Notre Dame shut out the Boilermakers 17-0.

Whereas the Boilermakers had scored five points in the 1906 season while allowing 86, the numbers weren't much better a year later when L.C. Turner replaced M.E. Witham as Purdue coach.

Turner's only team scored 10 points while allowing 108. Three of its five losses were by shutouts, meaning Purdue had lost 10 straight games over a two-year period, seven by shutouts, and the most points it scored in a single game during that span was six (in a 12-6 loss to Wisconsin).

Notre Dame Coach Thomas Barry had witnessed the Purdue-Wisconsin game and came away fairly impressed with the then 0-4 Boilermakers.

"Purdue is stronger than at any time this season," he told the *Notre Dame Scholastic*. "But," he added, "if Purdue wins it will be after a great battle."

For the fifth straight time, Notre Dame was forced to meet Purdue on Lafayette's Stuart Field—not that it made much difference since Purdue couldn't mount an offensive attack at home or on the road during this two-year drought.

Strange as it may seem, the Purdue fans had actually taken somewhat of a liking to the power-laden Notre Dame team. The *Lafayette Journal* reported that when Notre Dame players appeared on the field, the entire crowd applauded, showing the friendly feeling which "exists between the universities."

Chances are L.C. Turner and his boys weren't doing much cheering.

For the first half, Turner's Boilermakers put on an excellent show. While Purdue failed to score, it held Notre Dame to a single touchdown.

While college rules were altered slightly prior to the season in an attempt to accent the pass, neither team had perfected the new mode of transporting the football to the extent that they could damage the opponent sufficiently.

Notre Dame scored following a Purdue punt. Dom Callicrate, one of the Notre Dame players who had a touchdown called back a year earlier in Notre Dame's 2-0 win over Purdue, began the drive with a 17-yard run to the Purdue 18. Fullback Paul McDonald burst around the end for 15 yards to the Purdue three.

Reserve Jim O'Leary then went to the half-yard line before McDonald plunged over for the touchdown. McDonald missed the conversion, making Notre Dame settle for a 5-0 lead that they nursed into halftime.

Purdue's best opportunities came in the first half. J.W. McFarlane intercepted a pass for Purdue and moved within range of a field goal attempt by W.H. Hanna. Hanna shanked the kick.

Later in the half, R.M. Forsythe also missed two kicks for the Boilermakers. On nine occasions, Purdue moved the ball into Notre Dame territory only to come up empty.

Early in the second half, McDonald and Callicrate engineered another drive climaxed by a one-yard dive by McDonald, who also made the conversion, giving Notre Dame an 11-0 lead.

The afternoon didn't improve for Purdue. The last points were scored when Frank Munson punted for Notre Dame. Downfield awaiting the kick was Art Hutchens who apparently misjudged the kick. Hutchens fumbled, allowing the ball to roll over the goal line. Notre Dame's Henry Burdick recovered for the touchdown. McDonald followed with the final point.

And to think it could have been worse. Billy Ryan would have given Notre Dame additional points if a mistake on the part of the officials hadn't occurred. Ryan set off on a fabulous 70-yard run only to have it called back because of an official's laxity in moving the yard sticks early in the first half.

The second half was not without its moments off the field as well. As Notre Dame's dominance became apparent a few of their fans began taunting the Purdue fans.

"Three men dressed in Notre Dame colors were seen waving dollars in their hands trying to coerce Purdue students into betting," a student editorial in the *Purdue Exponent* alleged.

Other than that incident the game went off without any sign of foul play or, for that matter, offensive play by Purdue, outside of the one opportunity when R.S. (Newt) Shade was stacked up inside the two by Notre Dame's premier lineman Bob (Smousherette) Donovan.

"This game should go down in history as one of the cleanest wins Notre Dame ever had," the *Scholastic* reported.

The *Scholastic* also went out of its way praising Purdue for its sportsmanship.

"There is no team Purdue would rather play than Notre Dame, no team the Boilermakers would rather defeat, no team the old Black and Gold would rather lose to, if lose it must."

Again, it is difficult to imagine L.C. Turner and his boys nodding their approval.

Especially when Purdue and Notre Dame severed football relations following the 1907 game until 1918. What exactly transpired isn't crystal clear.

In January, 1908, the annual meeting of the Intercollegiate Conference was held in Chicago. There were nine teams represented, those from the Western Conference (later to be known as the Big Ten).

Some interesting developments included the expansion of the schedule back to seven games from five, the dropping out of conference, at least temporarily, of Michigan and the questionable ethics pointed out by the member schools against some of their non-roster brethren, including Jim Thorpe's Carlisle School.

The *Purdue Exponent* reported the following:

"The St. Louis University team came under criticism because they are made up of an aggregation of ineligibles gathered from all parts of the country. And that several members of the Carlisle school are not attending the Indian school but are paid salaries for playing football. While no action was taken ... they will find it very difficult, if not impossible to obtain places upon the schedules of conference colleges."

The report went on to say that Notre Dame was also adversely criticized.

Whatever the feelings, Notre Dame did not play Purdue again until 1918. Also conspicuous by its absence was Indiana from the Notre Dame schedule after 1908. Michigan dropped Notre Dame after 1909 and didn't play the Irish until 1942. Indiana played Notre Dame in 1919, a year after Purdue and Notre Dame patched up their differences.

Also of ironic note, Notre Dame played both Carlisle and St. Louis University in the years following that intercollegiate meeting.

Thomas Barry's last Notre Dame team went undefeated (6-0-1) including four shutouts. One of the shutouts came against Indiana in a 0-0 decision giving Notre Dame its only tie.

Perhaps, more than anything, it was Notre Dame's success over the last two seasons that caused the 11-year break. While Notre Dame was shutting out Purdue twice and totalling a 12-1-1 record including 12 shutouts, the Boilers were putting together matching 0-5 seasons and were barely scoring enough points to make their appearances worthwhile.

Regardless of the underlying reasons, one thing was certain: After eight meetings and back-to-back Notre Dame shutouts, the rivalry was put on hold.

Section II
1918-1923

Rockne
And The
Gipper

They are locked together forever in college football lore.

Knute Rockne and George Gipp.

"The Rock" and "The Gipper."

Unarguably, Rockne was the greatest coach to lead a team into battle during the Notre Dame-Purdue rivalry. Without question, the greatest all-around athlete ever to grace the stage of Indiana's greatest football rivalry was George Gipp.

The impact both left on the game is still being felt more than 60 years later. Both lived lives that continued to grow in fable-form long after each died tragically; Gipp at the age of 25 of an illness; Rockne in a plane crash at the age of 43.

Rockne and the Babe, George Herman (Babe) Ruth, were perhaps the first two American sports heroes who became identifiable by one name alone.

In encounters with Purdue, Rockne never lost a game. In fact, Purdue never came close to beating some of the greatest football teams ever assembled.

The legendary Babe Ruth with the incomparable Knute Rockne. (Photo courtesy of Notre Dame University)

Rockne's Irish played and beat Purdue six times beginning in 1918 and ending in 1923 when the rivalry was shut down for a decade.

Notre Dame outscored Purdue 174-36, an average score of 29-6. The most points a Purdue team could score off a Rockne-coached team was in 1919 when Purdue lost 33-13. From 1920-22, Notre Dame blanked the Boilermakers three straight seasons, 28-0, 33-0, 20-0.

By 1923, Gipp had died. In his place, rode the famed "Four Horsemen" of Harry Stuhldreher, Elmer Layden, Don Miller and Jim Crowley. There was obviously no letting up on Purdue.

The game itself had undergone massive changes since the 1907 meeting. In fact, the world had undergone a major upheaval following the four-year battle known as World War I.

America was looking for a new beginning. Baseball was still growing into the national pastime when it was sent stumbling to its knees in 1919 with the infamous Black Sox Scandal.

All the while, Rockne kept building team after team at Notre Dame.

In 1920, Gipp pulled off an 80-yard run against Purdue, the longest rushing play from scrimmage in the series history. He could run, throw and kick.

He scored 24 points in the series on three touchdowns, six extra points. Not included in his personal point total are the three touchdown passes he threw to Bernie Kirk, one in 1918 and two in 1919.

Legend has it that in the 1920 game, Gipp's heart may not have been in playing. He was supposedly loafing through the motions when a Purdue player sneered at him. Shortly thereafter, he scored on the 80-yard run knocking out a Purdue player in the process.

It was Rockne who found Gipp kicking a football on a deserted field in 1916. Then an assistant coach, Rockne couldn't believe the distance and the accuracy of Gipp's kicks. He persuaded him to join Notre Dame.

As they say, the rest is history. Beautiful, poetic history.

1918

Gipp Causes Purdue Fits

LAFAYETTE, IND.—The world was a different place when Purdue and Notre Dame patched up the differences that had kept the two from playing football since 1907.

A day before Notre Dame met Purdue on Stuart Field the German naval fleet surrendered, bringing to a close the first World War.

In the interim, the game of football had also shifted gears, undergoing a metamorphosis. The equipment changed. The passing game became an integral part in the offensive thinking. In 1912, the point value for touchdowns was increased from five to six and in 1909 a field goal was devalued from four to three points.

Notre Dame had also changed. Dramatically. A rookie coach was running the Irish.

His name was Knute Rockne.

His playing career ended in 1913. For the next four years he sat at the feet of Jesse Harper, perhaps the first great Notre Dame coach. Harper took over in 1913; his captain was Rockne. The 1913 Notre Dame team finished 7-0 and increased an unbeaten streak to 25 games. In 1911, Rockne's sophomore year, Notre Dame finished 6-0-2. In 1912, the Irish, with John Marks coaching and the famed Gus Dorais quarterbacking and captaining the Irish, Notre Dame finished with a 7-0 record.

The streak ended three games into the 1914 season when Yale whipped Notre Dame 28-0. During the streak the Irish compiled a 22-0-3 record and outscored the opposition by a staggering 1,131 to 85.

The Rockne years were well underway and his tenure as college football's most famous coach was just beginning.

The 1918 Notre Dame team finished with a 3-1-2 record marking the fourth straight year that the Irish had only lost one game. The loss that season occurred on November 16 to Michigan State. The Irish lost 13-7. Purdue was their next opponent.

While Notre Dame was constructing the most famous of teams, Purdue spent the years away from Notre Dame dwelling in mediocrity. In 1915, Harry B. Routh became Purdue's first recipient of the Big Ten Medal of Honor. A year later Elmer Oliphant, a former Purdue halfback, was selected to Collier's All-America team while playing for Army. Purdue, nevertheless, considers Oliphant its first All-America player.

The *Indianapolis Star* reported that this "Purdue team was the best it had since the days of Oliphant."

Maybe so, but it still was a few cuts below the Rockne-trained Irish.

Needless to say, Rockne was preparing his troops with a little extra whip following the loss to Michigan State. The *Purdue Exponent* reported that Rockne had drilled his players long and hard during the preceeding week, constantly repeating new plays he had put into the game plan especially for the Boilers.

A crowd of 7,000 bordered Stuart Field. What they saw was a 26-6 Notre Dame victory conducted by Knute Rockne and orchestrated by the great George Gipp, one of college football's early standouts.

The legendary Gipp had been questionable after rupturing a blood vessel in his face and injuring a leg earlier. But he played anyway. In fact, he was outstanding.

Edgar Murphy gave Purdue the lead on a three-yard run breaking a Purdue scoreless streak against the Irish of eight quarters and 13 years.

According to the *Lafayette Journal,* that drive was the one and only time Purdue had any momentum. From then on the Irish parlayed a scoreless first quarter into complete and utter dominance.

Notre Dame scored twice in the second quarter and on both touchdowns Gipp played a primary role. The first touchdown came when Gipp put together a pair of 18-yard runs. The touchdown coupled with the flubbed extra point left the score tied at six.

With three minutes left in the half, Gipp connected with Bernie Kirk for 18 yards and a touchdown. Gipp's kick failed but as Purdue Coach Butch Scanlon was to admit a year later, the Boilers were finished.

In reference to the 1918 defeat Scanlon said, "Defeat was not due to an inferior team representing Purdue but due to a team 'quitting' the game as lost after Notre Dame's first touchdown."

Early in the second half, Gipp continued his disheartening role by scampering 55 yards. It appeared as if Gipp would score the third Notre Dame touchdown, but Purdue's Fred Roth, the fastest man on either team, caught Gipp from behind at the 22. Earl (Curly) Lambeau went 10 yards and Gipp, no longer winded, finished the job with a 12-yard touchdown run off tackle. Gipp added the extra point giving Notre Dame a 19-6 lead.

The most spectacular play of the day was still to come. In the fourth quarter, Purdue's J.H. Quast punted. Bill Mohn, playing in the place of Frank "Abbey" Lockard, caught the punt at the Notre Dame 27. He weaved his way through the entire Purdue team on the way to a 73-yard touchdown. Gipp followed with the conversion.

A Rockne-coached team had its first victory over Purdue, 26-6. Perhaps Purdue wished it had waited a while longer before trying the rivalry back on for size—11 years later it still didn't fit right.

ANDERSON
End

BARRY
Halfback

HAYES
End

KILEY
End

THREE GREAT LEADERS

CAPTAIN BAHAN of the undefeated 1919 Varsity has had the honor of leading the greatest Notre Dame machine in over thirty years of football history. The Gold and Blue gridiron teams of 1912 and 1913, led by Dorais and Rockne, the mentors of last year's triumphant eleven, equaled in many ways but did not surpass Bahan's crew. "Pete" Bahan has been acclaimed "a Notre Dame man," the highest tribute of two thousand student-fan admirers. The press has named him the "wizard Irish general," and his teammates know him as a peerless leader to be depended upon entirely. Captain Bahan's generalship reflected the thoroughness of his team's perfections and the personal mental poise exhibited under stress gave Notre Dame many advantages in turning the tide of battle to victory. The captaincy of the 1919 team could not have been given to a more consistent and worthy man than Leonard Bahan.

CAPTAIN-ELECT COUGHLIN of the 1920 Varsity is the man to whom every follower of the Gold and Blue gridiron fortunes will look this fall. "Little Willie" has a big job on his hands to be able to toe the mark set by his predecessor of 1919. The students

DOOLEY
Guard

SMITH
Guard

ANDERSON
Guard

The 1919 Irish. (Photo courtesy of Notre Dame University)

1919

Rockne's Irish Achieve (9-0) Perfection

LAFAYETTE, IND.—The feeling early in the season was that Purdue stood a chance at derailing one of Knute Rockne's great Notre Dame teams.

Even as the game approached and the Boilers were a woeful 2-3-1 prior to their season finale against the Irish, the feeling was still alive that Purdue could provide a stumbling block to an unbeaten Notre Dame squad.

Sports writers from all parts of the country were writing about the game. After watching Purdue earlier in the season the consensus was the Boilers could indeed knock off a Rockne team.

Purdue Coach A. "Butch" Scanlon worked feverishly in the final days preparing the Boilers. He instituted new formations, blackboard sessions and "dummy" scrimmages. Mentally, the Boilers were prepared. As it turned out, it was all for naught. The Irish prevailed 33-13 in front of 7,000 at Stuart Field.

One of the reasons for the Irish success was they, too, were taking the meeting seriously.

"The coming game with Purdue," the *Lafayette Journal* reported, "is the sole topic of conversation at the Catholic institution and hundreds of students are planning to make the trip to Lafayette."

The Irish also had pride and a midwestern mythical ranking at stake.

"It's Rockne's aim," the *Journal* contended, "to run the score as high as possible so as to secure a rating among teams of the western conference.

"If Notre Dame wins by more than Ohio State did over Purdue (20-0)

54

then Notre Dame figures to rank with the best of the Big Ten."

With Rockne coaching, the great George Gipp quarterbacking and Bernie Kirk receiving, the Boilers really had little chance. The combination was responsible for half the total yardage of the 1919 Irish.

Gipp passed for two touchdowns and completed 12 of 20 passes for 162 yards. He used Kirk, Arthur "Dutch" Bergman and Frank Coughlin as his receivers. One of the touchdown passes went to Kirk, another to Bergman, who had returned to the lineup after being hospitalized. Scanlon had dreaded the Gipp and Bergman combination.

Purdue did score first when John Meeker ran for the touchdown and C.C. Stanwood converted.

The Irish failed to score during the opening period but quickly tied the game when Bergman scored from seven yards out on a double pass play orchestrated by Gipp. Gipp's conversion attempt failed. Following a Purdue punt and an Irish drive Kirk plunged over giving the Irish the lead for good. Gipp did make the conversion giving Notre Dame a 13-7 halftime lead.

In the third quarter, Gipp and Kirk combined for another touchdown on a pass play. The point after attempt by Pete Bahan failed but Notre Dame still had a 19-7 lead and put the Boilers in the unenviable position of playing catch-up.

Purdue did not possess the deadly passing potential of the Irish. Rockne had placed three defenders on Purdue's best threat, Ferdinand Birk. Purdue's captain and quarterback/fullback Kenneth Huffine did manage to bring the Boilers back within six points with a touchdown plunge after leading a long drive full of end sweeps. But later he threw a pair of interceptions leading to the final two Notre Dame scores.

George Trafton returned one 17 yards for a touchdown and Hartley "Hunk" Anderson returned another interception 20 yards for the fifth and final touchdown.

While the victory was Notre Dame's the Purdue fans were greatly satisfied in the Boilers efforts against a superior team. As the game ended, the Purdue fans carried the Boilers off the field in a salute to a valiant if not victory-filled season.

The loss was especially devastating to Purdue captain Huffine who was playing his final game for the Boilers after receiving several offers to turn professional including one from the nearby Pine Village Eleven.

"Closing a season with no conference wins," Huffine is quoted as saying in the *Purdue Exponent,* "is in no way due to a lack of coaching, but lack of material to compete with against conference schools."

The victory enabled the Irish to claim the Indiana state championship. Five days after playing the Boilers, the Irish completed the season on Thanksgiving with a 14-6 win at Morningside.

Rockne, in his second year as head coach, had produced his first unbeaten team (9-0). He would have four more perfect seasons.

The victory also gave the Irish their first breathing room in the series. In the nine previous meetings, the Irish were only 4-3-2 against their neighbors from the south.

Purdue Coach A. "Butch" Scanlon. (Photo courtesy of Purdue University)

1920

And The Band, And Gipp Played On

NOTRE DAME, IND.—Not since 1907 had a Purdue football team set foot on Cartier Field. The return of the Notre Dame-Purdue rivalry to South Bend brought out a homecoming crowd of 12,000, the first homecoming in Notre Dame history.

As had been the case previously, George Gipp ran wild and produced another outstanding passing effort, helping to crush Purdue 28-0.

One observer said, "It was a case of a splendid fighting team being outclassed by a better one."

The talk in the newspapers prior to the game regarded Notre Dame's chances at playing in a bowl game as outstanding. Knute Rockne quickly squelched that possibility. "That talk is very premature," he said.

Notre Dame was forced to play without three starters against the Boilermakers. Unfortunately for Purdue, the three didn't include the great Gipp, who was playing his third and final game of the series.

Purdue Coach A. "Butch" Scanlon surveyed what lay in his team's way and said the only way Purdue could possibly stand a chance was to stop Gipp and his primary receiver Roger Kiley, a pair of potential All-Americas.

No such luck. Gipp not only pulled an 80-yard touchdown run out of a punt formation but also threw to Kiley and Eddie Anderson for a total of 130 yards. If that wasn't enough he finished off three touchdowns with extra points. He did all that in less than 30 minutes of action.

The scoreboard wasn't the only statistic that Notre Dame dominated. The Irish threw for 161 yards, Purdue 41. Notre Dame had 18 first downs,

George Gipp, the Gipper. (Photo courtesy of Notre Dame University)

Purdue seven, including four late in the game against Rockne's second string.

"The Boilermakers will be up against a wonder team," the *Lafayette Journal* reported. "(Notre Dame) has drawn the praise of every eastern critic and it has defeated good teams as far west as Nebraska and as far toward the Eastern seaboard as West Point."

The Notre Dame fans were nothing but hospitable toward the visitors from Purdue which included a 25-man traveling squad plus nearly 1,000 Boiler backers. And why not? Notre Dame was on the road to another unbeaten season finishing the same as 1919, 9-0. Purdue, meanwhile, finished with a 2-5 record beating only DePauw and Wabash. Four of the losses were by shutouts.

After arriving by train, the Boilers were welcomed by the Notre Dame band and escorted to the Jefferson Hotel. The celebration continued long into the night with the Notre Dame band reportedly serenading the Boilers into the wee hours. A "celebration" that wasn't actually music to Purdue Coach Scanlon's ears. The eve of the game also marked the first appearance of a Notre Dame cheerleader, Al Slaggert, who performed at the Oliver Hotel.

The overflow crowd, which included Louis "Red" Salmon and Ray Eichenlaub, two of Notre Dame's former great players, came early to Cartier Field.

Notre Dame's Cartier Field in 1920. (Photo courtesy of Notre Dame University)

"The attraction was a football game between the greatest football team of all, and the courageous warriors of Purdue."

Purdue took the offensive almost immediately. Using a passing game that began on a successful note, the Boilermakers drove to the Notre Dame two. At that point, the Notre Dame defense stiffened, snuffing out Purdue's best opportunity.

After a scoreless first quarter, the Irish forged back. Paul Castner connected with Chet Grant for 50 yards and the first points of the afternoon. Castner followed with the conversion. Grant had quarterbacked the 1916 team but went into the service missing the 1917-18-19 seasons. He played in 1920 and again in 1921.

Later in the first half, Purdue threatened again. The Boilers advanced to the Notre Dame eight before turning the ball over. Notre Dame edged its way out to the 20-yard line where, on a fourth-down play, Gipp faked a punt and raced 80 yards for the second touchdown and then kicked the extra point.

The half ended with Notre Dame holding a 14-0 lead. The Irish added another touchdown in the third quarter when Notre Dame's Norm Barry broke free for 15 yards only to fumble. Eddie Anderson picked up his teammate's miscue and rambled the final 20 yards for the touchdown. Gipp converted the extra point.

The fourth and final touchdown was nearly a carbon copy of the third. A Purdue fumble bounced into the arms of Lawrence (Buck) Shaw who went five yards for the touchdown. Gipp added the conversion completing the rout.

"Gipp's sensational open field running and his passing coupled with Notre Dame's stone wall defense featured the game," the *Purdue Exponent* reported.

"The New York papers were warm in their praise for the Catholic squad, especially George Gipp, whose sensational work against the Army practically clinched an All-America berth for him this year."

The extra point that gave Notre Dame its 28th point that November 6th day was the last point Gipp scored against the Boilermakers.

One week later, in helping Notre Dame beat Northwestern 14-0, Gipp contracted the incurable streptococcic throat infection that would kill him three weeks later. He died on December 14 at the age of 25.

What ensued eight years later was perhaps the most touching locker room scene in the history of college athletics.

While on his deathbed, Gipp made his historic plea to his coach Knute Rockne.

"I've got to go, Rock. It's all right. I'm not afraid. Some time, Rock, when the team's up against it, when things are wrong and the breaks are beating the boys—tell them to go in there with all they've got and win just one for the Gipper. I don't know where I'll be then, Rock. But I'll know about it, and I'll be happy."

In November, 1928, Notre Dame, saddled with injuries and a 4-2 record, met the powerful Army in Yankee Stadium. According to Francis Wallace of the *New York News,* Rockne made his famous pre-game speech to his underdog Irish:

"The day before he died, George Gipp asked me to wait until the situation seemed hopeless—and then ask a Notre Dame team to go out and beat Army for him. This is the day and you are the team."

Notre Dame rallied for a 12-6 victory over the Army in what football experts considered the most inspired football ever played.

Even today, the legacy lives on. On a wall inside the Notre Dame locker room is a cross bearing the name George Gipp. The inspirational message lives on.

1921

An Upset Notre Dame Rolls On

LAFAYETTE, IND.—Iowa 10, Notre Dame 7. It was a major upset that occurred the week before Purdue was scheduled to play host to Notre Dame.

Notre Dame had lost for the first time in 22 games. What were the chances that Purdue, still struggling, still losing, would hand the Irish a second straight upset?

"It is tradition that Purdue always fights hardest against Notre Dame," the *South Bend News-Times* warned in its October 14 edition. "No other game means so much to them."

Purdue was coming off what amounted to a moral victory in a 9-0 loss to Amos Stagg's Chicago Maroons.

The chances, however, for victory over Notre Dame were slim. Consider that Notre Dame still was coached by Rockne and still possessed one of the most powerful teams of the era. Consider that Purdue was reeling. And also consider an amazing quality of Rockne's teams: only once in his 13 years as a head coach did Rockne watch his team lose as many as two straight games. And that was in 1928, not 1921.

Author Francis Wallace wrote in his book, "Notre Dame From Rockne to Parseghian," that the Irish were not about to be denied twice in one season: "That Iowa-Notre Dame game in 1921 became one of the landmarks of football...The 10-7 defeat was the only one Rockne sustained in three years. He wasn't happy about it. I doubt if anyone smiled on campus all that week. The squad took it out on a good Purdue team by 33-0, a big score in those days. Hunk Anderson was so mad that he blocked two punts and scored two touchdowns within three minutes—which must be an all-time record for a guard."

Notre Dame continued its sheer mastery over college football in general and Purdue in particular. In front of 7,500 Stuart Field fans, Notre Dame pummeled the Boilermakers 33-0. It was the second straight Notre Dame shutout over Purdue and fourth in their last six meetings, all Irish victories.

"Rarely," the *1921 Notre Dame Football Review* proclaimed, "has a better brand of football ever shown on a foreign gridiron and never has a team ever come back as Notre Dame did after that setback (against Iowa)."

The Boilers had hoped to catch the Irish down after the loss. And they were buoyed by the fact that for the first time in three seasons they were not meeting an undefeated Notre Dame team.

Minus the late, great All-America George Gipp, the Irish began quickly. Paul Castner, a left-footed kicker, booted a 29-yard field goal in the opening minutes of the contest. Before the quarter was history, John Mohardt scored on a five-yard run after Purdue had fumbled on its own 35. Lawrence Shaw missed the conversion, keeping the score at 9-0.

Purdue put itself in further trouble when it was forced to punt from deep inside its own territory. Edwin Rate shanked the kick, giving Notre Dame possession at the Purdue 12.

On a double pass, Mohardt scored his second touchdown from seven yards out and Shaw converted, increasing the Notre Dame lead to 16-0.

The second quarter continued to be a Purdue nightmare, especially for Rate. Forced to punt again, Rate's kick was blocked by Irish Captain Eddie Anderson. "Hunk" Anderson recovered in the end zone, improving the lead to 22-0. Shaw's conversion made it 23-0.

Purdue quarterback Don Field finally was able to move the Boilers. However, while returning a punt by Castner he fell and was kicked by Castner. He was knocked unconscious by the blow. Anderson scooped up the loose ball and rambled in from 25 yards for another touchdown. Shaw's conversion increased the lead to 30-0 at the intermission.

Anderson, a guard, had the distinction of scoring two touchdowns from his usually non-scoring position in a span of three minutes.

The final points were delivered by Castner in the third quarter when the Irish stalled and Castner was called in to kick a 24-yard field goal.

Purdue's fumbles were frequent and the team lacked the drive it had exhibited a week earlier against the University of Chicago. "Bad habits, like bad money," the *Notre Dame Scholastic* wrote, "are hard to get rid of."

The Notre Dame kicking game was also superior to that of Purdue. Castner averaged 43.5 yards a punt and added the two field goals.

Overall, Notre Dame had only nine first downs compared to four for Purdue but they outrushed the Boilers 231 to 88 and ran nearly 100 more plays (145-48).

"Greatly superior to the Boilermakers in the kicking game, the Irish gained most of their ground in an exchange of punts," the *Purdue Exponent* noted.

The shutout was one of six that the Irish pinned against their opponents that season. The loss to Iowa was the only mark against the Irish who outscored their oponents 375-41. Besides Purdue, Notre Dame shut out Kalamazoo (56-0), Nebraska (7-0 a week after the Purdue game at the Irish homecoming), Army (28-0), Rutgers (48-0) and Michigan State (48-0). The win over Rutgers came in New York at the famed Polo Grounds and occurred on the day that Warren Gamaliel Harding was elected as the President of the United States.

Purdue limped home with a 1-6 record in William "Lone Star" Dietz' only season as its coach. Purdue scored a total of nine points in 1921 while allowing 95. Their only win came against Northwestern (3-0) and they were shut out in five of their six losses.

All the while, Rockne's men continued to roll on.

1922

0 0 0 Is All They Wrote For Purdue

LAFAYETTE, IND.—If Purdue ever had an opportunity to defeat a Rockne coached team it was in 1922. Opportunity certainly appeared to knock, but as usual behind the door was yet another superior Notre Dame team.

After shutting out Kalamazoo and St. Louis University to open the season, the Irish were beginning to pile up the injuries. Rockne had six players out when Notre Dame traveled to Purdue. Among the missing were halfbacks Gus Desch and Will Maher along with linemen Ed DeGree and Bill Voss. During the game, Notre Dame lost tackle Tom Lieb with a broken leg. Other players who weren't 100 percent were Forrest (Fod) Cotton, the diminutive (5-7) Harry Stuhldreher, Don Miller and Elmer Layden. The latter three were sophomores, all reserves and soon to be revered in football lore along with Jim Crowley as the famed "Four Horsemen."

Purdue was primed for the occasion. The Boilers had themselves a new coach, a man out of the Rockne school, James Phelan. The rebuilding of the Purdue football tradition, once proud but lately tattered and torn, had begun.

The *Purdue Exponent* called the students to attention with a blaring headline THAT PEP SESSION CALLS YOU. TEACHER VERSUS PUPIL.

In 1914 Phelan was a student at Notre Dame under Rockne. Both men were great football players. Both had enjoyed success in coaching but Rockne had the upper hand. Rockne was a brilliant student and star end and captain on the football team. Phelan was a three-year starter at quarterback and served as the 1917 captain in coach Jesse Harper's final year.

"He is a true sportsman and a hard fighter," the *Exponent* wrote. "Phelan was on the Notre Dame varsity for three years. His gameness was one of his great assets and in one instance he refused to leave the field during the game with Army although he was suffering with a broken collarbone."

Before joining Purdue he had spent two seasons as the Army coach. He also coached at the University of Missouri.

The scene on the eve of the game was incredible. The Purdue student body had whipped itself into a frenzy.

"Notre Dame can be beaten and will be," said Purdue's Dean Coulter, according to the *Exponent*. "The student body takes an oath: 'I believe in Jimmy Phelan; I believe in that team; I'll do my bit.'

"Enthusiasm ran rampant in Eliza Fowler Hall last night," the *Exponent* reported on game day, "when the biggest student turnout in history appeared and threatened to blow the roof off the building in the literal sense of the word.

"After several yells, the band played the new fight song, 'Let's Go Purdue' several times. Dean Coulter's yell was, 'Notre Dame can be beaten, Notre Dame will be beaten eventually. Why not now.'"

Why not now? There were at least four good reasons—the yet to be named Four Horsemen.

Notre Dame threw only four passes in handing Purdue its third straight shutout of the series, 20-0. The Irish shutout string had reached four games dating from the final game of the 1921 season when they blanked Michigan State 48-0.

The shutout was not only the third straight Notre Dame had dealt Purdue but also the fifth in seven years. The Irish had a seven-game winning streak over Purdue, improving their series record to 8-3-2. Purdue hadn't won since 1906.

Of the "Four Horsemen" only Don Miller failed to have a part in the scoring.

After a scoreless first quarter, Elmer Layden connected for 15 yards with Paul Castner for the first touchdown in the second quarter. Castner's conversion attempt failed.

Neither team could score the remainder of the half. But Notre Dame broke the game open at the outset of the third quarter on a great effort by Jim Crowley. Crowley replaced Layden at the start of the second half and went 45 yards, finally capping the touchdown drive with a three-yard plunge. Castner's conversion made it 13-0.

In the fourth quarter, Stuhldreher was back in punt formation. He started to run and scrambled toward the sidelines, avoiding two tacklers before spotting Gene Mayl for a 20-yard touchdown pass. Layden booted the conversion, making the final score 20-0.

Rockne's Irish ripped through the remainder of their schedule, allowing only 27 points while registering six shutouts on the way to an 8-1-1 record. Only a 14-6 loss to Nebraska in the season finale kept Rockne from his third undefeated season.

Phelan, who served eight years as the Boilermaker head coach, ranking third behind Jack Mollenkopf and Stu Holcomb, suffered through the same miserable season that his predecessors had experienced. The Boilermakers finished with a 1-5-1 record after beating James Milliken 10-0 in the opener. The only other bright spot came in the final game of the season when the Boilers tied Indiana 7-7 in their homecoming game.

While there was no glimpse of daylight for Purdue, there was no sign of faltering on the part of Rockne's fine-tuned machine.

The famed Four Horsemen—(L-R) Jim Crowley, Elmer Layden, Don Miller and Harry Stuhldreher. (Photo courtesy of Notre Dame University)

1923

Purdue Just Doesn't Have The Horses

NOTRE DAME, IND.—In the foreground on a crisp November day, the fearsome foursome of Crowley, Miller, Stuhldreher and Layden rolled and rambled over Purdue 37-4.

With deep apologies to the great *New York Times* wordsmith Grantland Rice, the yet-to-be-named Four Horsemen of Notre Dame ran roughshod over Purdue. It marked the eighth straight time the Irish had buried Purdue.

The moniker would be attached a year later on October 18, 1924 when Rice wrote:

"Outlined against a blue, gray October sky the Four Horsemen rode again.

"In dramatic lore they are known as famine, pestilence, destruction and death. These are only aliases. Their real names are: Stuhldreher, Miller, Crowley and Layden. They formed the crest of the South Bend cyclone before which another fighting Army team was swept over the precipice at the Polo Grounds this afternoon as 55,000 spectators peered down upon the bewildering panorama spread out upon the green plain below."

A homecoming crowd of 20,000 filled Cartier Field peering across at another great Notre Dame. The players at Army had nothing on Notre Dame that Purdue didn't already know.

Before the 1923 Purdue game, Notre Dame had warmed up by defeating some of the great teams of the east—Army, Princeton and Georgia Tech. Purdue had lost to Iowa, Chicago and tied Wabash.

There was a moment or two that Purdue backers would take solace in. Reserve quarterback Joe Prout cut the lead to 14-7 with a 65-yard gallop through the Notre Dame defense. It was no small accomplishment considering Prout was only the second player to score off the Irish that season and would be one of five before the season ended.

It was also the first Purdue points off Notre Dame since the third quarter of the 1919 game. Since then 14 quarters had passed without Purdue scoring so much as a safety. The Purdue conversion was kicked by Mel Taube.

During the intermission a pennant was presented to Purdue coaches Jim Phelan and Eddie DeGree, both former Notre Dame stars. The biggest crowd in the series' history applauded two of its former heroes.

Notre Dame opened the scoring on a 10-yard run by Willie Maher in the first quarter. The Irish used a variety of long passes and end runs on the long drive. Miller scored his first touchdown on a four-yard run just before Prout set sail on his shutout breaking romp.

In the third quarter, Miller broke loose for an 18-yard gain that served to set up Crowley's 10-yard touchdown run. Before the quarter was history, Stuhldreher had thrown 24 yards to Miller for yet another touchdown, giving Notre Dame a 28-7 lead.

With Phelan and Rockne both using their reserves, the Irish completed the scoring when third-stringer Rex Enright carried 11 yards after Notre Dame had recovered a Purdue fumble by captain Ralph Claypool. The conversion failed, leaving Notre Dame 34-7 victors.

The loss ruined an otherwise festive trip for the Purdue players and fans who ventured north to South Bend.

"The Boilermakers were treated to a grand reception with a snake dance. They will be able to visit either a series of boxing bouts or a vaudeville show on campus," the *Purdue Exponent* reported.

"Saturday there will be a big barbeque at the gymnasium and a big parade of all monogram men before the game."

Once that was over, Purdue watched a parade of Notre Dame's best monogram winners dash past.

A week after the Purdue game, Rockne's troops watched as another undefeated season was ruined by Nebraska. Notre Dame was again outstanding, finishing with a 9-1 record.

Purdue continued to experience the worst of times, finishing with a 2-5-1 record. For the fifth straight season Purdue failed to win three games.

It was time for Purdue to regroup. Notre Dame had proven itself as a college football power on a national scale. The Irish had improved their schedule with some of the best teams in the midwest and the east. They no longer appealed to the Western Conference for acceptance. On the contrary, they were far from it. Purdue was removed from their schedule.

The two schools did not meet again until 1933, 10 years later. By then the Four Horsemen had graduated, Notre Dame had its first National Championship (1924), its first bowl victory (a 27-10 victory over Stanford in the 1925 Rose Bowl), both schools had new stadiums. Ross-Ade Stadium (seating 18,200) was dedicated in Lafayette in 1924 and Notre Dame Stadium was dedicated in 1930.

The changes were many. But the most tragic of all occurred on March 31, 1931 when Rockne and seven other persons were killed in a plane crash near Bazaar, Kansas. He was 43.

Section III
1933-1947

*Notre Dame's
Reign Roars On*

Thanks in part to the coaching and organizational abilities of two former Notre Dame players, James Phelan and Noble Kizer, Purdue's program began rising from the ashes.

The Boilermakers had talked themselves back onto Notre Dame's national schedule. The Irish were going big time by now. They had become a national rival with any school in the country that played major college football.

Purdue had returned to face Notre Dame at just the right time. The interest throughout the state was ripe and for the first time in more than a decade the Notre Dame talent had worn slightly thin.

Purdue came storming back into the picture with a running back named Duane Purvis, a great all-around athlete. Purvis played a part in the folklore by undergoing knee surgery (obviously minor) just days before the game against Notre Dame. He was far from questionable. The doctor's reports left no doubt that he would do the Irish no harm.

Miraculously, or rather mysteriously, Purvis returned to lead Purdue to a 19-0 victory over Notre Dame breaking an eight-game losing streak that dated to 1905.

The teams met the next year also with Notre Dame's magic returning. After a five-year break, the teams met in 1939 with Johnny Kelleher, virtually an unknown and unaccomplished Notre Dame player, kicking the winning field goal in a 3-0 Notre Dame victory.

Another World War was spreading over the globe. Purdue and Notre Dame would not meet again until a six-year struggle for peace had ensued and the world was forever changed by the atomic bomb.

In 1946 the rivalry returned and Notre Dame, under the direction of the great Frank Leahy, was atop the collegiate sports world. Leahy was a devout Catholic who would speak of "Our Lady" time and again in his pep talks. "Our Lady" could have been the Virgin Mary; it could have been Notre Dame. It may have been both.

It was the closest thing to Rockne and that is what he strove for. His record at Notre Dame speaks for itself. It was he who engineered a 39-game unbeaten streak that began in 1946 and lasted until 1950. It was he who coached the four National Championship teams from 1943-49.

Rockne won three National Championships, Leahy four. His 1946 and 1947 teams were among the greatest to have ever played. Both won National titles.

A total of 42 players from those two teams played professional football. An example of how talented and how deep Notre Dame's squad was can be found in the story of Vince Scott. Scott was a reserve guard who rarely saw game action. Yet, he went on to play pro football in the old All-America Conference and the Canadian Football League.

Purdue was obviously overmatched both years. Of the eight teams that had the misfortune to play Notre Dame both years, only Purdue and the University of Southern Cal were able to score off the Irish in the two meetings. That in itself was an accomplishment.

After 19 meetings, Notre Dame held a commanding 13-4-2 record over Purdue.

1933

Phenom Purvis Produces For Purdue

NOTRE DAME, IND.—Ten long years had passed. Since 1923 Notre Dame and Purdue shared only a common statehood.

The Irish under Knute Rockne had rocked American collegiate athletics and Purdue was left to stand idly by to wait for an opportunity to coax Notre Dame into letting the Boilers back on its schedule.

Purdue would have the last laugh in the first reunion in a decade. The Boilers shut out Notre Dame 19-0, breaking an eight-game losing streak against Notre Dame that carried back to 1905. The Notre Dame program was feeling the aftereffects of Rockne's tragic death in an air crash three years earlier.

Heartley (Hunk) Anderson had been called to lead the Irish, to follow in Rockne's footsteps. Anderson was the first of many to discover that there would only be one Knute Rockne.

While Rockne's death shadowed the glitter of the Irish, the Boilers were enjoying their finest winning streak in Purdue history.

The victory increased Purdue's unbeaten streak to 20 games. The loss was Notre Dame's fourth straight and the fifth time it was shut out that season. Overall, the Irish were blanked a team record six times and finished with 32 points scored—the lowest total of any Notre Dame team since 1889. Simply, it was Notre Dame's worst season.

Yet the rediscovery of one of football's great state rivalries was a beauty.

"All Indiana threatens to turn out for this game," Ralph Cannon wrote in the *Chicago Daily News.* "in spite of the fact that it is not the representative conference vs. Notre Dame battle it started out to be."

Wilfred Smith wrote in the *Chicago Tribune*, "Notre Dame to Purdue alumni and students is still the team which they most desire to take to the cleaners.

For one victory over the Irish, Purdue would trade a couple agricultural buildings in West Lafayette and riparian rights on the Wabash River. Notre Dame affects Purdue that way.

"Back in the old days," Smith continued, "Notre Dame was always assured of winning one game each season. That game was the Purdue game."

The resurrection of the Purdue program had begun in the late 1920s. In 1922, Purdue hired Jim Phelan away from Notre Dame. Along with Phelan came Noble Kizer, who would ultimately lead the Boilers out of the darkness.

"But by that time (mid-1920s)," Smith penned, "Notre Dame like some of their (Purdue's) conference brethren had decided the Boilermakers were small potatoes. They couldn't land on Notre Dame's schedule."

In 1929, Purdue won the Big Ten title with an 8-0 record under Phelan. In 1931, Purdue tied Michigan and Northwestern for the title and won it again in 1932 with a 7-0-1 record under Kizer.

"Up popped the Purdue alumni asking for another chance to meet the Irish who in a second-hand fashion had taught Purdue how to play football," Smith wrote.

The Irish, with everything to lose, accepted Purdue's challenge.

The week leading to the game was full of spirit. When Purdue arrived in South Bent the Boilers were welcomed by banner after banner:

"Purdue is still the second best team in Indiana."

"Show Purdue."

But as spirited as the Notre Dame fans were, they also realized their own situation had become an unenviable one. Another Notre Dame banner proclaimed:

"You're doing a great job 'Hunk'; stick to the youngsters and fire yourself."

Purdue fans came to Notre Dame in trainload after trainload. More than 6,000 of the 27,476 fans were from Lafayette. The Purdue administration had to ask Notre Dame officials twice for additional seats after two allotments were sold weeks in advance of the game.

The Purdue faithful didn't expect their best player, Duane Purvis, to see any action. The reports all week long never gave any indiction that Purvis would be available for the Notre Dame game after developing a leg infection.

When he underwent surgery on the Wednesday before the game, the entire population of Indiana was certain that Purvis would be lying on a Lafayette hospital bed Saturday.

"An operation was performed by Dr. Gordon A. Thomas, team physician," a report claimed. "Purvis was hurt in the Carnegie Tech game (the week before). An incision was made in the leg about six inches above the ankle and drains (were) inserted. 'He won't play,' the doctor said. 'But he may make the trip.'"

During Purdue's final workout on Friday, Purvis was on the sidelines wearing street clothes. He returned to the hospital following the practice and remained there until the train left for South Bend.

In what should be considered as a medical miracle or simply a grand set-up, Purvis, who had been averaging six yards a carry, was in uniform for Purdue. He not only played, but he scored the third touchdown on a 50-yard pass play from Paul Pardonner, the ambidextrous quarterback and kicker.

Purdue All-America Duane Purvis. (Photo courtesy of Purdue University)

By the time Purvis had "fully recovered" and scored, the Irish were well on the way to suffering their worse loss in five years. Purvis, who was also the Big Ten javelin champ, played 58 minutes.

Purdue opened the scoring with an interception by guard Fritz Febel who picked off a Nick Lukats pass and returned it 16 yards. Pardonner converted.

The second Purdue touchdown came on a 35-yard touchdown toss by Pardonner to Fred Hecker. Pardonner shanked the extra point.

Purvis, who had made one of the greatest one-hand catches in Big Ten history two weeks before against Wisconsin, followed with his 50-yard dash through a surprised and demoralized Irish unit.

Notre Dame had actually threatened first. Lukats completed two long passes to Hugh Devore and another to Steve Banas, carrying Notre Dame to the Purdue 10. Notre Dame's passing game then went sour. Lukats' next two passes were incomplete and the Irish ended up relinquishing the ball.

In the fourth quarter, Lukats had the Irish sitting on the Purdue three. The Irish tried running the ball every which way against the Purdue line. They made it as far as the one before the Boilers once again took over.

Purdue and Kizer has been extremely wary of the Irish. Notre Dame was still considered a national power. But in its five previous games it managed only 12 points, all coming in a 12-2 win over Indiana.

"If ever a team was on the spot," Kizer said, "It will be us on Saturday. You can't keep a good team down Saturday after Saturday. And the Irish after three straight shutouts are due to collect in a big touchdown way with the power they've developed. It's time to look out."

His words must have been taken seriously by his players. The Boilers had an unbeaten streak of their own on the line and had scored a touchdown in 44 straight games. Plus, they had fought long and hard to regain the opportunity to play and ultimately beat Notre Dame.

It was also Kizer's first coaching appearance against his alma mater. Ten years earlier, Kizer was a star guard for the Irish when they beat the Boilermakers for the ninth time in 12 decisions (not counting two ties). When Kizer was a freshman at Notre Dame, "Hunk" Anderson was a senior. When Kizer was an upperclassman he was a member of the famed "Seven Mules" front line which blocked for the "Four Horsemen." At one point, Kizer was later considered as a successor to Anderson. Indeed, it was a game Kizer wanted to win badly.

His Boilers finished with a 6-1-1 record. Halfback Purvis was selected as a consensus All-America, becoming only the seventh Purdue player so honored.

Anderson suffered through a 3-5-1 season, the worst at Notre Dame since the 1888 squad finished 1-2 in the second year of Notre Dame football. Anderson continually found the Notre Dame position to be extremely demanding. It sapped the fire from the man who was a teammate of George Gipp, who brought Anderson to Notre Dame in 1917. He had coached under Rockne and had witnessed the power of the program. But his own personal magic was fading.

The Irish did salvage an emotional 13-12 win over Army in front of 73,594 at Yankee Stadium in the season finale. The victory did not however, salvage Anderson's job. After three seasons he bowed out and was replaced by Elmer Layden.

Meanwhile, Purdue not only had its rivalry with Notre Dame back, it also had recast the first stone.

1934

A Quarter's Worth Of Trouble

NOTRE DAME, IND.—The smile did not rest long on the collective face of Purdue. One victory over Notre Dame in 1933 after eight losses and 28 years was quickly forgotten.

In front of 34,263 fans at Notre Dame's Memorial Stadium, the Irish suppressed Purdue for most of four quarters and built an 18-0 lead before allowing Purdue one touchdown.

The roster first-year Notre Dame Coach Elmer Layden had at his disposal was 75 players strong. Purdue still had its 'Touchdown Twins,' Duane Purvis and Jim Carter. And Coach Nobel Kizer had been successful at keeping the Purdue program strong. But against Notre Dame, Purdue again appeared to have the same troubles as it had experienced against the great Rockne teams of the late teens and early 1920's.

After a scoreless first quarter, Layden suddenly pulled his first string and inserted the second unit with Wally Fromhart going in at quarterback.

Within five minutes Notre Dame had scored two touchdowns. A barrage of Notre Dame points fell in the second quarter. Just two minutes into the quarter, George "Mink" Melinkovich scored the first touchdown on a 60-yard run. Fromhart's conversion failed.

Undaunted, the Irish came right back to score again. Mike Layden threw 35-yards to Melinkovich down to the three. "Mink" capped off the drive with a one-yard dive.

Purvis began moving the Boilers from their 15. With time eluding Purdue at the half the Boilers reached the Notre Dame 28. Purvis went to the air on the last play of the half. Notre Dame's Fred Carideo picked off the pass and went 74 yards for the touchdown. The crowd went wild and Purdue slid out of sight into the seclusion of the visitors' locker-room.

It took Purdue nearly the entire game to break the shutout. With just a couple minutes remaining, after Layden had played nearly the entire roster, Purdue's Carter led a 63-yard drive. He plunged over from the one for the only Purdue score. Dan Toriello's kick added the seventh point.

While Purdue had managed 11 first downs to Notre Dame's five and had rushed for only 26 fewer yards (200-174), the Boilers could not hold off the flurry of Notre Dame points in the second quarter.

The victory was Layden's first as a head coach, having watched his team lose the season opener a week earlier to Texas 7-6. Ironically, when Layden was gaining fame as a member of the "Four Horsemen" it was Kizer who blocked for him.

The celebration of Layden's first victory carried on well into the night. The Notre Dame University band began the festivities with a parade down Notre Dame Avenue to a giant bonfire in the hollow. A crowd of 3,000 joined in.

Layden's first year turned into a success with the Irish finishing at 6-3. It was far from the perfection that Notre Dame fans had been accustomed to, but at the same time it certainly improved upon the 3-5-1 record turned in by "Hunk" Anderson's 1933 team.

Layden had recruiting restrictions put on him that he didn't realize were coming when he assumed the position. But he was too much a Notre Dame man to ever question the rules, let alone bend them.

Kizer's Boilers finished with another respectable record at 5-3. All five wins came in rapid succession following the loss to Notre Dame. Once again, Purvis was named All-America.

Kizer's record at Purdue stands alone among Boilermaker coaches who coached more than two seasons. Overall, his record was 42-13-3 with a winning percentage of .764 from 1930-36. His health began failing and forced him to retire in 1937. He died three years later at the age of 39.

In 1958, Purdue inaugurated an award named in Kizer's honor. The award goes annually to the player who earns the highest academic excellence.

Following the 1934 game, the rivalry again cooled for five years. It wasn't until 1939 that Purdue and Notre Dame met again.

Purdue Coach and former Notre Dame player Noble Kizer. (Photo courtesy of Purdue University)

1939

Irish Get
A Kick Out Of
Kelleher

NOTRE DAME, IND.—The pre-game hoopla raged on. For the first time in five years Purdue would play Notre Dame and Purdue president Elliott was making certain the Purdue student body was charged.

"All we ask," he told a pep rally of 3,000 students on the eve of the game, "is one simple thing. That is that Purdue makes one more touchdown than Notre Dame."

The pep rally coincided with the Boilers' opening game and commemorated the 50-year anniversary of Purdue's first championship.

"Fifty years ago in November, 1889," Elliott said. "Purdue defeated Wabash and brought back with them the distinguished title of nobility, Boilermaker. The game is not only an athletic contest, it has great historical significance."

While Elliott spoke, the Purdue students raised banners proclaiming, "Let's fill the Old Oaken Bucket with Irish Stew" and "11 Men After One (Notre) Dame."

Veteran quarterback Ted Hennis added, "the coaches don't know what goes around in the huddle, but we're going up to South Bend to bring back the stew."

Elliott closed the ceremony by stating, "Come home carrying your shield, or on your shield."

Among the other festivities was the Purdue campus mixer featuring Bill Morton and his campus band. The *Purdue Exponent* reported the following: "The backdrop (for the mixer) in keeping with the sports season will depict the Notre Dame football mentor (Elmer Layden) clad in his gridiron armor seated on the sidelines industriously jerking his hair."

Much to the dismay of all involved, the Boilers were not able to "make just one more touchdown than Notre Dame." In fact, the Boilers weren't even able to score. Not that Notre Dame would fare that much better. The Irish also had trouble making yards meet. But when it came down to the final score, Layden had third-string quarterback Johnny Kelleher to call on. It was Kelleher's 17-yard field goal at the outset of the fourth quarter that gave the Irish a 3-0 win over Purdue.

The victory was Notre Dame's 10th over Purdue in the last 11 meetings.

A crowd of 31,341 made its way into Rockne Stadium to watch the two Indiana rivals begin the 1939 season. Kelleher was a senior whose varsity career included just one previous appearance. As the game began, his place on the Notre Dame bench was secure, his place in Notre Dame history was just ahead.

The game developed into a punting duel with both teams managing just five first downs apiece. The Irish had mounted the longest scoring drive of the afternoon but had run out of momentum just inside the Purdue 10.

As the Irish went nowhere in three plays, Layden called upon Kelleher, who with one swift kick lifted himself from anonymity to prominence.

"There's the boy that did it," Steve Sitko, the No.1 Irish quarterback was saying later in reference to Kelleher.

Long after all the other players had left the confines of the Notre Dame locker room, Kelleher, according to a *Chicago Daily News* report, stood holding onto the ball.

"My dad," he said, "gets this one for the mantel. He played here from 1911-14."

Indeed, Bill Kelleher had played at Notre Dame with then-captain Knute Rockne and for Coach Jesse Harper.

Following Kelleher's kick into prominence, the Boilers staged a rally that threatened to seal Kelleher's name back into a tomb of anonymity.

Late in the fourth quarter, Mike Byelene nearly broke free on a run. He was finally hauled down from behind by Milt Piepul. Byelene kept the Boilermakers moving by connecting with All-America end Dave Rankin. The completion gave Purdue its third straight first down and put the Boilers at the Notre Dame 37.It was there that the drive finally stalled.

The Irish went on to post a 7-2 record by winning nearly every close encounter. In nine games the Irish only outscored their opponents 100-73. Notre Dame had won six straight to open the season before losing a 7-6 decision at Iowa. Notre Dame concluded its season with a disheartening 20-12 defeat to Southern Cal.

After a promising 5-1-2 record the season before, Mal Elward's Boilers dropped to 3-3-2.

Purdue All-America end Dave Rankin. (Photo courtesy of Purdue University)

1946

Irish Bombard Purdue

NOTRE DAME, IND.—The War had ended. But the Purdue-Notre Dame battles raged on.

For the first time in seven years, the schools met. The Boilers entered South Bend tattered and torn with no less than six backs in sickbay. Among the missing were quarterback Bob DeMoss, who separated a shoulder the Wednesday before in practice. Also gone from the Purdue attack were Bill Canfield, the team's best running threat, star end Ned Maloney and halfback-punter George Buksar.

The Boilers had lost two of their first three games and Notre Dame would make certain there would be a third. There was no question. Notre Dame won handily 49-6.

There were a few other questions, one of which dealt with a national magazine article printed earlier in the week that claimed the Irish were violating rules. The article alleged that Notre Dame was giving players room, board and tuition in return for menial labor. The report infuriated Notre Dame Coach Frank Leahy and no doubt didn't sit too well with the rest of the Irish.

It's just terrible," Leahy fumed regarding the report.

On the positive side, the Irish unveiled Ernie Zalejski on this Columbus Day afternoon. Zalejski's name will never rest with Rockne, Gipp or Don Miller, but he was a hometown hero back safe and sound from the War.

He had been back from duty in Tokyo just long enough to enroll in school and put in two days of classwork before the Irish brought the South Bend native into the game late in the first half.

He had been the most talked about Indiana high school football player since Tom Harmon.

His appearance did little to change the outcome but it did wonders for the 55,452 fans at Notre Dame Stadium. What the Irish couldn't give them in their rousing 49-6 victory, Zalejski's presence did.

The offensive star for the Irish was John (Pep) Panelli who had been switched to the right halfback position with freshman Emil Sitko sidelined. Panelli rushed for 118 yards in just nine carries. He had six runs of 10 yards or better scurrying for runs of 42, 18, 17, 15, 14 and 10 yards against the fired-up, but inferior Purdue defense.

The Irish started slow, taking nearly 10 minutes to record their initial first down. But just five plays after their first down they had broken a scoreless deadlock.

Jim Mello, Leahy's acting captain this day, was responsible for a majority of the acreage chewed up on the first Irish drive. He gained 33 yards on the first down. Then, after Panelli had consecutive runs of 17 and 10 yards, Mello plunged over for the touchdown. Fred Earley's first of seven extra points gave the Irish a 7-0 lead.

It took nearly another quarter before the Irish could score again. This time Terry Brennan gained 31 yards on two carries setting up Cornie Clatt with a two-yard touchdown run.

Notre Dame's John (Pep) Panelli. (Photo courtesy of Notre Dame University)

The Irish were just two minutes away from breaking the Boilers hearts. Notre Dame's Gerry Cowhig broke a Purdue punt 51 yards to the Boilers 29. When the first two plays failed, Leahy reinstated quarterback Johnny Lujack and Brennan. All it took was one play for Lujack to hook up with Brennan for a 29-yard touchdown, giving the Irish a 21-0 intermission lead.

Purdue received the opening kickoff only to fumble it away. Jim Martin recovered Dick Bushnell's fumble, giving the Irish a near free pass to another seven points. With a second-and-nine at the Purdue 18, Panelli broke loose for the fourth Irish touchdown.

Panelli was also responsible for the fifth touchdown. After the Irish took over on the Purdue 30, Panelli went 14 yards on the first broken field jaunt of 42 yards to the Purdue 14. From the eight-yard line Lujack passed to Jack Zilly for another touchdown.

The Boilers finally broke through on the ensuing possession. John Galvin, who alternated with Jim Walley as DeMoss' replacement at quarterback, raced 52 yards on the first play of the final quarter for the Purdue touchdown. Ed Cody's extra point try was wide.

The Irish scored two more touchdowns before it was over. Freshman Leon Hart jolted Galvin on the next Purdue possession. The ball popped out of Galvin's arms and into Bob Skoglund's who rambled in for the touchdown. The final touchdown came with 45 seconds left when Bill Gompers, a fifth string back, went 20 yards.

The loss was especially disheartening to three Boilermakers. Receiver Eddie Ehlers, left end Bob Heck and lineman Joe Kodba were all formerly of South Bend before heading south to Lafayette and Purdue.

The Boilers finished with a 2-6-1 record, their poorest mark in five seasons. The margin of defeat was the widest, 43 points, of any of the previous 17 meetings. It was Purdue coach Cecil Isbell's only decision against Notre Dame.

The Irish had not only whipped Purdue for the 12th time in the history of the rivalry but they were putting together what would be Leahy's greatest era.

The win over Purdue was the Irish's third since losing the last game of the 1945 season to Great Lakes 39-7, a game that historians would one day mark time with.

The only mark against Leahy's 1946 team was the famous 0-0 decision against Army in front of 74,122 at Yankee Stadium. The Irish finished 8-0-1 and earned a National Championship just ahead of the Army. George Connor and Johnny Lujack were consensus All-America. And all the while, Leahy was planting the seeds of a faked unsatisfaction that would spur the Irish to greater heights.

"Some folks," Leahy said following the Purdue game, "think Notre Dame is better than we really are."

1947

Boilers Can't Rise To The Defense

LAFAYETTE, IND.—The streak had reached double figures the week before as Notre Dame ravaged Pittsburgh 40-6 in the season opener.

Still Frank Leahy wouldn't let up and neither would the press. Granted, the Irish had their hands full with Purdue the next weekend, winning 22-7 thanks to All-America quarterback Johnny Lujack. But the masterful psychology that Leahy preached had been inbred within the media who expected nothing less than scores demonstrative of the ranking National Champions.

"For the second straight week," Jim Costin wrote in the *South Bend Tribune*, "Notre Dame's football team, in another winning effort, was made to look like anything but the national champions the boys have been writing about."

The Irish were considered more than five touchdown favorites against a Purdue team that would finish 5-4 under new coach Stu Holcomb.

It was Holcomb who the Boilers put their faith in, largely because of his success at Army. Holcomb had coached the Army defense for three seasons and his teams' results over Notre Dame were staggering.

Consider: 1944 at Yankee Stadium. A crowd of 74,142 fans watch the Army humiliate the Irish 59-0, the most lopsided loss in Notre Dame football history.

Consider: 1945 at Yankee Stadium. A crowd of 74,621 witnessed another Irish pounding. Army crushed the Irish 48-0.

Consider: 1946 at Yankee Stadium. A crowd of 74,121 is on hand. The good news for the Irish is they don't lose. The bad news is they don't score for the third straight time against Holcomb's defense. They settle for a 0-0 draw.

Considerations made, whatever magic Holcomb possessed, the Purdue administration wanted a portion of it. He had been an Army coach on two straight National Championship teams in 1944 and 1945. The 1946 team finished second in the polls to Notre Dame.

Obviously the talent Holcomb was now working with was less bountiful than what he had encountered at West Point. Yet, on this day in front of an overflow crowd at Ross-Ade Stadium, Holcomb's Boilers were more than respectable.

As Costin wrote in the *South Bend Tribune*, had Johnny Lujack been absent this day, a victory may have never been carted back to South Bend.

Notre Dame quarterback Johnny Lujack. (Photo courtesy of Notre Dame University)

Lujack passed 21 yards for the first touchdown and raced 31 yards for the second when he couldn't find anyone open.

The Irish caught a break on the first play from scrimmage when quarterback Bob DeMoss, relegated only to the offense because of a shoulder injury, threw wild on an attempted lateral.

John Panelli recovered on the Purdue 21 for the Irish. On the seventh play following the fumble, Lujack connected with Brennan for the touchdown. Kicker Steve Oracko missed the first attempt at conversion, but when the Boilers were offside he was granted a second opportunity and converted.

DeMoss brought the Boilers back and was helped tremendously by a pass interference call. Receiver Ned Maloney was interfered with deep in Notre Dame territory, putting the Boilers in business at the nine.

Momentarily, the Boilers stalled. The drive was frozen at the nine until DeMoss threw to Harry Szulborski on fourth down for the touchdown. Art Haverstrock kicked the first extra point against Notre Dame since the end of the 1945 season when the Great Lakes kicker converted in the most recent Notre Dame defeat.

Another Purdue fumble set the Irish up again. With the Irish in possession at the 31, Lujack went to work. Faking a pass, Lujack kept the ball himself and dodged traffic for 31 yards and the second Notre Dame touchdown. Oracko failed to convert.

Only once in the second quarter did the Irish threaten. With a fourth-and-one from the Purdue 11, Leahy wasn't prepared to gamble with the Notre Dame running game. He opted for Oracko who kicked an 18-yard field goal—the first Notre Dame field goal since October 31, 1942 when the Irish beat the Navy 9-0. The half ended with Notre Dame leading 13-7, thanks almost entirely to the passing of Lujack and the fumbling of Purdue.

The defensive play of Purdue's Maloney, Clyde Grimenstein and Bob Heck bottled up the Irish's outside running attempts. The Boilers actually outgained Notre Dame on the ground 128-80 but Lujack and quarterback Frank Tripucka combined for 184 yards, completing 16 of 26 passes.

The final Notre Dame touchdown came in the third quarter when Coy McGee returned a Purdue punt 43 yards to the Purdue 17.

Eventually, Floyd Simmons scored from three yards out. Oracko missed the conversion.

An example of how futile the Irish running attack had been can be seen during a third quarter Irish drive. With Notre Dame handed a first down on the Purdue six, the Irish could gain only five yards in four plays, leaving the Boilers pinned at the one but also leaving Leahy unsatisfied with the victory.

"These Notre Dame boys tried to stuff themselves with all the newspaper, magazine and motion picture publicity," Leahy said, "but they weren't quite successful. Like most everyone else they began believing all the nice things said about them."

The furor in Leahy's statements even caught the ear of Lujack who reportedly had been unamused by the length and severity of the scrimmages Leahy was conducting before and after the Purdue game.

Leahy, a master of mind manipulation, responded, "Lujack, a wholesome, clean-cut young man, is the finest quarterback college or professional in the country."

What could Lujack's reply be to that?

With a 2-0 record and an unbeaten streak of 11, Leahy had laid the ground work for the Irish's second straight National Championship season.

Following the Purdue game he said, "I'll promise football fans that Notre Dame will get better and better, week by week. I predict we will make a day-to-day gain. We'll get better, I'll promise you."

With All-Americas Lujack, George Connor and Bill Fischer leading the way, Notre Dame finished with a 9-0-0 record, even finding a way to defeat Army 27-7.

Irish All-America tackle George "Moose" Connor. (Photo courtesy of Notre Dame University)

Section IV
1948-1953

Upsetting Purdue
Has Last Word
On Irish Streak

The game that serves as the cornerstone to this rivalry was the 1950 meeting that matched the defending National Champions from Notre Dame against a young Purdue squad.

The Irish were only defending champions in name. Graduation had caused more havoc to Notre Dame than any foe could. Only four prominent players from the 1949 team, quarterback Bob Williams, center Jerry Groom, end Jim Mutscheller and tackle Bob Toneff returned for the Irish.

They set forth carrying a 39-game unbeaten streak, the longest in their history, into a season that would leave them reeling.

Before Purdue and sophomore quarterback Dale Samuels could write history that October 7th afternoon, Purdue and Notre Dame would have to do battle in 1948 and 1949 to further set the stage.

The 1948 game was also a classic. Notre Dame hung on for a valiant but nearly disastrous 28-27 win. The game was considered one of the most exciting in the series history and was the best thing to happen to the rivalry since the early days.

The victory in 1948 increased the Notre Dame unbeaten streak to 19 games. A year later the Irish had an easier time with the Boilers for Notre Dame's 31st straight game without a defeat.

On a cold, drizzly day in South Bend, sophomore quarterback Dale Samuels began a Purdue tradition. He came out throwing more than any previous Purdue quarterback. From Dale Samuels came the Purdue quarterback. The Len Dawsons, Bob Grieses, Mike Phippses and Mark Herrmanns.

"In the past we had geared ourselves up with a high, emotional desire to win," Purdue Coach Stu Holcomb said. "This time, with a sophomore quarterback, I told the boys to go out and throw the ball and to have themselves some fun."

For the first time in five years, Notre Dame had been beaten.

Make no mistake. The Irish took it out on Purdue the next three seasons. The loss to Purdue, however, had started the Irish off on the way to a 4-4-1 season—the worst record by far of any Leahy-coached team at Notre Dame.

"It was Leahy's only down team," former Notre Dame player and sports historian Chet Grant said. "He couldn't understand that. He asked me many times 'Do you think I'm losing my touch?'"

Leahy's teams rebounded the next three seasons both in terms of beating Purdue and defeating most of the competition.

He finished his coaching career in 1953 with a 9-0-1 squad and 37-7 win over Purdue. Notre Dame's record over Purdue remained overpowering at 18-5-2.

1948

Irish Escape DeMoss, Boilers With 28-27 Win

NOTRE DAME, IND.—It was a tribute to college football and all that this great rivalry would be built on. Notre Dame and Purdue spent the afternoon in front of a Notre Dame Stadium record crowd of 59,343 building a monument to champions as well as one for challengers. It was a game to cherish forever.

"This game," Notre Dame Coach Frank Leahy proclaimed, "was the greatest game I ever saw."

It was indeed marvelous. Notre Dame survived for a 28-27 victory in a game that saw 14 points hung on the board in the final two minutes.

As would be the case in most of the teams' meetings, the Irish had the most at stake. Notre Dame came into the game with an 18-game unbeaten streak and wore the crown of National Champions for a second straight season. A glimpse of their 1948 schedule led them to believe that Purdue would offer the major roadblock to another National Championship as well as the continuation of the unbeaten streak.

Purdue also was aware of its special place in history. If the Boilers could knock off the Irish at Notre Dame Stadium, they would have captured the national spotlight. The Boilers had defeated the Irish once since 1933. Before that Purdue had beaten Notre Dame in 1905. Just two victories in 43 years over a state rival. Enough, Purdue said, was enough.

Boilers Coach Stu Holcomb, opening his second season as their head coach, kept the Boilers' practice sessions secluded during the final three weeks leading to the season opener against Notre Dame.

ACTION AS NOTRE DAME EDGED PURDUE, 28-27

Emil Sitko attempting to circle his own right end. Other Notre Dame men in picture are: Ralph McGehee (26); Capt. Bill Fischer (72); Leon Hart (82); Mike Swistowicz (55); Marty Wendell (58) and Jack Fallon (68).

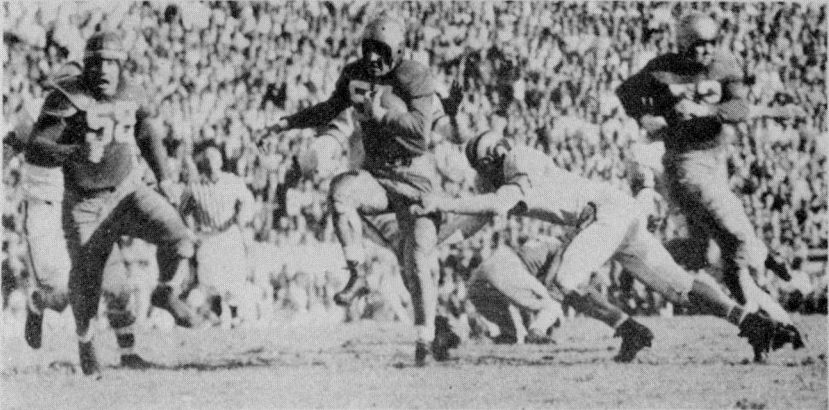

Mike Swistowicz going through middle of Purdue line. At left is Marty Wendell (58) and to the right, Capt. Bill Fischer (72).

The Boilers were prepared, as were the Irish. But as unpredictable as this game turned out, no team could have suspected or prepared for the proceedings.

Consider that a fourth-string tackle scored what proved to be the winning touchdown. Consider that a third-string guard, who doubled as a kicker, missed three point after tries before connecting on a 35-yard field goal and the one extra point that spelled the difference.

Consider that one team held a decided edge in rushing yardage (151-123), passing yardage (143-102) and first downs (13-10) and lost. Consider that a blocked punt produced yet another vital touchdown.

"Purdue," wrote Greg Halpin in the Notre Dame Scholastic, "played this game as if their personal reputation and those of their school depended on it. They outfought and outgained the Irish. They tore the vaunted Notre Dame forward wall into neat little chunks and galloped between the pieces for appalling gains. Their quarterback Bob DeMoss looked like a collegiate reincarnation of Johnny Lujack. They did everything but win the ball game. But look what they were up against."

The Irish broke the game open with a pair of touchdowns. Climaxing long drives, Emil Sitko procured the points with a pair of plunges through a determined Purdue line. The first touchdown came on Sitko's fourth attempt at penetrating the Boilers' defense.

The second Sitko touchdown resulted from a six-yard punt by Purdue's George Punzelt. The Irish traveled 36 yards for the second touchdown. But kicker Steve Oracko began building the suspense by missing the first two extra points.

The Boilers never lost faith. After a long drive of their own was thwarted by an interception in the end zone by Frank Spaniel, the Boilers in turn picked off a Frank Tripucka pass at the Irish 35.

Purdue quarterback DeMoss hit Norb Adams, who had intercepted Tripucka moments earlier, with a 19-yard touchdown pass. Rudy Trbovich's kick cut the deficit to 12-7 just before time expired in the first half.

The Boilers took the opening kickoff for a 74-yard drive that finished with Bob Agnew covering the last two yards for the score. The Boilers led 13-12, but Trbovich followed Oracko's lead and missed what turned out to be a very crucial extra point.

Still, the Boilers led and it appeared as if Notre Dame would have a difficult time mounting an attack against Purdue's inspired defense. For the first time since the final game of the 1945 season, Notre Dame found itself trailing. After 19 games and nearly three years, could the Irish find the magic to come from behind?

After Purdue recovered a Notre Dame fumble, the answer appeared to be no. The Boilers were set up at their 46. Purdue's offense finally stalled, bringing forth a punt. Punzelt was back at the Irish 35 when he received the snap from center.

In came Notre Dame's Jim Martin who got nearly his entire chest in front of the kick. Martin blocked Punzelt's kick and John Panelli recovered at the 30. Panelli outraced a stunned Purdue offense-turned-defense and scored the touchdown, giving the Irish an 18-13 lead. With 3:10 remaining in the third quarter, Oracko missed another extra point.

Leahy, perhaps in a move of desperation, inserted both quarterback Tripucka and sophomore quarterback Bob Williams into the backfield. The attempt to confuse the Boilermakers worked once but the Irish were still forced to punt.

Purdue took over deep in its own territory. DeMoss, throwing from his own end zone, was intercepted again. This time Mike Swistowicz picked off the pass and carried the ball 10 yards to the Purdue 20.

The Boilers dug in and forced the Irish into a fourth-and-five decision from the 15. Leahy went with Oracko even though the kicker had missed three attempts from a better angle and closer range. Oracko came through with a 24-yard field goal, giving the Irish a 21-13 lead and forcing the Boilers into a position in which they had to score twice to win. There was 10:50 left to play.

The Boilers were running out of time and apparently first down yardage when DeMoss was stopped on a pair of plays setting up a third-and-six from their own 38. DeMoss went for the distance and collaborated with Neil Schmidt. Schmidt, who was being covered by Terry Brennan, came down with the ball and was tackled at the Notre Dame 11. The Boilers forced their way to the Irish one, thanks in part to a pair of offside calls on Notre Dame. From the one, DeMoss scored. Trbovich converted, leaving Purdue down 21-20 with 7:30 remaining.

Disregarding a conservative approach, Leahy's Irish came out throwing again despite a one-point lead. The Irish marched downfield for four first downs before Purdue intercepted, a pass on its own seven. Only two and a half minutes remained.

DeMoss, again throwing from his own end zone, let fly with a pass that was batted in the air. Fourth-string tackle Al Zmijewski crossed the path of the ball and intercepted, taking it into the end zone. Zmijewski's touchdown gave the Irish another seven-point margin, 27-20. Oracko converted, leaving the Irish out of reach 28-20.

DeMoss wasn't finished yet, though. He put together a quick drive, connecting on another touchdown pass to Harley Jeffery with just seconds remaining. Without the option of a two-point conversion (a choice that was still 10 years away from becoming part of the rules), the Boilers had only one choice and that was for Trbovich to kick the one-point conversion, leaving the Boilers one point shy of one of the greatest upsets in college football history.

"I said all along that I would settle for a one-point margin," Leahy said. "Purdue has a great team and I'm proud of my team being able to come back."

The loss proved to be devastating to Purdue. The Boilers were shutout the next two games, losing 21-0 to Northwestern and 40-0 to Michigan, the latter being the widest margin of defeat against a conference opponent in Ross-Ade Stadium history. Purdue finished with a 3-6 record, but at least had the feel for what it would take to upset the Irish.

The Irish went into the final game of the 1948 season against Southern Cal with a 9-0 record and a 26-0-1 record through the last three seasons. The Irish needed an 86-yard kickoff return by Bill Gay for a tying touchdown with time running out to salvage a 14-14 decision. Notre Dame's unbeaten streak had reached 28, but a National Championship slipped away that season to Michigan. Notre Dame finished the season ranked second.

As if it were any consolation, Notre Dame could look back on its season opener and know that it had survived Purdue's best shot at an upset.

"It was one of the fiercest opening games in football history," the *Chicago Daily News* reported.

"Purdue at least," wrote Jack Clarke in the *Chicago Sun-Times*, "must be convinced there is more truth than poetry in the words of that famous war chant which reads, 'What though the odds be great or small, old Notre Dame will win over all'."

For Purdue those words were indeed sad and, for the time being, true.

Bob DeMoss, Purdue quarterback. (Photo courtesy of Purdue University)

1949

Sitko Sends Irish To 31st Straight

LAFAYETTE, IND.—The show Frank Leahy's Notre Dame team put on was complete by intermission and 52,000 fans, the largest crowd to that date to ever watch a game in Ross-Ade Stadium, knew they were watching a team of incredible power and talent.

Leahy had voiced open concern about the Irish's lack of depth, but his words were lost on Purdue and its Coach Stu Holcomb. Notre Dame ran long and wild on the way to a 28-0 halftime bulge that couldn't be equalled. A third touchdown gave the Irish a commanding 35-0 lead. Finally, with Notre Dame easing up on the peddle, the Boilers scored twice.

The 35-12 trouncing by the Irish was their 31st straight game without a defeat. Purdue had followed Indiana, a 49-6 loser, and Washington, a 27-7 victim, with little more than a hope and a prayer.

Neither could offset the Irish's outstanding running game headed by Emil (Six-Yard) Sitko. By day's end, Sitko had scored three touchdowns and Howie Roberts wrote the following Monday in the *Chicago Daily News* that "Six-Yard" should have been upgraded to at least "Seven-Yard."

The Irish front line offensively opened holes large enough to transport convoys. The Irish broke no less than eight runs for 20 or more yards.

The Boilers were in the game only at the outset when they drove to the Notre Dame four. One would have thought the Boilers were prepared to capitalize, especially since Holcomb had drilled the team extensively in two areas the week before: 1) not fumbling (the Boilers had fumbled twice against Northwestern and had lost seven of eight to Iowa in a pair of defeats), 2) scoring from inside the opponent's 10-yard line.

The good news is the Boilers didn't fumble away that first drive.

The bad news—you guessed it—the Irish held the Boilers at the four.

Frank Spaniel, the hard-nosed Irish halfback, quickly ran the Irish out of danger with an amazing 55-yard dash down the sidelines. On the next play, Sitko took the Irish the remainder of the distance, 41 yards. Just that quick, Notre Dame had snuffed out a long, tedious Purdue drive and turned it into its own points.

Stunned, but not completely shattered, the Boilers didn't collapse until later.

In the closing moments of the first quarter, the Boilers punted to the Irish 42. Sitko and Larry Coutre then exchanged the honor of running through gaping holes left courtesy of the well-fortified Irish line.

From the Purdue 48, Coutre broke another long gainer for 39 yards to the Boilers' nine. Coutre got the ball again and scooted to the five. Sitko came back to pick up the final five yards and the touchdown early in the second quarter.

A determined Purdue squad drove back into Notre Dame territory. Once at the Notre Dame 33, Norb Adams fulfilled the rest of the bad news for Holcomb—he fumbled. Coutre, Spaniel, junior quarterback Bob Williams and Leon Hart, on his way to becoming the third Notre Dame player in seven years to capture the Heisman Trophy, hammered their way to the Purdue nine.

Once again, Sitko finished the drive.

Sitko's final touchdown of the day was perhaps the prettiest. Williams rolled out and began running with the ball. When the right end came up to make the tackle. Williams lateralled to Sitko. It was the 1949 version of the option play. As was the case this afternoon, the Irish left the Boiler with no option.

Prior to Sitko's final touchdown, the Boilers tried to resort to an air attack after falling behind 21-0. Purdue quarterback Ken Gorgal discovered that the Notre Dame pass defense was at least paramount to their offense. Bill Gay picked off a Gorgal pass deep inside Notre Dame territory and returned it 61 yards for a touchdown.

The final Irish touchdown came thanks to another interception. Again, the Boilers were deep in Notre Dame territory. Gorgal's pass was picked off by Tommy Helwig at the 18. Helwig returned it to the Purdue 46. Williams, who only threw four passes, completed his only toss of the day, a 12-yarder to Jim Mutscheller. Jack Landry and Billy Barrett, a pair of Irish reserves, carried to the six before Barrett went over for the final touchdown. Steve Oracko kicked his fifth.

If Williams wasn't hurting the Boilers enough with his astute play calling and execution, he was killing Purdue with his punting. He punted five times for an average of 48.4 yards a kick. One of his kicks went out of bounds on the Purdue 16, another on the seven and a third on the two.

The Boilers, who nearly outrushed the Irish 398-395, broke the shutout in the final quarter. John Kerestes, who would have his say one year later, scored from the five and Harry (Hurricane) Szulborski climaxed a 98-yard drive with a 15-yard run for a touchdown. The long drive was highlighted by a 31-yard run with a fake punt by Bill Skowron, who later went on to star with the New York Yankees and Chicago White Sox.

The Boilers were playing in an enlarged Ross-Ade Stadium that season. The added fans did nothing positive for the Boilers, however. They finishe I with a 1-3 record at home. Overall, Holcomb's team went 4-5, an improvement over the 3-6 record of the 1948 team.

Leahy's Irish were still riding the crest of an incredible unbeaten string. The Irish had quite a team that season. Besides Hart winning the Heisman Trophy, Williams finished fifth in the voting and Sitko sixth. By the time the Irish played and beat Southern Cal 32-0, the writers and sportscasters were calling "Six-Yard" Sitko, "Eight-Yard" Sitko. How good was Emil Sitko?

Consider that there are only three other Notre Dame football players who bettered his 2,226 yards gained. Those three are Vegas Ferguson, Jerome Heavens and George Gipp. Sitko is the only running back in Notre Dame history to lead the team in rushing four seasons.

In 1949, he also paced the team in scoring with 54 points. It was the second straight season he led the team in scoring. Along with captain Jim Martin, Sitko was named to the All-America team. Barrett also scored 54 points in 1949.

Williams passed for 16 touchdowns, the most any quarterback has thrown at Notre Dame. He also passed for 1,347 yards, the most to that date of any Notre Dame quarterback.

The Boilers also had nothing to be ashamed of even in defeat. Notre Dame would go on to complete another undefeated season and wrap up its third National Championship in four years. Its unbeaten streak had risen to an unprecedented 38.

Purdue could always look to next year. For the first time in a few years Notre Dame rivals would catch a partial break—the Irish were graduating 10 starters and 10 reserves.

Purdue ultimately did a lot more than just look to next year.

The upset quarterback—Dale Samuels. (Photo courtesy of Purdue University)

1950
Upset

NOTRE DAME, IND.—Perhaps the greatest day in Purdue football history was October 7, 1950. It was the day when Notre Dame's 39-game unbeaten streak, the longest of its glorified history, came to pass. It was the day 5-9, 160-pound Dale Samuels captured the spirit of America with his passing and execution. It was the day Purdue beat Notre Dame 28-14.

Whenever and wherever the Notre Dame-Purdue rivalry is recalled, the 1950 meeting is the one the historians use to mark time with.

In the four seasons prior to 1950, Notre Dame Coach Frank Leahy had produced three National Championship teams. Since losing to Great Lakes 39-7 on December 1, 1945, the Irish had not suffered defeat. Midway through the 1946 season Army had tied Notre Dame 0-0, due in part to the wizardry of an Army assistant coach—Stuart K. Holcomb. The Irish won 21 straight before being tied by Southern Cal 14-14 in the final game of the 1948 season. The Irish stormed through 1949 in unbeaten and untied fashion. Notre Dame was simply tremendous. During the 39 games preceding the second game of the 1950 season, Notre Dame had outscored the opposition 1,256 to 262 or a per game average of 32-6.

Then came Purdue.

It would be unjust to consider Leahy's 1950 team on a par with his previous Notre Dame teams. Graduation had depleted the ranks noticeably. Most of his backfield and all of his offensive line had graduated. Notre Dame's depth was very suspect. The freshman class was considered one of the weakest in decades.

Notre Dame would finish with a 4-4-1 record. Purdue, amazingly enough, won only one other game that season, finishing with a 2-7 mark, ultimately one of its worst seasons in history. Except for October 7 that is.

While it is right to set the record straight, it is also necessary to honor and praise Purdue, for it was the Boilermakers who would write *finis* to one of college football's greatest chapters.

A mist lingered over Notre Dame Stadium that afternoon, pressing against the stained glass of Sacred Heart Church and caressing the 56,748 fans who came to witness history.

In the previous 39 Notre Dame games you could count the close calls on one hand. The tie games could have gone either way—0-0 to Army in 1946 and 14-14 against Southern Cal in 1948. Northwestern had threatened to end the streak twice, losing 26-19 in 1947 and 12-7 in 1949. The other close call belonged to Purdue which dropped a 28-27 decision in 1948.

In the week prior to the Purdue game, Leahy was sensing the end of the streak. "When Notre Dame's streak is stopped, I have only one hope. That is, that the team that does it will be a team with which we have had fine relations over a period of years."

In the 22nd meeting of the two schools, that is just how it worked out.

With destiny entrenched in Purdue's corner, the Boilers began the drive to an upset. Early in the game Samuels directed a Purdue drive that stalled at the Notre Dame one.

While missing a chance to gain an early lead, Purdue did come back to score on its next possession. The drive began at Purdue's 26. With fullback John Kerestes leading the way, the Boilers moved to midfield.

Samuels hit Mike Maccioli and Bernie Flowers with passes before Neil Schmidt broke loose for 18 yards to the Notre Dame 32. Samuels went back to Schmidt again. With Schmidt trying to make the catch at the Notre Dame two, an Irish player was called for pass interference, giving Purdue the ball at the two. Kerestes went over for the first touchdown. Samuels kicked the extra point with less than two minutes remaining.

It was Schmidt, Samuels and Kerestes that were also responsible for the second Purdue touchdown.

In the second quarter, Samuels directed Purdue inside Notre Dame territory. From the 42, Samuels and Schmidt hooked up for 36 yards to the Notre Dame six. Two plays later, Kerestes carried for the touchdown.

Notre Dame began to try a comeback. The Irish made it out to the Purdue 45 but were forced to give up the ball because of a reception by an illegal receiver. From there Purdue began a third touchdown drive.

Kerestes and Schmidt brought the Boilers to the Notre Dame 30. With 65 seconds left in the half, Samuels went deep to Schmidt for the touchdown.

Purdue had a 21-0 halftime lead. It had outrushed the Irish 128-115 and Samuels had passed for 104 yards compared to All-America quarterback Bob Williams who had completed only four of 13 passes for 24 yards and two interceptions.

The Notre Dame locker room at halftime was quiet. Frank Leahy searched for something to say.

"This is the first time I've ever talked to a team behind 21-0," he told his players.

He concluded by saying, "If you can come back you will probably be remembered as the greatest fighting team in Notre Dame's colorful gridiron history."

Notre Dame did return a different team. The fire was in their eyes, but it was already too late. There was no way they could persuade defeat to leave them be.

"We were still pretty confident," co-captain Kerestes said, "But the second half was rough. Notre Dame was a different team. The middle of their line was tough."

Notre Dame took advantage of a Purdue fumble to break the shutout early in the third quarter. Dick Cotter recovered at the Purdue 12. Bill Barrett and William Gay carried to the three. Williams then threw a three-yard pass to Jim Mutscheller, cutting the deficit to 21-7.

Notre Dame had capitalized. Purdue was now faced with a crucial series. If Purdue couldn't prove that it had more left than the Irish, the Boilers would be doomed.

The Boilers drove long and hard and reached the Notre Dame two. At that point, the Boilers fell short. Notre Dame took over. A roughness penalty against Purdue and a 33-yard gain by Barrett were the key plays leading Notre Dame to the Purdue 22. John Petitbon and Jack Landry brought the Irish to the 10 before the third quarter expired.

Just 15 minutes remained.

On the opening play of the final quarter, Petitbon raced the 10 yards for the second Notre Dame touchdown. Joe Caprara converted his second extra point.

The pressure now rested squarely with the sophomore Samuels and Purdue. Notre Dame was reaching down as deep as it could. It was now Samuels' turn to prove Purdue's persistence.

Samuels moved Purdue out to the 44 behind the rushing of Kerestes and Maccioli. With a first down at the 44, Samuels tried going to the air.

His first pass was incomplete. His second pass was incomplete. With a third-and-10, he dropped back again. He found Macciioli behind the Notre Dame defense. Maccioli, who was a questionable starter earlier in the week, made the reception and sprinted 56 yards for the final touchdown. Samuels' conversion put Purdue back in front by 14 points, 28-14.

With Leahy's halftime words still in mind, Notre Dame came right back looking for its third touchdown. Williams led Notre Dame deep into Purdue territory quickly.

The final blow to the Irish came with 10 minutes to play. Jack Landry was busting in at the Purdue 16 when he fumbled. Schmidt, one of the heroes on offense, pounced on the loose ball.

It was over.

As the mist developed into a steady drizzle the final gun sounded. The Streak was history. The Boilers were victorious. And a nation wanted to know how it had come about.

In the *Minneapolis Tribune* Bernie Swanson wrote, "Anything can happen. It did here Saturday afternoon as Purdue's gallant band of swashbuckling youngsters ended a gridiron Notre Dame sage with a smashing 28-14 victory under skies as bleak as the Fightin' Irish's dashed hopes."

Arch Ward, writing in the *Chicago Tribune's Wake of the News*, wrote, "Their (Purdue's) courage in playing Notre Dame year after year paid rich dividends. Purdue may carry on to the Big Ten championship but, come what may, it will be remembered as the team that whipped Notre Dame, an achievement none of the latter's 39 previous opponents had been able to say."

Moments after the game ended the Notre Dame Stadium turf was taken over by the Purdue band. While the band played, "Hail, Hail to Old Purdue," the Boilermaker fans did a snake dance across the field.

In the Purdue locker room, Holcomb was telling an array of reporters what pre-game doubts he had washed away.

"For once we had the squad speed necessary to worry Notre Dame at more than one or two spots," he said. "Then our squad came up remarkably fast for the game after our tough early test down in Texas (a 34-26 loss). The furious spirit was heart-warming and the boys supported our new quarterback right up to the hilt. Dale Samuels directed this zeal and speed into the right channels.

"Our coaching staff had confidence in Samuels being able to do this. We have studied Notre Dame habits for years and they have concentrated on ours. Always our offense was much stronger, both passing and running, to the right than to the left. The same situation prevailed at Texas. We felt that Notre Dame defensive plans would consider this fact. Therefore, we banked heavily on plays to the left, hoping to find weaknesses in the defense. Passes to Mike Maccioli, our injured left halfback who couldn't play against Texas, and runs by Neil Schmidt were in order."

"I didn't think we could do it," Holcomb said. "I just hoped."

"We could have licked the whole state of Texas today," Samuels said. "The whole week long I had a feeling we were going to win. We were up for this game."

The *Purdue Exponent* filled no fewer than eight pages with the quotes of the heroes:

"Ever since I was a kid all I ever heard was Notre Dame, Notre Dame, Notre Dame," said fullback Norman Montgomery. "And I have always wanted to be on a team that played Notre Dame, much less beat them. I don't think I've ever been so happy in my life."

"It is the greatest thing that ever happened," said end Leo Sugar. "I always wanted to play for them or beat them."

"We should have done it in 1948," said Neil Schmidt. "But now we have done it. I had the feeling we could do it today. So did everyone else." Schmidt, who wore No. 40, rushed for 80 yards, caught one pass for a touchdown and two other passes that set up touchdowns. He had been the Purdue hero in the 28-27 loss in 1948. He suffered a knee injury in that game that made him useless the remainder of the season and for most of 1949.

"One of the reasons I came to Purdue," halfback Phil Klezek said, "was to play on a team that would beat Notre Dame."

"I've hated Notre Dame for 21 years," said Lafayette's Dick Schnaible, the backup quarterback. "I've waited four years to beat them. Those were four long years, but we finally made it."

The Purdue celebration continued long past the weekend. On Monday morning with 6,000 students filling the Hall of Music, Purdue President Frederick L. Houde, a former Minnesota quarterback, said, "Officially the university is in session. Unofficially, it is yours."

The parade in Lafayette swung down Columbus Street and up Main. The students and Purdue fans were wearing black and gold tags proclaiming "40-Never."

In the quiet of the Notre Dame locker room, Leahy was absorbing his worst defeat as Notre Dame coach. The cold drizzle was still falling outside as Leahy addressed his players following a defeat for the first time in nearly five years.

"Men," Leahy said, "a lot of people will be watching to see how we take this adversity. It's a test of real men to be able to lose like champions . . . If we had to lose, I am glad it was to a time-honored opponent like Purdue. That Purdue team was great. They didn't make any mistakes. We were outcoached and outplayed, but not outfought."

The defeat was only the fourth under Leahy. It was also Purdue's first victory over Notre Dame since 1933. Besides being the first loss since 1945, it was also the first loss in Notre Dame Stadium since 1942.

"What is there I can say?" asked quarterback Bob Williams, the only returning starter from the 1949 National Champions. "What is there to say?"

"It was bound to come," said Notre Dame athletic director Ed "Moose" Krause, who had begun negotiations with Purdue on a 10-year contract the evening before. "We can't win them all."

"We'll always play Notre Dame," Purdue athletic director "Red" Mackey had said a couple days earlier. "If we don't play them, we can't beat them and the day is coming when we will beat them."

"And now," Krause continued, "he is right."

The Notre Dame locker room remained silent except for the hissing of the showers.

1951
Revenge

NOTRE DAME, IND.—In the history of the Notre Dame-Purdue rivalry, there was no game that dictated as much need for revenge as the 1951 encounter.

The rivalry had been one-sided in Notre Dame's favor for most of the first 20 games. The Irish had a commanding 15-4-1 lead prior to the 1950 game. The meeting of the teams was a rivalry only in the sense that both teams were from Indiana and one team had constantly rubbed the other's nose in the dirt.

After 1950, all had changed and this game would be the first true glimpse of a rivalry suddenly burning anew.

There were nine starting members, five from Purdue, who had taken part in history the year before. Ends Bernie Flowers and Darrell Brewster, guard Joe Skibinski, center Clint Knitz and, of course, the quarterback Dale Samuels returned for Purdue. Skibinski pulled a groin muscle during the pre-game warm-up and was lost for the afternoon.

The Irish starters who had played major roles a year earlier were ends Jim Mutscheller and Chet Ostrowski along with halfbacks John Petitbon and Bill Barrett.

As if the Irish needed an historical parallel to remind them of what happened a year earlier, on the eve of the game, Rocco Marchegiano, better known as Rocky Marciano, KO'ed the great Joe Louis in the eighth round of a fight at New York's Madison Square Garden. Louis, at 37½ years old, was finished. Notre Dame, another great champion, would prove that it wasn't.

After a scoreless first period, Notre Dame set sail to a rousing 30-9 victory over Purdue.

The momentum swayed back and forth in the early going. The ball changed hands eight times before Notre Dame could mount a successful offensive.

Taking possession at the Notre Dame 25, Neil Worden and Barrett rambled through the Boilers' nine-man defensive line to the enemy 36. Freshman Paul Reynolds bolted loose for 14 yards to the 22 and followed with a five-yard spurt to the 17. Quarterback John Mazur passed to Ostrowski at the nine, giving Notre Dame a first down. Reynolds carried twice and Worden once. On Reynolds' second carry from three yards out, he scored. He had accounted for 50 of the 75 yards traveled.

As prepared as the Irish were for a return meeting in front of many of the same 57,800 Notre Dame Stadium fans who had witnessed the upset of a year earlier, the Irish couldn't have been ready for Purdue's return.

Notre Dame Heisman Trophy winner Johnny Lattner. (Photo courtesy of Notre Dame University)

Purdue recovered a Neil Worden fumble and began a drive that stalled at the Irish 34-yard line. Kicker Jim Reichert didn't let the Boilers' drive go for naught. He kicked a 41-yard field goal, cutting the Irish lead to 7-3.

Seconds later, Notre Dame fumbled again. This time it was Reynolds who lost possession. Once again, the Boilers turned the miscue into points. Samuels fired a 43-yard touchdown pass to Darrell Brewster, giving Purdue a 9-7 lead. Samuels' point after attempt failed.

Purdue had an unexpected chance to stifle the once fired-up Irish. But John Petitbon, who had been beaten a minute earlier on the touchdown pass, returned the kickoff to the 32.

On third down, Mazur, who would finish the day leading scoring drives of 75, 68, 66, 42 and 44 yards, connected with Barrett for 50 yards down to the Purdue 12. The drive stalled but not before Minel Mavraides kicked a 16-yard field goal, giving the Irish a 10-9 lead and putting the momentum squarely in the middle.

Notre Dame didn't know it at the moment, but it was home free. It would erupt for 23 second-half points while holding Purdue scoreless.

The Boilers would stage one final attempt at pulling out another upset. Samuels led Purdue to the Irish 43. Samuels was looking to go deep and did. Notre Dame linebacker Dan Shannon intercepted at the Irish 26. It was that play that launched the next Notre Dame touchdown drive.

Six minutes after grabbing a one-point lead, Johnny Lattner ripped through the Boilers' line on a fourth-and-one from the 39. The future Heisman Trophy winner and two-time All-America went 39 yards for the score. Mavraides' conversion gave the Irish an eight-point lead, forcing the Boilers to score at least twice to regain the lead.

With a 23-9 lead, Barrett continued the scoring from the one and Mazur finished off the Boilers with an eight-yard toss to Mutscheller.

"I've no complaint," Purdue Coach Stu Holcomb told Harry Monahan of the *South Bend Tribune*. "My boys played their best. They were a threat every minute and never gave up."

The Boilers were forced to play three new backs. John Durham, Max Schmaling and Jim Whitmer were seeing their first action after the usual starters were besieged with injuries.

Across the way from the Purdue locker room, the Notre Dame players were in a state of jubilation.

"It was our best game of the season," said athletic director and former All-America Ed "Moose" Krause.

"Yeah, I thought so, too," Irish Coach Frank Leahy said.

"We had to play our best to beat Purdue. That was a good Purdue team and this was a typical Purdue-Notre Dame game with a lot of contact. I was surprised by the margin of victory. but if Purdue had been at full strength it could have been easily a lot closer."

"We did the best we could with what we had," Holcomb said. "We just don't have one of those backs that we can shake loose for that quick touchdown. You have to have one in a game like this."

Phil Klezek would have matched Holcomb's description, but he was also one of the Boilers in sickbay.

At that point in the Purdue season, it looked as if the Boilers were in for a dismal year. However, they rallied from a 1-4 start to win their last four games and finished on the upbeat with a 5-4 record.

Leahy's Irish rebounded from the mediocre 4-4-1 record of 1950 to finish 7-2-1, following a 5-1 start. Three games and two victories after beating Purdue, Notre Dame won its 400th game by defeating North Carolina 12-7.

No doubt win No. 398 was also highly thought of that season. While a reborn rivalry had no doubt been sprung the year before, the Irish made certain they returned to the top as soon as the opportunity was available.

1952

Fumbles Humble Purdue

LAFAYETTE, IND.—For once, it was time for Notre Dame to stomp out a Purdue winning streak. The Boilers had put together an impressive seven-game unbeaten streak since losing 30-9 to the Irish the year before.

Primed and ready to make it eight, Purdue Coach Stu Holcomb went on record in the days prior to the game proclaiming that diminutive senior quarterback Dale Samuels was without equal.

"There isn't a better quarterback in college football than our little Dale," Holcomb told the *Chicago Daily News*.

No doubt, Holcomb had his evidence. Best remembered for leading the upset over the Irish two years earlier, snapping Notre Dame's 39-game winning streak, Samuels had passed for 2,342 yards, 20 touchdowns in completing 188 of 292 passes through the first 21 games of his collegiate career.

If, indeed, there were doubters among the 49,000 fans that failed to fill Ross-Ade Stadium this particular afternoon, Samuels didn't exactly convince his detracters any.

The Boilers not only dropped a 26-14 decision, they also spent the afternoon dropping the football. The Boilers fumbled 11 times, including two by Samuels, and Notre Dame recovered eight. On two occasions, the Irish turned the recoveries into points. Ironically, the Irish had recovered eight of its opposition's 11 fumbles coming into the game.

Notre Dame also had its troubles. The Irish fumbled 10 times, but lost only three. Notre Dame did, however, also give up four interceptions, bringing the turnover total a little closer to Purdue's.

What this game was was an advertisement for footballs with handles.

As the *Chicago Daily News* report so aptly penned, "Stu Holcomb will conduct an intensive course this week in 'The Football and How to Hold on to it'."

Besides Samuels losing two, fullback Max Schmaling fumbled four times, losing two in scoring territory and Rex Brock had the dubious distinction of fumbling away Purdue's first possession of each half. Back-up quarterback Roy Evans and safety Phil Mateja also fumbled for the Boilers.

Brock fumbled the opening kickoff, setting the Irish up at the Boilers 24. Jackie Lee recovered. Four plays later, Notre Dame's Joe Heap fumbled at the four-yard line. The ball squirted into the end zone where Joe Bush recovered for the Irish touchdown. It would be that kind of game.

Following Metaja's first of two interceptions, Samuels, who would complete only five of 16 passes thanks to Notre Dame's non-stop pass rush, found end Bernie Flowers on a 27-yard touchdown play tying the game at seven.

Still in the first quarter, the Irish drove inside the Boilers' 10-yard line. Twice inside the five, the Irish shifted into their box formation and twice the Boilers jumped offside. Finally, from the two-yard line Neil Worden scored, giving Notre Dame a 14-7 lead following the second PAT by Menil Mavraides.

Deep into the second quarter Mateja, who would go on to set a Purdue interception record that season with seven, came down with a Ralph Guglielmi pass. Mateja's record stood until 1979 when Bill Kay matched it.

Not only fame was fleeting, however, for Mateja. The ball was also skirting away. He fumbled and Notre Dame regained possession. With a second left in the half, Guglielmi rifled a 41-yard pass to Johnny Lattner for another touchdown.

Purdue was crushed. The Irish had turned out twice the offensive plays (50-25) and had managed to turn a potential momentum stealer into six points of their own.

Brock opened the second half, the same way he opened the game. He fumbled and Notre Dame's Dave Flood recovered at the Purdue 23. Luckily for the Boilers, Mavraiders' field goal attempt was wide.

After a scoreless third quarter, the Boilers caught a break when Notre Dame's back-up quarterback Tom Carey fumbled at his own 35. Evans, who played the last 20 minutes after Samuels had fumbled for the second time, needed only two plays to jump on the opportunity. On second down, he combined with Flowers for a 32-yard touchdown pass. Samuels' extra point attempt narrowed the Irish lead to six, 20-14.

Suddenly, all the Purdue fumbles seemed to be washed away. The Boilers defense came on. On a second down play, the Boilers threw Johnny Lattner, on his way to his first All-America season, for a huge loss, resulting in a third-and-15 situation. Carey, who played behind Guglielmi most of the season, came up with the biggest play of the second half. Down the sidelines he found Art Hunter for 41 yards. The play not only killed the Boilers' defensive purge, but also set up Worden's second and final touchdown of the afternoon with 3:10 remaining.

The Irish, who had come off a loss to Pittsburgh, finished the season with a 7-2-1 record after a 1-1-1 beginning. Leahy, who had privately said that 1952 could have been one of the worst seasons, had his fears overturned.

One of the reasons for Leahy's apprehension was the schedule Notre Dame was playing. When it was over the Irish had defeated four conference champions, including Purdue whichshared the Big Ten crown with a 4-1-1 conference mark.

The Boilers finished with a 4-3-2 record overall.

Samuels, a pre-season choice to complete his days at Purdue as an All-America player, didn't make it to that lofty standard of greatness. He left Lafayette with credentials unmatched by any previous Purdue quarterback.

He had a career total of 260 completions, 517 attempts and 3,154 yards. The yardage total still ranks fifth in Purdue history through the 1982 season, another standard of greatness that has been surpassed by only a few of Purdue's truly outstanding quarterbacks.

Samuels' passing did have one more benefit to it in 1952. Bernie Flowers caught a team-high 43 passes, a mark that stood until Bob Hadrick caught 47 in 1965. Flowers also scored seven touchdowns and earned All-America honors. Without Samuels, Flowers' All-America award may have never materialized.

The great Notre Dame backfield of (L-R) Ralph Guglielmi (quarterback), Johnny Lattner (right halfback), Paul Reynolds (left halfback) and Neil Worden (fullback). (Photo courtesy of Notre Dame University)

1953

Leahy Leaves A Legacy

WEST LAFAYETTE, IND.—Frank Leahy coached Notre Dame 11 seasons and in this, his last, the Irish were reaching a peak. He would later call the 1953 Notre Dame squad the most talented Irish team he had the privilege of coaching. It was quite a statement from a man of intense, Irish pride who patterned himself and his methods as close to Knute Rockne as possible.

But then again, it was quite a team also.

Purdue was struggling in the wake of the graduation of quarterback Dale Samuels. Coach Stu Holcomb's crew could have done better by not showing up against Leahy's fired-up Irish.

Notre Dame destroyed Purdue 33-7, the biggest margin of victory in the series since the 1946 game in which Notre Dame bombed Purdue 49-6.

Many pre-season experts called the Notre Dame backfield a corps of All-Americas. There were no weak links, just leaders and outstanding players. Quarterback Ralph Guglielmi was on his way to the all-time statistic leadership among Notre Dame quarterbacks. Guglielmi still ranks fifth on the all-time list. Right halfback Johnny Lattner was on his way to the Heisman Trophy, the fourth in Notre Dame football history. Left halfback Joe Heap led the team with 22 receptions for 335 yards. Fullback Neil Worden paced Notre Dame with 11 touchdowns and 859 yards rushing.

One Notre Dame historian went as far as to claim that this backfield was the equal, if not better than, the famed "Four Horsemen" of the

Rockne era. It was another example of poetry in motion.

On this steamy day at Ross-Ade Stadium a capacity crowd of 49,135 gathered to watch one of the best Notre Dame teams in history take another step toward an undefeated season as well as the ending of an era.

Just two plays after the Irish had taken a 3-0 lead on Minnie Mavraides' 29-yard field, Notre Dame got back into position to add to the lead. Max Schmaling fumbled for Purdue and Heap recovered at the Boilers' 29. Heap carried on first down for four yards. Guglielmi went to Lattner for 14. Worden went the final 11 for the touchdown.

With the Irish's second team in possession moments later, Dick Fitzgerald went around the right end, reversed his field and carried 46 yards to the Boilers' nine. Only an Irish penalty and fumble kept Purdue from falling further behind.

The lone success enjoyed by Purdue came shortly thereafter. Quarterback Roy Evans connected with end John Kerr for a 75-yard scoring strike. Notre Dame would get its victory, but not a shutout. The touchdown toss kept the Boilers from suffering their first shutout of the series since 1939.

The Irish still led 10-7. Following the Purdue touchdown, it would have been natural had the momentum shifted. Lattner made certain that it didn't. On the ensuing kickoff Lattner fielded the ball at the 14 and set off on an 86-yard touchdown run.

On Purdue's next possession, Notre Dame's back-up quarterback/safety, Tom Carey, picked off the first of his two interceptions.

Again with Leahy's second team in, Dick Washington rambled 32 yards for the third Notre Dame touchdown of the first half, giving the Irish a 23-7 lead.

In the third quarter, both teams exchanged fumbles, giving Purdue the ball at its 18. Schmaling broke loose for 45 yards to the Irish 37. Evans then connected with Rex Brock for an apparent touchdown. A holding penalty nullified the score and put the Boilers back at their 48.

On the play following the holding call, disaster again struck Purdue. Evans fumbled and Don Penza recovered at the 42. Guglielmi, who combined with Heap for three receptions, found his multi-talented running back for 31 yards. Lattner went six yards, bringing the ball to the five. At that point, Guglielmi called his own number and scored from five yards out on a quarterback sneak.

With more than four minutes remaining in the third quarter, the Irish would put the finishing touches on the Boilers. Eddie Neves' punt traveled meekly to the Purdue 17, giving Notre Dame excellent field position again.

Guglielmi threw seven yards to left end Dan Shannon. After two plays failed to gain, Guglielmi handed off to Worden who bolted the 10 yards

Paul Hornung, right, with Coach Frank Leahy and right halfback Sherrill Sipes. (Photo courtesy of Notre Dame University)

for the touchdown. Mavraides, who had begun the point deluge with his field goal, finished it with his extra point conversion.

Leahy went with his second team from that point on, giving his prized backfield a respite. Purdue could still only manage one other first down the remainder of the game.

The big plays for the Irish according to Leahy were Lattner's 86-yard kickoff return for the touchdown and the holding penalty that cost Purdue a second touchdown.

Holcomb's Boilers would go on to win only two games while losing seven. The Irish would finish off the Leahy legacy with a 9-0-1 record, the great leader's sixth undefeated season.

While the National Championship that season went to Maryland and Coach Jim Tatum, the Irish did finish second in the polls. Lattner was selected as a concensus All-America for the second straight season along with tackle Al Hunter and end Don Penza. Lattner, as previously mentioned, also won the Heisman that season.

Leahy's health continued to fail and ultimately forced his retirement following the season. Just three weeks after beating the Boilers, the Irish were in the process of ending Georgia Tech's 32-game unbeaten streak when Leahy was rushed to the hospital at halftime. It was feared he had suffered a heart attack. The halftime pep talk turned into an emotional prayer vigil.

Leahy was given the last rites of the Catholic Church that afternoon by Father Joyce. Prior to his death, Leahy was reportedly given last rites more than 20 times.

On January 31, 1954, Frank Leahy, only 45 years old but suffering with ileitis, stepped aside as the Notre Dame football coach. He remained a vocal influence, however, in the years that followed.

On February 1, 1954, Terry Brennan, a former player under Leahy, was selected to lead the Irish.

The baton had been passed.

Another great era had flickered out.

Section V
1954-1969

*Purdue Throws
Notre Dame For
Loss After Loss*

What the 16-game stretch from 1954 through 1969 reflected was the shocking realization that Purdue could indeed dominate an era and that Notre Dame could struggle.

There was Purdue Coach Jack Mollenkopf leading the Boilers to six victories in eight games beginning in 1956. There was the 1967 game matching National Champion Notre Dame and Big Ten and Rose Bowl Champion Purdue. In 1968, Notre Dame was ranked No. 1 by one poll and Purdue was selected for the top spot in the other.

In both cases, Purdue throttled Notre Dame behind Mike Phipps.

In 1969, Phipps completed the three-year sweep of Notre Dame that put him head and shoulders above any quarterback that ever dueled the Irish.

For Notre Dame there was embarrassment and humilation. Nothing so illustrates the plight of Notre Dame as the 1960 game. Purdue scored 31 points in a 10:52 second-quarter stretch on the way to a 51-19 victory. The loss did more than shake down a little Irish thunder.

While Purdue was enjoying its success, Notre Dame was churning in turmoil.

Its coaching situation turned into a shambles. First, Terry Brennan replaced Frank Leahy. For five years the young and brilliant Brennan toiled in the shadow and within critical earshot of Leahy.

Following Brennan was Joe Kuharich, the only coach in Notre Dame history to lose more games than he won. After four years, Kuharich was replaced by Hugh Devore. Devore served for one season before the arrival of Ara Parseghian. The arrival of Ara led to the revival of Notre Dame.

There were many great match-ups and outstanding combinations during the 16-game span. In 1954 and 1955, Len Dawson of Purdue and Notre Dame's Paul Hornung met head on. Dawson and Hornung both went on to great careers in the professional ranks.

In 1964, Notre Dame had the great passing combination of John Huarte and Jack Snow. Two years later, it was Terry Hanratty and Jim Seymour.

Following the Dawson years, Purdue produced quarterbacks Ron DiGravio, Bob Griese and Phipps. Dawson, Griese and Phipps all had outstanding pro careers, as did running back Leroy Keyes.

In 1957 the series took on additional merit with the introduction of the Shillelagh Trophy.

By winning 11 of the 16 games, Purdue closed the gap. After 40 games, Notre Dame had a 22-16-2 edge. It was truly a grand era for Purdue.

1954

Soph Dawson
Jinxs Notre Dame

NOTRE DAME, IND.—If there was anything unsettling for a visiting sophomore quarterback playing in front of 58,256 leather-lunged Irish backers in Notre Dame Stadium, then somebody forgot to tell Purdue quarterback Len Dawson what it was.

The only unsettling Dawson did was of the Notre Dame defense. He completed four of his first six passes for 92 yards, leading the Boilers to a 14-8 halftime lead and finally to a 27-14 upset over the No. 1 ranked Irish.

The loss was the Irish's first in 14 games and also the first for 25-year old Coach Terry Brennan. Another era in Notre Dame football was beginning.

The footprints Brennan stood in that day at Notre Dame Stadium belonged to Frank Leahy, who had resigned begrudgingly on January 31, 1954. Brennan was named the next day to replace a man he had played halfback for only seven years earlier. He was replacing the closest thing Notre Dame had to another Rockne. Only the great Rockne had a better winning percentage at Notre Dame than Leahy and the margin wasn't much (.897-.887).

Brennan was the choice of Father Theodore Hesburgh, who in 1947 had taught Brennan philosophy. Brennan won out over Bill Earley and former All-America Johnny Lujack, both assistants to Leahy. Lujack had wanted to succeed Leahy but the argument was that he was just a seasonal coach. His other interests included an insurance agency and a sporting goods company.

The man who would lead the Irish on would be Terry Brennan. But in this, his second game as the Irish coach, it would be sophomore Len Dawson that would send the Irish to disaster.

A week earlier, Dawson had thrown for four touchdown passes against Missouri, leading the Boilers to a 31-0 rout. Knowing that, the Irish geared for a deluge against its pass defense.

All Dawson could accomplish against the Irish was four more touchdown passes despite only completing seven of 12 passes. It wasn't the quantity that mattered. It was the quality and Dawson with four touchdown passes and 216 yards (30 yards per catch) was Grade A.

Purdue's Len Dawson. (Photo courtesy of Purdue University)

Notre Dame gave Dawson his first opportunity almost immediately after Jim Peters recovered a Don Schaefer fumble on the Irish 34. It occurred on the first play from scrimmage.

Moments later Purdue held a 7-0 lead. Boiler fullback Bill Murakowski barreled through for eight yards on first down. Dawson went to the air for the first time. He connected with Bob (Choo-Choo) Springer for 20 yards. From the six, Dawson threw over the head of defender Jim Morse and into the arms of end John Kerr. Dawson finished the damage with the first of his three extra point conversions.

On the Boilers next possession, following a shanked 21-yard punt by Ralph Guglielmi, Dawson threw 41 yards to Rex Brock for the second Boilermaker touchdown.

To make matters potentially worse, Dawson picked off a Guglielmi pass in the second quarter. He led the Boilers 50 yards to the Irish one. It was there that Jackie Lee stopped a possible rout by recovering Murakowski's fumble.

The Irish offense, despite the presence of another promising sophomore quarterback, Paul Hornung, couldn't budge the Purdue defense. Finally, Notre Dame caught a break when Purdue center Don Fife snapped the ball over punter Rex Brock's head. Sam Palumbo and Ray Lemek caught up with Brock before he could escape the end zone. It wasn't pretty, but the Irish had themselves two points.

On the ensuing free kick, Hornung was finally able to move the Irish. He did most of it himself, carrying 59 yards to the Boilers one. Nick Raich carried from the one but Hornung's kick was wide. Purdue still led 14-8 at halftime.

Notre Dame continued its effort to change the momentum. On its first possession of the second half, senior quarterback Guglielmi moved the Irish to the Purdue 43. A 41-yard reception by co-captain Dan Shannon set up Schaefer for a two-yard touchdown, tying the score. Again, the conversion failed.

Suddenly, the Irish were right back in the game. Or were they?

Just as suddenly, Purdue regained possession after the kickoff 73 yards from the end zone. On the first play, Dawson found sophomore Lamar Lundy. The 6-7 end lumbered 73 yards for the touchdown, out-racing two Notre Dame defenders. Dawson's kick gave the Boilers back a seven-point lead.

The Irish had one last opportunity to come back. After leading the Irish 50 yards to the Purdue 26, Guglielmi fumbled. After each team exchanged punts, Dawson went to the air again with the typical results.

After six straight running plays and a 10-yard completion put the ball on the Notre Dame 38, Dawson set the Irish up for a screen pass.

With the Notre Dame line rushing frantically, he laid a pass off to Murakowski. Murakowski was gone and so were the Irish hopes. Dawson missed the extra point, the first challenge he had missed all afternoon.

"That Dawson," Brennan said, "should be pretty tough in the Big Ten. He's a fine quarterback and the Purdue line was just as tough as Texas' (a 21-0 victim of Notre Dame in Brennan's opening game a week earlier), except quicker."

"If we're going to do well," Brennan said, "We're going to have to come up with some depth. Right now we don't have it."

Purdue had the depth, but Coach Stu Holcomb, who had enjoyed his finest moment four years earlier in the same stadium against the Irish, wasn't sure what to make of his young, but prone-to-be-sensational Boilers.

"I'm reserving judgment," Holcomb said, "I can't believe this team is that good. But if this isn't a test than there is no test," he told the *Chicago Daily News*.

"Dawson was great, our line was tremendous. We should be No. 1 in the nation now. Notre Dame was No. 1 last week.

"Seriously, I suppose we'll be in the Top Ten."

Dawson, who in his first two collegiate games had completed 18 of 29 passes for 401 yards and eight touchdowns, finished the season with 87 completions in 167 attempts and 15 touchdown passes. While it was his best collegiate season as far as touchdown passes were concerned, it was his poorest in terms of pass completion percentage even though it was a mighty impressive .521.

The Boilers went on to a 5-3-1 record but Holcomb nearly got his wish the week following the Notre Dame victory. United Press International had the Boilers ranked third, the Irish ninth. The Associated Press had the Boilers fifth, the Irish eighth.

In the long run, though, it was the Irish who ultimately hit their stride and found the needed depth. They turned Brennan's first season into a dream.

Their record was 9-1 with Purdue being the only team to keep Brennan and the Irish from an undefeated season and a possible National Championship, shared by Ohio State and UCLA that season.

The Irish had presented Brennan with what would be his best season. It proved to be only a momentary resting place before denouement.

1955

Hornung Horns In On Holcomb's Final Series

WEST LAFAYETTE, IND.—Round 2 of the Paul Hornung-Len Dawson duel went to Hornung. This time it was he who would direct an offense to victory and it was he who would do the intercepting defensively.

A crowd of 55,500 came to Ross-Ade Stadium, christening the arena's fourth expansion since 1924 when it first opened. What they saw was Notre Dame gain revenge on the Boilers for the 1954 upset that ultimately ruined a perfect season.

The Irish came away with a 22-7 victory in a game that was nearly the mirrored-image of the previous meeting.

A year earlier, Jim Peters had fumbled away the ball on Notre Dame's first possession, first play. The Boilers recovered and deposited the turnover for seven points.

This time it was Purdue who coughed up the ball. On its second play from scrimmage, Bill Murakowski, one of the 1954 heroes, gave up the ball.

Jim Morse helped the Irish take advantage with a 23-yard burst. Dean Studer, in his first start, picked up 19. With a fourth-and-three at the Purdue eight, Don Schaefer drove for six to the two and scored on the next play.

The Boilers and Dawson, facing Notre Dame's "umbrella defense" in which the Irish rushed seven men and had four pass defenders in a half circle, couldn't get untracked in the first quarter.

Only after Hornung's pitch out to Morse was fumbled and recovered by the Boilers on the Irish 42 did Purdue mount an offensive.

Dawson needed just six plays. He tied the game with a 13-yard pass to Len Zyzda.

Notre Dame was held scoreless through the remainder of the half, sending the teams into the locker room tied at seven.

Just a few plays into the second half was all Notre Dame needed to regain the lead. Bob Scannell and Dick Prendergast sacked Dawson, forcing a fumble at the Purdue 26. Five plays later, Studer scored from a yard out. Hornung's extra point was unsuccessful.

Dawson tried leading the Boilers back and it looked as if the junior might pull it off. The Boilers were at the Irish 34 when Dawson's pass fell barely incomplete at the Irish five. On the next play, Morse intercepted Dawson at the 25, returning it 21 yards to the 46.

The Irish went to work on a drive and the clock. After a sustained drive, Aubrey Lewis scored from the 10. From then on Dawson was in trouble.

Hornung followed with his interception. After Purdue and Dawson regained possession, he was sacked for losses of three, 14 and 10 yards. Finally, faced with a fourth-and-52 from their own 12, Purdue went back to punt.

Dawson, the Boilers' punter, had the ball snapped over his head and through the end zone, giving the Irish their final two points and a 22-7 victory.

Dawson, who had completed 11 of 22 passes for 104 yards, paid dearly for every completion. More than half of those passing yards were lost to sacks. The Irish sacked Dawson for 59 yards.

"We've used that defense before," Brennan said. "It has worked well for us right along but on this occasion it was practically perfect."

Coming into the game it was obvious the Boilers would try to beat the Irish the same way they had the year before—through the air. The Boilers had passed for 483 yards while rushing for only slightly more (503). In comparison, the Irish had rushed for 976 yards and passed for just 260 yards. The Irish maintained their game plan, rushing for 20 first downs and completing only one of five passes for eight yards.

The senior-laden Irish, who had been beaten the week before by Michigan State 21-7, finished with an 8-2 record, giving Brennan a 17-3 record for two seasons. The 1956 team, loaded with underclassmen and beset with injuries, would turn into one of Notre Dame's darkest.

The loss marked the end of the Stu Holcomb coaching era at Purdue. He had directed the Boilers for nine seasons, five of the seasons were winning ones including the 1955 record of 5-3-1. In those nine years he only beat the Irish twice, but both times the defeats hurt the Irish deeply.

It was he who led them into Notre Dame Stadium in 1950 and broke a 39-game unbeaten streak along with the Irish hearts. In 1954, the Boilers again went into Notre Dame Stadium and stopped another unbeaten streak of 13 games and also kept Brennan and the Irish away from a perfect season and possible National Championship.

While seven of Stu Holcomb's losses at Purdue were against the Irish, it will be his two wins over them that will live forever at Purdue.

Boilers Coach Jack Mollenkopf had Notre Dame's number. (Photo courtesy of Purdue University)

1956

Molly Wins His First Of Many

NOTRE DAME, IND.—The Official Associated Press Almanac lists 13 disasters/catastrophies that occurred during 1956—the Notre Dame defense was not included.

Make no mistake, the numbers don't lie. If the kind people who publish the almanac didn't see fit to call 286 points allowed a disaster, rest assured, more than a few Irishmen did. Little did they care that 22 of the 38 players were merely sophomores.

All the Irish backers cared to point out was that no Notre Dame team before 1956 and no Notre Dame team since 1956 allowed as many as 200 points. In the 55 seasons since the turn of the century, the Irish had amassed 18 undefeated seasons, 17 one-loss seasons and 15 two-loss seasons. The most losses in one season before 1956 was five. Notre Dame lost five games in 1933, Heartley "Hunt" Anderson's final year as coach.

The results of that season were no more appealing. The Irish, in coach Terry Brennan's third and middle year of his five-year problem, finished with a 2-8 record. One of the eight was a 28-14 loss to the Boilermakers.

In front of 57,778 proud but tentative Irishmen, the Irish dropped their second game of the season. It was also their second loss in the last three years against Purdue. To say the least, after a successful 8-2 season in 1955, it was a year of rebuilding.

With Jack Mollenkopf opening his rookie season as the Boilers coach, Purdue would not experience the best of years, finishing with a 3-4-2 record. But on October 13 they were at least twice as good as

Notre Dame on the scoreboard.

Purdue's 28-14 victory over Notre Dame was possible mainly because of fullback Mel Dillard. Dillard rushed for 142 yards and two touchdowns. The Irish rushed for 129 yards and two touchdowns.

"Maybe," Mollenkopf said boldly, "we proved that Notre Dame isn't that tough."

My, how that must have cut the Irish pride. Truth be told, he was right.

The Boilers had nearly three times the yardage (370-129) and nearly twice the offensive plays (86-48). The Irish still had Paul Hornung calling the signals while the Boilers had senior standout Len Dawson.

One day they would hitch their stars to championship pro football teams. On this particular day, they were shooting for survival.

The Boilers took it to the Irish from the outset. Purdue went 80 yards in 11 plays following the opening kickoff. From the beginning, Dillard made his presence felt. During the drive he caught a pass for 11 yards and broke off runs of 12, four and 18 yards. Dawson went to receiver Ken Mikes for 13 yards to the Irish two. Dillard finished the drive from there.

Purdue co-captain Mel Dillard rushed for 142 yards and scored two touchdowns in the 1956 game. (Photo courtesy of Purdue University)

On the following possession, Notre Dame and Hornung were faced with a fourth-and-one near midfield. They gambled and went for the first down. They lost.

Purdue took over and went 49 yards for the score. Dillard's 13-yard run capped off the drive. Dawson kicked his second extra point.

Before the half ended, Hornung had started a Notre Dame comeback. Using the pass and the run equally and with equal success, Hornung needed eight plays, four of them pass completions for 50 yards, to break the Purdue shutout with a 70-yard drive.

Dick Royer's seven-yard pass reception cut the deficit in half following Hornung's extra point. Hornung threw only three passes for touchdowns that season.

Facing Purdue for the final time may have inspired Hornung. He took Dawson's kickoff to open the second half and returned it to the Boilers 41. The Irish took the lead from Hornung and quickly began another drive.

Frank Reynolds circled the right end for nine yards. Captain Jim Morse carried eight yards to the 23. Chuck Lima picked up four and Morse went around the end for another eight to the 11.

One play later, Reynolds ripped off another 11-yard gain for the touchdown. Hornung's kick tied it at 14.

It was now up to the Irish defense to preserve the momentum. As evidenced by the points allowed during the season, the defense rested.

The Boilers responded with a 75-yard march, including 65 yards on the ground. Only once did co-captain Dawson throw and that was to co-captain Lamar Lundy for a 10-yard gain. Bill Jennings put the Irish back in a hole with a one-yard plunge.

Hornung had one last opportunity to corral Purdue. Early in the fourth quarter his punt set the Boilers back on their own three. Dawson, however, was able to respond to the challenge. He led the Boilers down to the Irish 18 before the drive stopped.

The Irish got as far as the 29 when on first down Sherrill Sipes fumbled away a reception and Purdue took over at the Notre Dame 17.

Given another chance, the Boilers took advantage of the fumble. Dawson moved to the eight where he was brought down by Ed Sullivan, who led the Irish defense with 20 tackles. A holding penalty against the Boilers dropped them back to the 28. But Ross Fichtner took a Dawson pitch-out with 2:09 remaining and scurried 28 yards for the touchdown that finished Notre Dame.

"What really hurt Notre Dame was the inability of their line to hold," Mollenkopf said. "They weren't charging out at all."

"We didn't react well defensively," Brennan admitted. "Plus Purdue was the best team we've seen lately. Hornung did an excellent job under the circumstances."

Hornung went on to win the Heisman Trophy, becoming the only player to win college football's greatest individual honor while playing for a losing team.

The circumstances would improve for Brennan and the Irish. But apparently not soon enough.

Before the season-ending game against Southern Cal, Frank Leahy blasted Brennan and the Irish. Leahy was quoted as saying it wasn't the losing that bothered him but the attitude. Leahy, who was replaced by Brennan, then a 25-year old and former Notre Dame player and philosophy student, had drawn the battle lines in full view of everyone.

Meanwhile, Mollenkopf had laid the foundation for the greatest success any Purdue coach would know against Notre Dame.

1957

Defense Returns Under The Dome

WEST LAFAYETTE, IND.—The beauty of survival is reaping the benefits of the disaster. When Notre Dame Coach Terry Brennan reviewed the 1956 season he knew immediately that the defense was the No. 1 area in need of rehabilitation. The 1956 team was young and lean.

Brennan sat back and waited to see what a year would do to his players. He also went out and added two new coaches strictly for the purpose of making sure the year of devastation wasn't for naught.

He brought in Bernie Crimmins, formerly the head coach at Indiana. Brennan also hired Henry (Hank) Stram, a backfield coach from Purdue.

Ironically, the first two games of the 1957 season were against Purdue and Indiana. The Irish shut out both.

The Boilers fell 12-0 and the Hoosiers were crushed 26-0. Suddenly, Brennan had a team that could play defense.

"It is amazing," Brennan said, "These are the same kids as last year."

The Boilers picked up a mere 113 yards, 257 fewer than the year before. Purdue had eight first downs, 19 fewer than last year. Purdue's All-America candidate Mel Dillard rushed 15 times for 51 yards, just barely more than a third of his rushing total of a year earlier.

The Boilers had even worse success through the air. Bob Spoo had replaced Len Dawson as quarterback. Spoo didn't complete a pass until the waning moments.

"Notre Dame's football team," Joe Doyle wrote in the *South Bend Tribune*, "defending its goal-line and once-famed reputation with equal tenacity ... struggled, stormed and finally stymied Purdue ..."

The shutout was the first in the series since the Irish nipped Purdue 3-0 in 1939 on third-string quarterback Johnny Kelleher's 17-yard field goal. The victory also gave Notre Dame first possession of the newly-created "Shillelagh" trophy, emblematic of the Purdue/Notre Dame rivalry.

While the Notre Dame offense didn't especially create a breeze for the defense with 12 points, the final six coming in the final three minutes, the Irish defense made certain that the Boilers' best bet would be a 0-0 deadlock.

The closest the Boilers came to erasing the zero on the board was in the third quarter. With Nick Pietrosante quick kicking the ball to the Purdue 49, the Boilers gave the Irish defense one scare.

With Dillard and Tom Fletcher beginning to find leaks in the Notre Dame defense, the Boilers drove to the 27. Bob Spoo decided it was time to open up the Irish defense and set up to pass. It was the first time that Purdue managed to tie together two first downs on one drive. Out of nowhere came Mike Muehlbauer to sack Spoo at the Irish 39.

Spoo had no recourse but to put the ball in the air at this point. His next two attempts hit nothing but the Ross-Ade Stadium turf. Ken Mikes was forced to punt, kicking away the only chance the Boilers would have.

The Irish had broken out on top on their second possession, going 77 yards in seven plays. The touchdown came on a pitch-out from quarterback Bob Williams to previously little-used Dick Lynch. Lynch went 22 yards, giving the Irish all the points they needed. With 7:26 left in

Terry Brennan, Notre Dame Coach. (Photo courtesy of Notre Dame University)

the first quarter, Aubrey Lewis missed the first of two unsuccessful conversion attempts.

The Irish squandered a few more scoring opportunities as time ticked on. All through it, the Irish defense kept the Boilers going nowhere. Before the final fruitless possession, the Boilers had the ball 14 times. They were forced to punt 11 times, were victimized by fumbles twice and an interception once. Suddenly, the Irish were giving lessons in stalwart defensive play.

"Our pursuit was the best it's been since 1955," Brennan said. "We covered well on wide plays, plays that really killed us last year. We made plenty of mistakes on offense but that's expected."

The Irish defense was led by tackles Bronco Nagurski and Frank Geremia, guard Bob Gaydos and linebacker Ed Sullivan, who had been called on to make 20 tackles in the Purdue game a year earlier.

The final Irish touchdown came with less than three minutes to play. Williams connected with Bob Wetoska for 59 yards to the Purdue eight.

After Chuck Lima lunged for two yards, Williams threw a six-yard touchdown toss to Frank Reynolds.

Lewis missed another conversion attempt but it didn't matter. Purdue was going nowhere fast offensively.

"You can't tell much about one game," Brennan said. "But in that one game we were improved defensively maybe as much as 100 percent.

"We made a few mistakes on defense but they really didn't hurt us. The important thing is we didn't make the mistakes that killed us last year."

The Irish rebounded from the injury-plagued season of 1956 to a 7-3 record, just one win shy of the 1955 team.

After losing its first three games, the Boilers recovered for a 5-4 season.

On the surface, it appeared that the complete reversal in record and defensive performance (the Irish allowed 153 fewer points than in 1956) had washed away the bad taste of the 1956 season under Brennan.

To Brennan's credit there were the overall results to consider, plus a pair of wins over Purdue and Indiana, Notre Dame's two biggest in-state rivals. There was also the thrilling upset of Oklahoma ending the Sooners' 47-game unbeaten streak, still the longest in college football history. The results seemed to be enough to clear Brennan's record.

While on the surface it appeared Brennan should have been retained, the decision had already been made. The alumni were already beginning the campaign to relieve Brennan of his duties in favor of Joe Kuharich. Kuharich, a South Bend native, was a former player at Notre Dame under Frank Leahy.

Time would tell.

1958

Purdue Jars Irish Behind Joltin' Jarus

NOTRE DAME, IND.—In 1958, sports turned the corner into a new era. In major league baseball, the Brooklyn Dodgers died and were reborn in Los Angeles, setting the stage for baseball's move west and forever changing the nature of the game.

In college football innovation interceded for the first time since 1912 when the value of a touchdown rose from five to six points. In 1958, the point after touchdown became optional. The two-point conversion was born at the college level.

It wasn't used in Purdue's thrilling 29-22 victory at Notre Dame Stadium that season. Had the Irish scored again in their furious fourth-quarter comeback and brought themselves within a 29-28 margin, Terry Brennan would have been faced with an opportunity to throw away a tie and go for victory. Unfortunately, we'll never know since the Irish ran out of thrilling plays before they could fulfill the comeback.

Led by junior quarterback George Izo, the Irish stormed back from a 26-7 fourth-quarter deficit to pull within 29-22 in front of 59,563 slightly hysterical fans.

Izo, using what later become known as the shotgun offense, opened the Boilers up with a pair of touchdown passes to Monty Stickles from 29 and 43 yards away.

It was one of the great Irish comebacks of the Terry Brennan reign, but it was thwarted when the Boilers stopped Ron Toth on a fourth-and-two from the Purdue 27. Only 1:21 remained at that point.

The Irish, playing without four players including starting guards Jim

Schaaf and All-America Al Ecuyer, were geared for stopping Purdue's running game. The Boilers had picked up 955 of their 1,202 yards on the ground and had run 255 running plays compared to 40 passes.

Purdue also had a formidable defensive alignment. The Boilers were simply great against the run with a 5-4 defense that practically placed nine-men on the line.

"Our first aim," Purdue Coach Jack Mollenkopf said, "is to stop the opposition's running game. Even against a passing team, I'd say we'd try and stop their run first. For without a running game, passing loses a lot of its effectiveness."

And Mollenkopf had proof: A 14-5 upset of Michigan State. The Boilers were on their way to an outstanding 6-1-2 record. They held the Spartans to 38 rushing yards. The last Purdue team to have a better record was Elmer Burnham's 9-0 team of war-torn 1943.

The Irish defense averaged 220-pounds and was allowing little more than 100 yards a game on the ground.

Nevertheless, the Boilers, behind the brilliant running of Bob Jarus, went strength against strength and survived largely due to Jarus, who scored three touchdowns.

Jarus' one-yard plunge followed by Ross Fichtner's conversion tied the game at 7-7, following quarterback Bob Williams 14-yard touchdown run for the Irish.

Playing through a steady drizzle, neither team could sustain anything offensively until early in the third quarter. It was then Purdue erupted for three touchdowns in the first eight minutes of the second half.

The momentum became Purdue's when they forced Jim Crotty to fumble the kickoff to start the second half. Richie Brooks recovered at the Notre Dame 21. It took seven plays, but Jarus finally broke the tie with another one-yard plunge. The conversion attempt failed.

Len Wilson, who had fumbled the snap from center on the conversion attempt, rectified his mistake by intercepting Williams' pass on second down of the ensuing series. Wilson brought the ball down to the Notre Dame five. Jarus again was called on to finish the task from five yards out. The two-point conversion failed.

The Irish defense was still stalled and forced All-America Nick Pietrosante to punt. The Boilers took over again at the Irish 43.

On a first down play, fullback Jack Laraway broke 28 yards for the final Purdue touchdown. This time Fichtner's conversion was good, giving the Boilers a 26-7 lead with 7:18 left in the third quarter.

With Izo replacing Williams, the Irish began the long road back. The first stop was the end zone after Izo, using a formation that was described as "a quarterback in a punting position with four receivers split wide," found Stickles between a pair of Purdue defenders. Stickles' kick cut the lead to 26-14.

*Bob Jarus scored three touchdowns in the 1958 game for Purdue.
(Photo courtesy of Purdue University)*

The Irish tried an onside kick that failed to go the required 10 yards. The gamble set up Skip Ohl's 21-yard field goal, increasing the Purdue lead to 29-14.

Izo took the Irish down to the Purdue two where he fumbled. Purdue recovered at the one but were caught for a safety when Pietrosante nailed Laraway in the end zone. After Purdue's free kick Izo again connected with Stickles for 43 yards and another touchdown. Purdue still led 29-22 with only 2:28 remaining.

This time the Irish pulled off the onside kick but had their hopes crushed when the Boilers stopped Toth inside their 30.

"That (defensive) spread caught us off guard," Purdue Coach Jack Mollenkopf said. "We knew nothing about it and we didn't do a good job against it. Our ends didn't know whether to rush or play soft.

"That Izo is a beautiful quarterback and Stickles, at 6-4, 225 pounds, is a beautiful receiver. Especially when somebody 5-10 tries to cover him."

"Next time," Brennan said, "we might use that spread in the first quarter."

For Brennan there was no next time against the Boilers. Despite a 6-4 season, Brennan was fired. The announcement leaked to the press just days before Christmas, creating a massive outburst.

The Rev. Theodore M. Hesburgh, the president of Notre Dame, notified Brennan, 30-years old and a father of four, that the faculty board in control of athletics had voted him out. It was no doubt a deed Hesburgh hated to carry out. Brennan had been his choice, his former student.

Famed *New York Times* columnist Arthur Daley wrote, "So Brennan is out and that matchless artist in public relations, Rockne, must be giving a whirling dervish performance in his grave. Never before has Notre Dame plummeted to lower esteem and it was the timing that made such an outrageous botch of the job. The damage is irreparable."

On December 22, 1958, Joe Kuharich, a classmate of Rev. Hesburgh, became the head coach at Notre Dame.

1959

Home Is Sweet
For Purdue
After 54 Years

WEST LAFAYETTE, IND.—Joe Kuharich had won the election and was entrusted with the Notre Dame football fortunes for the next four years.

In the stands at Purdue's Ross-Ade Stadium this fall day, presidential candidate John F. Kennedy, of Irish descent, took time out from his campaigning to watch Notre Dame.

Let history proclaim that had he lost the 1960 presidential election to Richard Millhouse Nixon he may have considered this afternoon wasted. As it turned out, he could have just claimed he wasn't a witness to the Boiler's 28-7 smothering of Kuharich's young Irish.

It was the first of 23 losses Kuharich would suffer as Notre Dame's coach. He, the local boy made good, had come back from the pro ranks and the Washington Redskins to lead the Irish out of the nowhere land they had been taken to during an era of football de-emphasis at Notre Dame.

Terry Brennan, who was unceremoniously fired just before Christmas, 1958, had produced winning seasons of 6-4 and 7-3 after a 2-8 mark in his third season, 1956.

If the Irish, Kuharich and the millions of Notre Dame backers realized anything that day, it was changing coaches doesn't change outcomes, at least not immediately.

Kuharich had the cards stacked against him from the outset. He was missing his two best backs, quarterback George Izo and halfback Red Mack.

Joe Kuharich began a stormy four-year term in 1959. (Photo courtesy of Notre Dame University)

Notre Dame was simply overmatched. Jack Mollenkopf's Boilers used 62 players compared to 24 for the Irish.

The Ross-Ade Stadium sellout crowd of 50,362 was able to see a stadium first. Since the Boilers moved from Stuart Field to Ross-Ade Stadium in 1924, they had never been able to beat the Irish in front of their hometown fans. In fact, the last time a Purdue team had beaten the Irish at Lafayette was in 1905 when D.M. Allen scored three times in a 32-0 romp. Enough was enough.

The Boilers, realizing they could be part of history, took off at the outset. Quarterback Ross Fichtner carried the first two plays for 38 yards. Two plays later he clicked off another dozen yards, setting the Boilers up at the Notre Dame 21. Fichtner's first pass was complete to Bob Jarus. From the five Jarus scored the first touchdown.

Mollenkopf used his second unit to start the second Purdue drive. With the second period just 44 seconds old, the Boilers were wrapping up a 77-yard eight-play drive. The key play was a 58-yard pass from quarterback Bernie Allen, an All-America Purdue shortstop and future Washington Senator infielder, to Len Jardine. Fitchner came in to complete the drive with a seven-yard pass to Dick Brooks. Allen converted his second extra point.

Purdue added to its lead when Jim Crotty attempted a lateral and lost possession. Purdue tackle Dale Rems recovered at the Notre Dame 22.

Again, Jarus got the call from a yard out, scoring his second touchdown of the game and his fifth against the Irish in two years. He would score only one more touchdown in 1959.

Crotty's touchdown narrowed the deficit to 21-7 early in the second half but Purdue's Allen stopped a second Irish drive with an interception at his own 14. Three plays later, Jim Tiller, a 150-pound scatback, had given Purdue the equalizer along with a 28-7 lead by scampering 74 yards.

Purdue outgained the Irish 398-202 and, unlike Boiler teams of the future, needed to complete only three of six passes (66 yards) against Notre Dame.

"When you're fighting an uphill game, you've got to throw the ball," Kuharich said, "And with an inexperienced team that means you're going to make a lot of errors and get in trouble."

There was no concealing what he was referring to. The biggest error Notre Dame made followed Crotty's touchdown. The Irish were driving for what would have been the touchdown to pull them within one touch-down of Purdue. It was then that Don White's pass was picked off by Allen. White was a reserve behind Izo for two seasons.

"We had the momentum," Kuharich said, "We had a couple good shots when a completed pass could have made a big difference."

The Irish finished with a 5-5 record but needed two strong games at the end of the season to resurface at the .500 level. Notre Dame stunned Iowa 20-19 at Iowa City and then beat Southern Cal 16-6 in the season finale. The Trojans were 8-1 at the time.

Purdue, which lost Fichtner with a separated shoulder during the third quarter, finished with a 5-2-2 record.

Ironically, one of the Irish defeats that season was to Northwestern. The Wildcats, coached by a gentleman named Ara Parseghian, beat Notre Dame 30-24.

Later that winter at a Notre Dame football dinner, the guest speaker was, you guessed it, Mr. Ara Parseghian.

1960

Purdue Punishes Irish 51-19

NOTRE DAME, IND.—If there is one game that points a coach to the door, it was this game for Joe Kuharich. Although the Notre Dame coach would return to the National Football League after two more seasons at Notre Dame, what transpired on October 1 against arch-rival Purdue would surely be remembered as the blackest eye in Irish history, especially where Purdue was concerned.

Purdue scored 31 points in a 10:52 span during the second quarter on the way to a 51-19 pounding of the Irish. The 59,235 fans that shoehorned into Notre Dame Stadium sat bewildered, belittled and stunned. They could not believe what they were watching.

"The Purdues never were better," Bob Collins wrote in the *Indianapolis Star.* "Notre Dame seldom had played so bad. The game was absolutely unbelievable."

It marked the third straight Purdue victory over the Irish. It also rewrote the Irish record book under the dubious section. The 31 second-quarter points were the most ever scored in one quarter against Notre Dame. The 51 points were the most ever scored against Notre Dame under the shadow of the Golden Dome. The point total was also the fourth highest allowed by a Notre Dame team.

The result acted as a measuring stick for Kuharich and the Irish. The concept of rebuilding the Irish into a national power was still nothing more than a dream. The road was suddenly longer than anyone decked out in green cared to travel. They would have miles to go before they could reap another successful season.

There really was no other way for the game to turn out when the Irish gave the Boilers the ball eight times in the first half and the Boilers parlayed seven possessions into touchdowns. Three Irish passes were intercepted, twice the Boilers turned them into touchdowns. Three times the Irish fumbled and three times the Boilers moved in for touchdowns.

Through one quarter, Notre Dame actually trailed by only a point, 14-13. Purdue scored first on a 44-yard pass from Maury Guttman to Don Elwall. Guttman had given Purdue possession after intercepting Daryle Lamonica.

Notre Dame's Bob Scarpitto countered with a 64-yard run off tackle. Joe Perkowski's kick was wide, leaving the Irish behind for the remainder of the afternoon.

Bob Wiater increased Purdue's lead with a 78-yard run for a touchdown. The Irish again stormed back with George Haffner catching Angelo Dabiero open for 24 yards and a touchdown. The quarter ended 14-13. Outside of the final stats—that showed Notre Dame with 18 first downs and Purdue 17 and 358 offensive yards per team—the balance ended after a quarter.

From then on the Boilers would score from 78 yards out on a lateral, 66 yards out on a punt return, pass plays of 44 and 30 yards, two short bursts through the Irish line and, finally, a 34-yard field goal.

Purdue's historic second quarter looked like this:

Don Mayoras scored from a yard out to open the quarter. Bernie Allen's third successful point after gave Purdue a 21-13 lead. Allen, who scored 15 points this day, picked up three more on a 34-yard field goal after Tom Yakubowski recovered an Irish fumble on the Notre Dame 20.

Next, reserve halfback Tom Bloom picked off Haffner's pass and returned it to the Notre Dame 13. Four plays later, Yakubowski scored from the one. 31-13.

The Irish at that point found themselves losing more than a game. Bill "Red" Mack, one of their leaders and great running backs, was injured in the end zone on a play in which he was called for pass interference. He was sidelined for the duration of the season.

Following the kickoff, Haffner fumbled and Forest Farmer recovered at the Irish 41. Allen then faked a handoff and let fly with a 31-yard pass to Jim Tiller who was unguarded at the five. Allen's successful kick made it 38-13. The clock had barely ticked past the halfway mark of the second quarter.

Notre Dame finally managed to hold on to the ball without fumbling or throwing an interception. No matter. Scarpitto's punt carried to the Purdue 34 where Tiller was waiting. Tiller took off on a 66-yard punt return.

45-13.

There was still 4:08 left in the half, but the Boilers were finished for now. The Irish, on the other hand, were simply finished.

Late in the second half Allen completed the massacre with a six-yard touchdown run after Purdue recovered a Denny Murphy fumble.

It was over.

On one side of the field the triumphant Boilermakers were hoisting Coach Jack Mollenkopf onto their shoulders.

Across the field, Notre Dame's John Powers buried his face in his hands.

Future pro baseball player Bernie Allen led the Purdue rout. (Photo courtesy of Purdue University)

"Sure we were beaten badly," Kuharich stormed. "and if it had been done methodically there would be reason to be alarmed. But it was a group of things—three fumbles lost, three interceptions lost, poor tackling.

"That all pieced together spells disaster."

"That win," Mollenkopf said, "was like a dream to all of us. We deserved to win but not by a score like that.

"We thought we could throw long on them. Young players are eager to get into the action. Notre Dame made so many mistakes, it just made it easy for us. It will be tough to judge just how good we are."

Mollenkopf held a 4-1 record over Notre Dame at this point. As the 1960 season transpired the Boilers proved to be nothing spectacular, finishing with a 4-4-1 record.

Purdue, which scored the first seven times they had the ball, were pre-game three-point underdogs. Besides adding a page to the all-time Notre Dame record book, Purdue also set series records.

It shattered the record for most points scored by a winning team (46 by the 1946 Irish). The win over the Irish was Purdue's fifth in seven seasons, fourth straight at South Bend and 10th overall.

Purdue also became only the fourth team to defeat Notre Dame three straight seasons joining Pittsburgh, Iowa and Michigan State.

"It was just one of those days," Kuharich told the *South Bend Tribune*. "You can't expect to win if you give the other team the ball six or eight times in scoring territory.

"But every game is different. You just can't predict what is going to happen. In all my life, I don't believe I've seen a game quite like this one."

While some historians point to Army's 59-0 victory over Notre Dame in 1944 and Oklahoma's 40-0 whitewashing of the Irish in 1956 as more devastating defeats, it must be remembered that the 1960 Irish were made up of quality performers. The Irish had 19 returning lettermen and players like Myron Pottios, Nick Buoniconti, Red Mack and a sophomore quarterback named Daryle Lamonica.

The loss staggered the Irish for a season. They lost the next seven games, including the second of four straight to Northwestern and Ara Parseghian. For the second time in five seasons the Irish had registered a 2-8 record.

The rebuilding turned into a massive task. There were those who believed Kuharich would not be the architect.

Those who doubted were proven correct.

1961

Win Is About Time For Irish

WEST LAFAYETTE, IND.—It was a Saturday afternoon of slump breakers. Notre Dame Coach Joe Kuharich watched sophomore place kicker Joe Perkowski give the Irish a 22-20 victory over Purdue with a 28-yard fourth quarter field goal ending Purdue's three-game winning streak over the Irish. It was also the first time Kuharich had beaten the Boilers in three tries.

A couple hundred miles to the southeast New York Yankees slugger Roger Maris had connected for his 62nd homer of the season and his first in the World Series, breaking an 0-for-10 slump against the Cincinnati Reds.

"About time, isn't it?" Roger asked.

No doubt the Irish and Kuharich were echoing the same line regarding their sudden success.

Perkowski, who had flubbed an extra point try and two field goals, one from 15-yards, fought the pressure just long enough to pull the Irish from a 20-19 deficit.

Perkowski's kick came with 11:50 remaining, putting the pressure on the Boilers and, ironically enough, their kicker, Skip Ohl. Ohl, who had helped Purdue take the lead with a pair of extra points and two successful field goals from 40 and 36 yards, nevertheless shanked the one that made the biggest difference.

With little more than three minutes left, his 36-yard attempt veered left, going out of bounds at the Irish three. For some reason, Ohl remained on the field during the next play, further damaging the Boilers' comeback attempt by being penalized as the twelfth man on the field.

Instead of the Irish starting from their three, they began at the 18, giving quarterback Daryle Lamonica more room to work. While the Irish failed to get a first down, the 15 yards kept the Boilers out of reach and Notre Dame's victory tucked away. It also meant Purdue missed finishing with its most wins since 1945 (7-3) by a mere field goal.

"It was a tough one to lose, but a nice one for Notre Dame," Purdue Coach Jack Mollenkopf said. "They showed us a lot more on offense. They did a few things we weren't ready for."

"I believe this is the best Notre Dame team we've played in years."

Joe Perkowski kicked the Irish to a two-point win in 1961. (Photo courtesy of Notre Dame University)

If the Irish surprised the Boilermaker defensive brain-trust, it wasn't with their passing game. Lamonica completed six of 10 passes for 77 yards but threw only three passes in the second half. The Irish made up the difference in the rushing yardage. The Irish gained nearly 100 more yards than the powerful Boilermakers (272-184).

"(Jim) Snowden and (Paul) Costa gave us a couple good runs," Kuharich said. "If any one gave us a lift it was Snowden."

Snowden and Costa were both sophomores and gave the Irish the running they needed to pull within range of Perkowski's decisive kick. Costa carried five times for 46 yards and Snowden eight for 45. They proved to be the needed thrust behind the reliable Angelo Dabiero, who had 66 yards in 14 attempts.

As it turned out the Irish needed every yard they could gather.

The Boilers took the lead on their first possesion following a Notre Dame punt. Quarterback Ron Digravio mixed the running efforts of fullback Roy Walker with the receiving of Dave Miller (38 yards on one reception during the drive) to travel 74 yards in nine plays. DiGravio gave the Boilers the lead with a one-yard dive.

With 4:23 left in the first quarter, Notre Dame had matched the Boilers' opening drive almost perfectly. The Irish went 73 yards in 10 plays. Faced with a fourth-and-one from the Purdue 27, Kuharich went against a field goal attempt and was paid well for his ambition. Gerry Gray took off on a 27-yard touchdown run, tying the score at 7-7 following Perkowski's extra point kick.

The Boilers, going with a two-platoon offensive system, roared to the Irish four behind second-string quarterback Gary Hogan. At that point, Mollenkopf reinserted the starting team. Roy Walker finished the drive from four yards and Ohl's second extra-point kick gave the Boilers a 14-7 lead.

Purdue took a 10-point lead when Notre Dame punter Frank Budka had his kick partially blocked. The Boilers took over at the Irish 37. Their drive got them as close as the 19. From there Ohl kicked a 26-yard field goal.

It was on Notre Dame's next possession that Perkowski missed a chip shot from 15 yards, severing the Irish momentum.

Undaunted, the Irish, behind Lamonica's 27-yard pass to Jim Kelly and two-yard burst by Snowden, cut the deficit to 17-13. Perkowski, however, missed the extra point.

The Irish attempted an onside kick. With less than a minute remaining, Purdue recovered and moved into position for another Ohl field goal—this one from 30 yards.

Both defenses took over at the outset of the second half. Notre Dame finally drove deep into Purdue territory where Lamonica and Kelly teamed up for a seven-yard touchdown pass, bringing the Irish within a point. With more than a quarter to play, Kuharich went for the two-point conversion, perhaps not wanting to ruin Perkowski's confidence altogether if he missed another chip shot.

Anyway, the two-point attempt went for naught. The Irish still trailed 20-19.

On the next Irish possession, Lamonica continued using his entire sophomore backfield of Budka, Denny Phillips, Costa and Snowden. Costa busted one play for 29 yards, bringing Perkowski forward to make or break the afternoon. His 28-yard kick was good although referee Rem Meyer kept the Ross-Ade Stadium crowd of 51,295 waiting while he looked long and hard before deciding so.

"When you come back to win people seem to think you were fired up to an unusual extent," Kuharich said. "That isn't so. We just played our usual game."

If, indeed, it was a usual game for the Irish, it wasn't the usual result. After opening with three straight wins, including one the following week, a 30-0 bombing of Southern Cal, the Irish went on to lose three straight. They finished the season with two more wins followed by two more losses. Finishing with a 5-5 record was nothing new for Kuharich's Irish teams. They had finished 5-5 his first season (1959) and would finish 5-5 in his last season (1962).

Purdue finished 6-3 losing the three games by a total of 7 points (22-20 to Notre Dame, 16-14 to Michigan, 10-7 to Minnesota). The Boilers opened the season with a 13-6 win over Washington, the 300th win in Purdue history.

1962

Purdue Win Opens Kuharich's Final Stand

NOTRE DAME, IND.—The final saga of the forlorn Joe Kuharich years was played out to the limit. Kuharich, the only coach in the history of the school's football program to finish with a below .500 career record (17-23), closed out his fourth and final year with a 5-5 record.

The first loss of the season came via Purdue and in front of a Notre Dame Stadium record crowd of 61,296.

Notre Dame had a newly re-gilded dome, the eighth re-gilding in 80 years; at a cost of $50,000. But the Kuharich team had the same old result.

Kuharich teams rarely had success over the Boilers. Only once in the four years did the Irish defeat Purdue. That victory, a slim 22-20 conquest, came in 1961, the year following the biggest black eye in Notre Dame gridiron history—a 51-19 humbling by the Boilers at South Bend.

The Irish, who averaged just under 16 points a game during the 1962 season, had difficulty putting any offense together in the 24-6 Boilers victory.

Despite the seemingly untapped potential of Daryle Lamonica, the Irish never had a chance against Purdue.

The first quarter was scoreless. On the first play of the second quarter, Skip Ohl converted a 27-yard field goal, giving Purdue a 3-0 lead.

During the two weeks preceding the Notre Dame game, the Boilers were concerned about the condition of quarterback Ron DiGravio. DiGravio hadn't worked in a contact situation for nearly two weeks. There was also concern surrounding end Forest Farmer. Both

155

quarterback and receiver had come into this game hurting.

You would have never sensed that, however, after watching DiGravio lead the Boilers on a 63-yard drive. The finishing touch was provided by DiGravio who connected with Forest for a 25-yard touchdown pass.

The partisan fans sat by and watched. Finally they could stand it no more. "A Lamonica punt on a fourth and seven situation drew boos from the crowd," Joe Ryan wrote in Notre Dame's *Scholastic*, "(They) felt the Irish had given up."

DiGravio and Purdue sensed they had the Irish mentally demoralized. DeGravio led a nine-play 94-yard drive finished off by his own one-yard run.

Purdue led 17-0 after three quarters. The Boilers would have Joe Kuharich to kick around only a little while longer.

At the outset of the fourth quarter, Notre Dame thought it had caught its first break. South Bend's Dennis Murphy picked off a Purdue pass and took it 55 yards for an apparent touchdown. A yellow flag said different.

From bad to worse to more disaster.

Later in the quarter, Kuharich replaced Lamonica with sophomore third-string quarterback Dennis Szot. On his first play as a varsity member, Szot fumbled.

Purdue took over at the Notre Dame 20. One play later, Gene Donaldson raced 20 yards for the touchdown that forever sealed Notre Dame's fate.

Down 24-0, the Irish broke the shutout against what remained of the Purdue defense. Szot threw a 17-yard touchdown pass to Don Hogan with 3:31 remaining.

The victory was Purdue's fourth in its last five outings against the Irish. Make no mistake, though, this Purdue team was far from overpowering. It finished with a 4-4-1 record.

Just four years earlier, Joseph Lawrence Kuharich had been the logical choice to succeed Terry Brennan. He had served in the pro ranks and was bringing with him a philosophy not yet accepted by the college ranks. Certainly Brennan's assistants, who came from pro ball, had already scratched the surface.

Again though, he seemed the clear cut choice. He was born in South Bend and played for the Irish from 1935-37. As a youngster, Knute Rockne had led him out to the Notre Dame practice field one day.

There were reports that the alumni had tried to buy out his contract and that the administration would not hear of it.

Finally, on March 13, 1963 Joe Kuharich dug up his roots and announced his was going back to the National Football League as its supervisor of officials. One year later, he became the head coach and later went on to become general manager of the Philadelphia Eagles.

Kuharich departed, but he left behind a quote for future Notre Dame coaches to examine. The *South Bend Tribune* quoted him as saying, "This insatiable appetite to win has become so strong it is ludicrous. The day of invincible college football teams, year after year, is gone."

Kuharich is quoted in Francis Wallace's book, "Notre Dame From Rockne to Parseghian" as saying the decision was the most heart-wrenching one he had ever made.

"The toughest thing I've ever had to do in my life," Kuharich said, "was to stand in front of those boys and tell them I was going to quit. It was absolutely my own decision. The thing that helped me make up my mind was that all the assistants will be retained and Hughie (Devore) will take over."

Devore, who had served as the Irish coach in 1945, came back for one more season before Ara Parseghian was called to lead the Irish back to respectability.

Joe Kuharich works with quarterbacks Daryle Lamonica, left, and Frank Budka. (Photo courtesy of Notre Dame University)

1963

Purdue Makes It 6 Of 8

WEST LAFAYETTE, IND.—Before you could applaud the fourth-quarter Purdue drive that meant a 7-6 victory, before you could marvel at the infallibility of Boilers' quarterback Ron DiGravio and before you came to realize the significance of Purdue's sixth victory over Notre Dame in eight tries, you had to shake your head and feel for Notre Dame Coach Hugh Devore.

No doubt when Devore opened up his inheritance left by Joe Kuharich, he must have smiled. It was Notre Dame. His alma mater.

The school, the Dome, the stadium where he played tight end for three years in the 1930's and captained The Irish as a senior. He was the head coach in one of the ultimate coaching positions in North American sports.

Then he looked again. If he wasn't wincing over the sad state of his newly-acquired football team he should have been. Notre Dame was still reeling, still caught in the depression of the Joe Kuharich years.

"I don't know why they picked me," Devore is quoted in Francis Wallace's book *Notre Dame From Rockne to Parseghian*, "but I'm going to make it the best football season I ever had."

By the time the Irish had slipped to 2-7 and were averaging a meager 12 points a game offensively, Devore's statement gave the world the ultimate example of naivete.

The Boilers had beaten the Irish five out of the last seven times. In one of the most exciting get togethers in the schools' long rivalry, the Boilers made it an amazing six out of eight.

Bob Collins of the *Indianapolis Star* wrote: "A full house—51,723 citizens sat here on a pleasant 78-degree autumn afternoon and watched a contest the temperature of which was at least 200. It was what people have come to expect at a Purdue-Notre Dame game—bang, boff, bang for 60 rugged minutes."

Make no mistake, the 7-6 victory was no easy accomplishment.

After a scoreless first quarter, the Irish got their six points in a hurry. With a first down on the Notre Dame 20, quarterback John Huarte threw a 39-yard pass to Alan Lobay. On the next play, Huarte connected with Jim Kelly for 41 yards and the touchdown.

In just 35 seconds the Irish had broken through but they had also inadvertently set up the play that would make the difference.

Huarte, who had a gimpy ankle when the game began, aggravated it on the touchdown pass to Kelly. Since it was Huarte who would normally kick the conversion, the Irish were forced to make a decision regarding the extra point or points.

"The boy (Huarte)," Devore said, "figured his arm was the next best thing."

The decision made, Huarte went for the two points. His pass to Tom MacDonald was off target.

For nearly two quarters, the play didn't outwardly affect the ultimate result. The Boilers had fretted away two good scoring chances in the second quarter—the first when kicker Jim Long missed a 20-yard field goal and the second when Dave Ellison fumbled on the Irish 14 following a reception.

It wasn't until early in the fourth quarter that the Boilers made the Irish regret their second-quarter gamble.

Notre Dame's punter Dan McGinn had felt the heat of the Purdue rush all afternoon. On this occasion, the Irish were kicking from inside their 20. The snap to McGinn was high. McGinn reacted quickly and ran toward the sidelines realizing he could not get the kick off from his standard punting position. While on the run, he let loose with a 48-yard punt setting the Boilers back on their 33.

From there DiGravio started the winning drive. His first two passes were complete to Bob Hadrick, moving the Boilers inside Notre Dame territory to the 39. A holding penalty against the Irish gave Purdue control at the 19.

Gordon Teter picked up eight yards on three carries but a Purdue illegal procedure penalty set the Boilers back at the 19. DiGravio, a senior who had beaten the Irish as a junior, threw a wobbly pass to Jim Morel who made an outstanding catch at the nine, setting up a fourth down and inches.

DiGravio nudged over for the first down. Two plays later, following a Tom Goberville sack of DiGravio at the 11, the Irish committed a personal

Ron DiGravio, Purdue quarterback. (Photo courtesy of Purdue University)

foul, keeping the Boilers alive. The penalty gave Purdue possession at the five.

The Irish defense stormed in again, knocking DiGravio for a two-yard loss. From the seven, DiGravio connected with Hadrick for the touchdown, tying the score 6-6.

Had the Irish kicked the conversion successfully in the second quarter, the burden would have rested entirely with Purdue Coach Jack Mollenkopf. If Notre Dame had kicked and if the kick had been successful, Purdue would have had to decide whether it wanted to kick for a tie or go for the victory with 9:15 remaining. When the Irish conversion failed, the Boilers had no decision to make. Gary Hogan kicked the conversion and the Boilers had a 7-6 lead and eventual victory.

The ensuing kickoff was returned by Ron Bliey to the 29. Huarte continued going to Bliey who carried five times for 47 yards to the Purdue 34. Huarte went to the air and found John Simon at the 21. Two plays later and Huarte had the Irish sitting pretty with a first down at the Purdue 11.

Purdue's defense stiffened. On third down the Boilers' Dave Ellison dropped Bliey back at the 21. From there Huarte tried a field goal of 28 yards.

The attempt was blocked by Purdue's Pete Dudgeon, giving the Boilers possession with just 2:10 remaining. If DiGravio could keep the Boilers on the ground and pick up one first down, the Irish wouldn't have a chance.

The Boilers didn't make it.

With the clock running down, Huarte had one play left. From the Purdue 38, Huarte dropped back and looked for Jack Snow. For a moment Snow was open and Huarte threw. The ball was heading directly for Snow when at the last moment Gordon Teter put his hand in the way deflecting the pass at the eight.

The gun sounded Purdue's victory.

It was only the second Boiler victory over the Irish in the last 10 years at Ross-Ade Stadium. Mollenkopf's squad finished with a 5-4 record and the knowledge that DiGravio's replacement would be well-suited for the job—Bob Griese.

The Irish and Devore were headed in a different direction. The Irish would finish with a 2-7 record, a record they have not come close to matching since.

For the remainder of the season, they would go most of the route without Huarte, who played only 45 mintues in 1963. Jack Snow, who would team with Huarte to establish one of the best passing combinations in the history of the school, was used mainly at halfback in 1963 playing 135 minutes away from his natural position.

Devore's second term and final season as the head coach ended.

Unfortunately, he was put into a no-win situation not only because of the young squad he had inherited but also because the coaching staff he had around him were Kuharich's men—a coaching staff that had not been associated with victory for some time.

Devore took the position of assistant athletic director. The influx of candidates poured into South Bend. He had earned a lifetime position at Notre Dame if he chose to stay. He did not. In 1966 he joined the Houston Oilers of the American Football League.

The man chosen to replace him had many of the same qualities as the famed Rockne. Like Rockne, Ara Raoul Parseghian was not an Irish-Catholic. Rockne was Norwegian-Lutheran before changing to Catholicism. Parseghian was Armenian-Presbyterian.

The similarities didn't end there—both were winners.

The great Notre Dame passing duo of Heisman Trophy winner John Huarte, right, with end Jack Snow. (Photo courtesy of Notre Dame University)

1964

Huarte's Passing Snows Boilers

NOTRE DAME, IND.—Somehow, someway, John Huarte had rubbed away the pain of a separated shoulder. After a spring practice experience that led first-year Notre Dame Coach Ara Parseghian and his staff to think Huarte was the answer, out went Huarte's shoulder.

Doctors said he had a 50-50 chance of recovering without surgery. Parseghian hated the idea of the kid undergoing surgery. Surgery was not performed, and John Huarte did nothing all season but perform.

On the list of Notre Dame Heisman Trophy winners John Gregory Huarte's name rests sixth. Above it are such examples of greatness as Paul Hornung, 1956; Johnny Lattner, 1953; Leon Hart, 1949; John Lujack, 1947; and Angelo Bertelli, 1943. There is no name below Huarte's. He is the last member of the Irish to earn football's most distinguished award. No school has as many Heisman Trophy winners as Notre Dame.

His march to the Heisman began a week before the Purdue game when he combined with receiver and long-time friend Jack Snow for a 31-7 romp over Wisconsin in Madison. Snow caught passes for 217 yards, a school record.

The jury was still out on Huarte who had labored in the shadows of Frank Budka in 1963 and Daryle Lamonica and Budka in 1962. His chance, in this his senior year, had finally arrived. But what, the experts wanted to know, would he accomplish against Purdue and its sensational sophomore quarterback Bob Griese?

What he did was take a second step toward the Heisman by leading Notre Dame to a 34-15 decision.

The win was also a giant step forward for the Irish and the capacity crowd of 59,611 that filled Notre Dame Stadium. For the first time since 1951 they witnessed first hand an Irish victory over the Boilers at South Bend.

The Boilers had also won five of the last six but Huarte and Snow wrote the end to that string.

At first there were those who had their doubts. Griese took the Boilers on a 75-yard tour of the stadium floor including 57 yards of his own doing. His one-yard quarterback sneak on the 12th play of the drive gave the Boilers a 7-0 lead.

Led by halfback Nick Eddy, the Irish almost followed suit. Eddy and Huarte moved the Irish to the Purdue three. From there sophomore Ken Ivan watched his chip shot of a field goal go up in smoke when the Boilers blocked it.

After Purdue lost possession, Huarte reloaded and began again. His primary target was Snow. They combined to move Notre Dame to the Purdue three. Bill Wolski blasted over the middle and the Irish tied the game at 7-7.

Griese's passing game was on-again, off-again. When Tom Longo picked off Notre Dame's second interception of the game, Griese and Purdue were about to fall into deep trouble.

Huarte delivered the Irish again. The touchdown was scored by Snow on a two-yard flip. Snow, who teamed with Huarte during the summer months in California, had perfected many routes running on the beaches.

In the third quarter it was time for the Notre Dame defense to do its part. The Irish had been pressuring Griese, who doubled as the Boilers' punter, during the first half. This time they'd succeed in blocking the kick.

Keven Hardy and Alan Page, a pair of huge defensive linemen, bore down on Griese. The kick dented Hardy's chest and bounded into the hands of Page. Alan rambled 57 yards with the third Notre Dame touchdown.

One Irish possession later and all Purdue hopes were finished. Pete Andreotti scampered around the end for 23 yards. Ivan's fourth extra point made it 28-14.

Snow was finished doing the Boilers damage with his receiving but he had one more destructive act left—a third-down quick kick. His kick traveled 70 yards to the Boilers' three where Purdue fumbled. Phil Sheridan recovered and Nick Rassas completed the rout with a three-yard touchdown run.

Unfortunately for the Irish and Huarte, he was already a senior. The success Notre Dame enjoyed that season ended a long dry spell. Ara's first team posted a 9-1 record, the school's first winning record since

1958 when Terry Brennan's last squad went 6-4. The only defeat came with 1:33 left in the season when a USC field goal beat the Irish 20-17 in Los Angeles. It was the first Notre Dame team to post a 9-1 record since Brennan's first squad of 1954, a long, tedious decade earlier. The Irish completed the season ranked third by the Associated Press and eighth by United Press International.

Huarte, whose boyhood idol was Lattner, captured the Heisman and Snow finished fifth in the balloting. Without each other, neither one would have stood a chance.

Griese, who completed 13 of 28 passes in his first Notre Dame experience, helped the Boilers to a 6-3 season under Jack Mollenkopf. Following the Notre Dame game, the Boilers did run off four straight wins including one against Michigan. It was the only loss suffered by the Big Ten Champions that season.

But the era under Ara was underway.

1965

Griese (19-for-22) Too Slick For Irish

WEST LAFAYETTE, IND.—He carved his own special place in Purdue history while he cut out a piece of Notre Dame's heart. Bob Griese, one year older and apparently a decade wiser, put on the most magnificent passing performance of this or any other rivalry.

On the way to Purdue's 25-21 comeback victory over the Irish, something amazing happened to Griese. He connected on an unbelievable 19 of 22 passes for 285 yards, both Purdue records. That's no misprint. 19-for-22.

He also picked up 39 yards in only eight carries averaging five yards per shot. He was simply at his best and the largest crowd in Indiana football history, 61,921, crammed its way into newly enlarged Ross-Ade Stadium to take part.

"Let's face it," Irish defensive coach John Ray said. "We were terrible."

If the Irish were indeed terrible, Griese was the major reason.

The suspense had been building long before the opening kickoff. A few days before the game, Dick Hackenberg of the *Chicago Sun-Times* wrote, "It's one of those games destined to become a permanent part of athletic Americana, to be replayed again and again for years and years to come in every Hoosier hamlet, in big city bars the breadth of the country.

"In this one game the three Horseman of Notre Dame may be born Nick Eddy, Bill Wolski and Larry Conjar. Or sports immortality may await Purdue's Randy Minniear or Gordon Teter or Bob Griese or Bob Hadrick."

The suspense continued to mount as the game approached. It continued to swell during the early segments of the contest finally reaching its apex when Notre Dame's Ken Ivan booted a 24-yard field goal that clanged off the crossbar and fell over breaking an 18-18 deadlock.

Purdue Coach Jack Mollenkopf must have felt like falling over after watching that.

If he did, though, he would have missed what he later told the *Chicago Tribune*, "was one of the finest comebacks he'd ever seen."

And it sure didn't take long. Just four plays and 100 seconds later found Purdue in the end zone. Griese had cut right through the Notre Dame defense and its heart for 67 yards and seven points.

Griese ticked the yards off quickly, throwing 32 yards to Jim Finley and then parlaying two catches by Jim Beirne for 12 and 19 yards to set up Teter's three-yard burst for the touchdown. As if he hadn't done enough, Griese kicked the point after.

Earlier Griese had passed the Boilers to their first three touchdowns. Beirne had been on the receiving end of two and Minniear one. Not to be forgotten was Bob Hadrick's contribution. Not only did he forsake his hometown of South Bend and head south to college, but he came back against the Irish with eight receptions for 113 yards.

In fact, one Griese to Hadrick pass left even Parseghian shouting the duo hosannas.

"It was the best pass I've ever seen thrown in 15 years of coaching. "How," he asked "can you stop that? Anytime a fellow completes 19 of 22 passes, it's sensational. That's tough to do in practice, let alone in a game."

"Nineteen of 22?" Griese questioned. "It seems like I missed more than that."

"We tried everything against him," Ara said. "We tried to rush him, we tried to put up a zone defense against him and we tried a different combination of rushes. He was just too good."

"I seemed to sense when they were going to blitz and I'd throw short passes over the blitzers," Griese said.

Despite the passing game of the Irish being limited to two passes through three quarters, Notre Dame matched Purdue point-for-point in a game that watched the lead volley back and forth no less than five times.

With less than three minutes remaining in the first quarter, Ivan kicked a 27-yard field giving Notre Dame the first lead.

Griese and Beirne came right back to better the Irish. Beirne worked his way behind Nick Rassas, who lost his footing and slipped. Griese threw over the prone Rassas to Beirne for 28 yards and a touchdown. Griese missed the extra point.

Notre Dame continued to set the stage by rallying immediately for a touchdown. Eddy completed a 11-play, 56-yard drive by scoring from the four. Ivan's kick gave Notre Dame a 10-6 lead.

Just before the half ended, Griese hooked up with Beirne again for 14 yards and a touchdown. With less than two minutes remaining the half, Griese went for the two-point conversion and had his pass fall incomplete. The touchdown drive did cover 75 yards in just nine plays. Purdue, despite two missed conversions, led 12-10 at halftime.

Purdue took the opening kickoff of the second half and turned it into more points. Griese led an 80-yard drive in 10 plays. Minniear scored the touchdown on a 12-yard pass. Again, though, Griese's two-point conversion failed. With 5:16 of the second half gone, Purdue led 18-10.

Notre Dame relinquished possession and Purdue suddenly appeared on the verge of blowing the game open.

Just as suddenly, Tony Carey intercepted Griese's only mistake of the afternoon. Notre Dame regained possession just outside Purdue territory.

It didn't take long for Notre Dame to completely squelch Purdue's momentum. Bill Wolski went 56 yards for the Notre Dame touchdown. When quarterback Bill Zloch connected with Tom Talaga, who made a great acrobatic catch, the Irish had pulled even in 18-18.

Notre Dame took the lead when Ivan's 24-yard field bounced off the crossbar.

By then Mollenkopf was at the end of his rope yet he knew he had the man out there who could make this game turn out right.

"The only thing I told him after Notre Dame went ahead," Mollenkopf said, "was just go out there and throw the ball."

Griese followed Mollenkopf's orders to the detail. Nothing more. Nothing less.

Parseghian rallied the Irish to six straight victories before finishing with a loss to Michigan State and a tie against Miami. A 7-2-1 record was good enough to be ranked eighth in the United Press International poll and ninth by the Associated Press.

The Boilers were turning the corner into their greatest five-year stretch. The 1965 team finished with a 7-2-1 record with three All-Americas, tackles Jerry Shay and Karl Singer and Griese, who had set a percent completed record (.864) against Notre Dame.

The Irish, along with the rest of the teams in the midwest, were in for some difficult times against the Boilers.

"Griese was simply sensational," Parseghian admitted. "He was fantastic. Anytime a kid can pass for 1,000 yards as a sophomore like he did a year ago proves he's a good one.

"He has a tremendously quick delivery. We're talking of fractions of seconds which mean the difference between a reception and negative yardage.

"And the frightening thing is we'll have to look at him for another year."

Two-time All-America Bob Griese completed an astonishing 19 of 22 passes to crush the Irish. (Photo courtesy of Purdue University)

1966

Boilers Seymour
Of Hanratty
Than They Care To

NOTRE DAME, IND.—There had been great combinations before in Notre Dame quarterback/receiver history. There had been Bob Williams and Heisman Trophy winner Leon Hart in the early 1950s. There was Daryle Lamonica and Jim Kelly in the early 1960s and Heisman Trophy winner John Huarte and Jack Snow as recently as two years earlier.

On September 24, Irish coach Ara Parseghian unveiled the newest duo, Terry Hanratty and Jim Seymour. The unfortunate guests the afternoon of the unveiling were the Purdue Boilermakers, winners of three of the last four meetings.

A national television audience watched the Hanratty-Seymour premier played in front of the usual 59,075 eyewitnesses in Notre Dame Stadium. It marked the 11th straight series sellout. What they saw was a combination to behold and, for the Irish fans, a final score to match. Without realizing it at the time, the crowd also watched two of the country's best collegiate teams. One would become the National Champion, the other a Rose Bowl victor.

Seymour set a school record with 13 receptions and was on the receiving end of three touchdown passes of 84, 39 and seven yards to lead the Irish past the Boilers 26-14.

"After looking at the films," Purdue Coach Jack Mollenkopf said, "I apologize to my pass defenders for getting mad at them. One guy defending Seymour just isn't in the cards."

Hanratty and Seymour accounted for most of the Notre Dame offense. Consider that Hanratty completed 16 of 24 passes for 304 yards and

170

Notre Dame quarterback Terry Hanratty. (Photo courtesy of Notre Dame University)

The great Irish receiver Jim Seymour. (Photo courtesy of Notre Dame University)

Seymour caught 13 for 276 yards. That left three receptions and 38 yards to be divided among the other Irish receivers.

"It's all just a big blur to me," Seymour said. "I look at the movies of Paul Warfield, Gail Cogdill and Bob Hayes whenever I can. They are the best. I wouldn't mind being like them."

On this particular day, the famous NFL trio Seymour acknowledged probably wouldn't have minded being Jim Seymour.

Hanratty, who wore No. 5—the same number as the great Paul Hornung—was as calm as could be considering Parseghian was trying to keep his pre-game exuberance and own nervousness bottled up.

He was afraid that Hanratty's nerves would get to the sophomore quarterback before the Purdue defensive line. No way.

"Sure I was nervous," Hanratty said. "I was keyed up but I was relaxed at the same time. I could feel the confidence coming on during the pre-game."

Not only did Hanratty and Seymour carry the show, they also managed to upstage the star of the 1965 game, Purdue quarterback Bob Griese.

The All-America selection had devastated the Notre Dame pass defense a year earlier, completing an amazing 19 of 22 passes for 283 yards. The last completion of the day a year earlier went for the deciding touchdown in a 25-21 Purdue victory.

Somehow, Griese got lost in the shuffle this time around. Bob was 14 for 26 for 178 yards. Outstanding totals, certainly, but nowhere near as stunning as a year earlier.

"The coaches," Irish tackle Pete Duranko said, "did not have to say a thing to get us ready for Griese."

Hanratty and Seymour didn't share the entire spotlight. Cutting in on the action was a pair of picturesque touchdown runs, one by Purdue's Leroy Keyes and the other by Nick Eddy. Both earned All-America honors that season.

With Hanratty and the Irish driving, Hanratty's pass to Rocky Bleier was caught then fumbled at the Boilers' six. Keyes picked up the fumble and raced 94 yards for the first touchdown. Griese's extra point gave the Boilers a 7-0 lead.

If the Irish were stunned by the Keyes' run they didn't show it. On the ensuing kickoff Eddy began at his own four. Behind a wedge of blockers Eddy found daylight and cut left along with Bleier and Larry Conjar. Eddy went the distance and Jim Ryan's kick tied the game at 7-7. Within 30 seconds, a scoreless game had grown to 14 points.

Both teams missed additional chances to score. Ryan and Griese each missed short field goal attempts.

With 5:38 left in the half, Hanratty went deep to Seymour. The ball traveled more than 55 yards in the air. Seymour brought it down near the Boilers 30 and took it the rest of the way for the go-ahead touchdown. The play covered 84 yards.

Griese was able to mount another drive. Once inside the Irish 25 he missed on three straight passes, giving the ball back to the Irish before the half ended.

After both teams had their opening drives of the second half snuffed out, Hanratty and Seymour went back to work. Faced with a third-down situation, Hanratty sent Seymour deep against Dennis Cirbes. Parseghian had hoped to isolate the 6-4 Seymour one-on-one as much as possible. Ara got his wish on this play.

Seymour beat Cirbes and the Irish had a 20-7 lead after Ryan missed the point after.

With plenty of time still remaining, Griese was far from finished. He led the Boilers on a 74-yard march climaxed by Perry Williams' one-yard plunge.

The pressure began building on Hanratty. He led the Irish deep into Purdue territory before throwing an interception to John Charles in the end zone. The pass was intended for Seymour.

Earlier in the week, the Irish defense had promised Hanratty they would win the game if necessary. The interception gave them a chance.

With Griese leading the Boilers to what would have been the tying touchdown, All-America end Alan Page stormed into Griese, forcing a fumble. Harry Alexander recovered the fumble and ultimately the victory.

There was 2:46 remaining when Hanratty completed the hat trick to Seymour with a seven-yard touchdown toss despite the close watch put on by defender Bob Mangene.

"I think we just beat a damn good football team," Ara said. "I feel wonderful about it because Purdue is so dangerous. Griese was again outstanding. We figured if we could stop Griese we'd be all right. We didn't quite accomplish that but we made certain he didn't force us into one-on-one coverage very often.

"We were awfully keyed up about this game."

The Boilers dressed quickly. Within 20 minutes only coach Jack Mollenkopf remained.

"That boy Griese was terrific," he said. "He took a real beating out there. He was battered and bruised but stayed in there.

"Our pass rush wasn't so hot. We gave Hanratty too long to unload. But the way he and Seymour were playing I don't know if we could stop them anyway."

The Hanratty-Seymour duo continued to be magnificent throughout the season. The only blemish on the Irish record was the infamous 10-10 decision against Duffy Daugherty's Michigan State Spartans on November 19.

Other than that, the Irish were unbeaten and untied in nine other contests, outscoring the opposition 362-38. The Irish blanked Army (35-0), North Carolina (32-0), Oklahoma (38-0) on three successive weekends. The Irish also blanked Pittsburgh (40-0) and Duke (64-0) before tying the Spartans and shutting out USC (51-0).

It may have been the most overpowering Irish team of the modern era. No less than 11 players earned All-America status through one publication or another. Eddy and linebacker Jim Lynch were concensus choices.

The 14 points scored by Purdue were the most allowed by Notre Dame all season. Northwestern and Navy each scored a touchdown and Michigan State scored 10 points.

In any other season the Boilers would have had more to be proud of than the Irish. After all, the Boilers' only other loss was to Michigan State. They posted a 9-2 record including a 6-1 record in the Big Ten. The Boilers were ranked 7th in the nation by Associated Press and 6th by United Press International.

For the first and only time in their football history they went to the Rose Bowl where they edged Southern Cal 14-13.

Mollenkopf would lose Griese to graduation. Waiting to write Purdue history was Mike Phipps.

1967

Champion Vs. Champion

WEST LAFAYETTE, IND.—For the first and only time in the long history of the Purdue-Notre Dame rivalry, the 1967 game pitted champion against champion.

The 1966 Irish finished with a 9-0-1 record and wore National Championship rings. The Boilers had finished 9-2 and claimed the biggest bowl victory of the winter pageant and the most prominent bowl win in their history. Purdue had won the Rose Bowl.

The anticipation had built through the winter, spring and summer. The week before the game was overflowing with expectations. It began boiling over in West Lafayette on the eve of the game.

"Friday night," Purdue Coach Jack Mollenkopf said, "was the biggest pep rally in history. They had more than 60 signs and banners. You know how emotional the students are."

The emotions went further than the students. On the morning of the game, Notre Dame Coach Ara Parseghian awoke at 6 unable to sleep any longer. One sleeping pill and two tranquilizers later, Parseghian still awoke at 7 a.m.

Rocky Bleier, the Irish captain and soon-to-be war hero, said, "When challenge is turned inside out it becomes opportunity. And we'll be mentally and physically prepared to accept both."

The record sell-out throng of 62,316 that descended on Ross-Ade Stadium came to see if Terry Hanratty, who passed for three touchdowns and 304 yards as a sophomore a year earlier, could do himself one better.

Hanratty didn't fail to measure up to his earlier standards. He set Notre Dame records for passes attempted (63), completed (29), and yards (366).

But Notre Dame didn't. The Boilers were led by a sophomore quarterback who would cause the Irish more heartbreak than any single performer in their history. Purdue turned four Hanratty interceptions into a 28-21 victory, breaking a 12-game Irish unbeaten streak.

It was Page 1 of the Mike Phipps historic record of devastation against the Irish. He completed only 13 of 35 passes but he connected with his receivers when the Boilers needed the yardage most. The Boilers gained 238 yards through the air, an average of 18 yards a reception.

On third- and fourth-down situations, Phipps connected on six of eight passes for a staggering 166 yards.

Mike Phipps was three for three against Notre Dame. (Photo courtesy of Purdue University)

In the same situations, Hanratty was equal to Phipps. The Irish junior was 9-for-14 for 96 yards. What did Hanratty and the Irish in was Phipps' awesome ability to convert under pressure.

Example I: On a third down play, Phipps and Jim Beirne collaborated on a 40-yard pass play to set up the Boilers' first touchdown. The play was the third offensive play of the day for the Boilers.

Following a Hanratty touchdown drive of 75 yards and eight plays, the Irish took a 7-6 halftime lead.

Example II: Faced with a fourth-and-six at the Notre Dame 37 late in the third quarter, Phipps scampered away from Chuck Lauck's rush and found Bob Hurst open. Hurst is tackled at the three. Fullback Berry Williams carried the final three yards for the go-ahead touchdown, giving the Boilers a 12-7 lead. Phipps combined with Jim Beirne for the two-point conversion.

Example III: After the Irish had tied the score at 14 with a 94-yard drive capped by a one-yard plunge by Bleier, the Irish had handed Phipps a third-and-13 situation. Phipps connected with Leroy Keyes on a play that ended 44 yards later. That play set up another Phipps-Keyes combination that produced another touchdown, giving the Boilers a 21-14 lead.

Example IV: Hanratty had brought the Irish right back for the tying touchdown three minutes later when he found Paul Snow open on a 27-yard reception. The ball was now on the Irish 31 and Phipps was looking at yet another third-down trek of 10 yards. Again, he got more than he needed. His 31-yard pass to Bob Baltzell produced the winning touchdown.

No matter how many times the Irish gallantly came back and put Phipps in a hoe, the sophomore survived. Time and time again, the Irish, the No. 1 team in the nation, forced him into obvious passing situations and still he conquered.

"This evening," *Chicago Tribune* columnist Dave Condon wrote, "that name (Phipps) shines as brightly in Purdue football lore as the names of Dale Samuels and Len Dawson, sophomore standouts of yesteryear whose passing opened Irish eyes."

As much as Phipps drew the attention of the nation, the Boilers' defense was also an integral part of the victory.

Cornerback Tim Foley picked off two of Hanratty's passes. Sophomore Don Webster stalled a potent Irish drive with an interception at the Boiler 15 and Keyes, playing both halfback and cornerback, intercepted Hanratty's final attempt of the game.

"This was awfully sweet," Mollenkopf said. "You've got a real football team when you've got a bunch of kids who never give up against No. 1.

"I don't think we can play any better than we played today. Notre Dame has such unbelievable size. Yet our boys made up their minds to win. That's what makes football such a great game."

The well-wishers and telegrams kept arriving late into the night at the Mollenkopf residence. Moments after the victory, Mollenkopf had placed in his hands a fresh copy of the *Purdue Exponent*. The headlines read: "PURDUE BEATS NOTRE DAME."

The lawn of Purdue athletic director Red Mackey's home was covered with fans. More than 300 people stormed his doorstep in celebration.

Purdue and Mollenkopf had beaten the Irish before and would beat them again, but never like this.

"This game against Notre Dame," Mollenkopf said, "always gets us."

The teams totaled 834 yards and at one point scored three touchdowns in little more than four minutes. It was a wide open affair with no room for error.

"How?" a stunned Parseghian asked, "can you gain 485 yards and get beat?"

One reason was Purdue's constant two-way ferocity. Keyes not only intercepted a pass but had nine catches for 108 yards plus a touchdown. He also rushed for 27 yards on eight carries.

"We used Leroy as much as we needed him," Mollenkopf said after Keyes had successfully defended against Jim Seymour on the 63rd passing attempt and 101st play for the Irish. "And that," he added, "was just about the entire game."

"I am somewhat angered that they ran so successfully against us," Parseghian said. "Sure, we knew Keyes would carry on those certain plays but we just couldn't do anything to stop him."

Defensive back Dennis Cirbes batted down five Hanratty passes and linebacker Dick Marvel contributed a dozen unassisted tackles along with eight assists.

Hanratty was able to connect with Seymour on eight occasions for 114 yards. Seymour had 13 receptions for 276 yards and three touchdowns a year earlier.

The Irish lost defensive lineman Kevin Hardy with a badly sprained ankle. Hardy had also missed the game two years earlier, a 25-21 Purdue victory, after undergoing back surgery. Ironically, that game too was played at Ross-Ade Stadium and the Irish had come in ranked No. 1 in the nation.

After taking out their frustrations the next week with a 56-6 blasting of Iowa, the Irish dropped a 24-7 decision to the Trojans of Southern Cal. Parseghian's team would not lose again that season, finishing with an 8-2 record. The Irish were ranked 4th by United Press International and 5th by Associated Press. On November 18, the Irish crushed Georgia Tech 36-3. It was the 500th victory in Notre Dame history.

Purdue also finished 8-2 and 6-1 in the Big Ten. The Boilers were ranked 9th by Associated Press and United Press International. Unfortunately for Mollenkopf's squad the final loss was to another arch rival, Indiana. That loss on the final afternoon of the season allowed the Hoosiers and Minnesota to tie Purdue for the Big Ten title. Indiana earned a Rose Bowl bid but lost to USC 14-3.

1968

No. 1 Vs. No. 1

NOTRE DAME, IND.—A year earlier it had been champion vs. champion. On September 28, 1968 it was No. 1 vs. No. 1 after the Associated Press ranked the Boilers first and United Press International went with the Irish.

By the time the Boilers had demolished the Irish 37-22 with quarterback Mike Phipps writing Chapter II of his heroics against the Irish, even Notre Dame Coach Ara Parseghian was ready to concur with Associated Press.

"Purdue," he said, "gets my vote for No. 1 this week."

There are those that would claim the great Irish potato famine didn't cause as much heartbreak as Phipps.

He guided the Boilers to five touchdowns and completed 16 of 24 passes for 194 yards. In crucial third-down situations he was just as potent as he was a year earlier—five-for-five.

Make no mistake, one man alone could not defeat the Irish. Phipps received plenty of help from Heisman Trophy candidate Leroy Keyes and newly discovered receiver Bob Dillingham.

Dillingham, who wasn't a starter, collected 11 passes and scored a pair of touchdowns. The 11 receptions tied a Purdue record and also set an unwanted one for the Irish. Dillingham became the first receiver to ever catch 11 passes in a game against Notre Dame.

Keyes had the opportunity to display his two-way talents to a television audience as well as to most of the nation's press which had descended upon Notre Dame Stadium along with the customary 59,075 fans. Keyes didn't disappoint anyone, except the Irish and their fans.

Leroy Keyes high-stepped it by the Irish. (Photo courtesy of Purdue University)

Keyes ran for two touchdowns and threw a 17-yard scoring pass to Dillingham, giving the Boilers a 23-7 lead late in the second quarter. That play climaxed a three-and-a-half minute living hell for the Irish who had watched the Boilers roll off three touchdowns.

The first score was a 16-yard jaunt by Keyes. A Bob Yunaska interception of a Hanratty pass and a Bill Yanchar recovery of a Bob Gladieux fumble set up the two ensuing scores—touchdown passes to Dillingham, one by Phipps and the other by Keyes.

Besides Keyes and Dillingham, Phipps also received some aid from the Irish themselves. The Irish drove within the Purdue 30-yard line seven times without scoring. The Irish also fumbled away possession on six occasions—three within the Purdue 30 and three times deep inside their own territory which served to plant the seeds of Boiler touchdowns.

For a majority of the first half, the Irish seemed to have Phipps and the Boilers under control. It was almost immediate disaster for Purdue when tackle Bob Jockisch sacked Phipps on the first Boiler play of the afternoon. Phipps limped off the field, leaving the offense in control of junior Don Kiepert. Phipps, nursing a leg cramp, watched Kiepert lead the Boilers in range of a 34-yard field goal by Jeff Jones.

The initial report was not encouraging on Phipps.

"I got a charley horse," he said. "When I went off I honestly didn't know if I'd make it back."

He did make it back in the second quarter, just in time to orchestrate the 20-point Purdue explosion in the 3½ minutes span. Before his reappearance, the Irish were only able to generate seven points.

Despite running off nearly twice as many plays (35-18), the Irish didn't take the lead until sophomore halfback Denny Allan went around right end for five yards and a touchdown. The Irish had already failed twice when field goal attempts went wide.

After recovering from the avalanche of Purdue points, Hanratty led the Irish on a drive that pulled Notre Dame within a 23-14 deficit. His adept passing found Jim Seymour, another Heisman candidate, Gladieux and Tom Eaton between the Boilers' defense. Between scrambling and finding his receivers, Hanratty led the Irish to the Purdue 17. He then drilled a pass to Eaton in the end zone, cutting the margin to nine and reviving the hopes of the Irish faithful.

While the Irish defense was able to contain Phipps for a quarter, the Notre Dame offense sputtered away another opportunity when a 70-yard drive flickered out on the Purdue 22.

Purdue had handed the Irish the only opportunity it would allow. On the first play of the fourth quarter, Keyes went 18 yards for a touchdown. Not long after, teammate Perry Williams equalled Keyes in both distance and result.

The Irish were still able to move inside the Purdue 50 four more times but only came up with one more touchdown when Hanratty and Allan combined for an eight-yard reception.

The 37 points represented the most scored against the Irish in 62 games (a 42-21 win by Iowa in the next-to-the-last game of the 1961 season).

The offensive show the experts predicted had indeed materialized. The Boilers rolled up 479 yards and the Irish 454. Hanratty, who became the all-time pass completion leader in the school's history when he surpassed Ralph Guglielmi, went to the air 43 times. While it was 20 times less than the year before, it was still about 20 more than Parseghian had hoped for. But the 20-point burst by the Boilers made Parseghian's game plan go up in smoke... partly because of Phipps and mainly because of Keyes. Leroy had stated prior to the game that winning this game was more important than capturing the Heisman ("There are a lot of guys who win the Heisman and you never hear of them again.") He not only gained yardage as a runner and receiver but he played well defensively against Jim Seymour. His presence also afforded Dillingham single coverage and Phipps used it greatly.

Purdue receiver Bob Dillingham caught a record 11 passes in the 1968 game. (Photo courtesy of Purdue University)

"He was catching the ball and he was open," Phipps said. "I figured I'd just keep throwing it to him."

Keyes, whose hero in high school was the great Lenny Moore, was the subject of the Notre Dame student newspaper earlier in the week. "Get this man," the headline called out above Keyes' picture. But it all went for naught.

Not even the appearance of actor Pat O'Brien, who portrayed the great Knute Rockne in the famous movie, could spur the Irish past Purdue.

"I think it will be awfully tough to beat Purdue," Ara said.

"We might be more explosive than last year," said Purdue Coach Jack Mollenkopf, the first coach to defeat Ara three times and also the first to win two straight from Parseghian.

"On two of our touchdowns it took us only four plays to go 50 yards and two plays to go 28 yards."

Mollenkopf was almost correct in his prediction. Purdue finished with its second straight 8-2 record, losing only to potential Rose Bowl champ Ohio State 13-0 and Minnesota 27-13. It was ranked 10th by Associated Press.

Keyes did not win the Heisman. He lost out to a gentleman from Southern Cal named O.J. Simpson. But Keyes and guard Chuck Kyle were named to All-America squads.

The Irish defense proved to be its biggest weakness, allowing 170 points, the most by any Parseghian coached team and the highest total in a 17-year span. Still the Irish were ranked 5th by Associated Press and 8th by United Press Internationl.

Hanratty and Seymour graduated into the pros, leaving a new passing duo of Joe Theismann and Tom Gatewood in their wake.

Hanratty, Seymour and tackle George Kunz earned All-America honors and Notre Dame finished with a 7-2-1 record and spent another summer trying to figure a way to stop Mike Phipps. For the third straight year Hanratty finished within the top 10 in the Heisman balloting. He placed third.

1969

Phipps Three Times A Charm

WEST LAFAYETTE, IND.—It was the closest statement to "Win One for the Gipper" a Notre Dame team had heard since Knute Rockne addressed the troops prior to the November 10, 1928 game at Yankee Stadium against Army, a 12-6 Notre Dame victory.

"Football," Ara Parseghian began in the *Notre Dame Scholastic*, "is insignificant to many and, in total view of the world today, very minute. But "Rocky" Bleier, our 1967 captain, just wrote a letter to me from his hospital bed in Tokyo. He was wounded in Vietnam action and near to losing his foot. Yet, he wrote and asked me to wish the 'guys' luck . . . before we invade Lafayette. Right now football and the people who play it crowd everything back. Unlike many things in our affluent world, a victory must be fully paid for with work and sacrifice. At this juncture, I hope we've paid enough. Rocky . . . he paid too much. But the 'guys' will know and care . . . and thank him for his remembrance."

As noble and touching as the scenario must have been, Purdue's Mike Phipps didn't witness it. He was on his own mission, one that would carry him and him alone onto a plateau never before reached. He was about to lead the Boilermakers to their third straight victory over the Irish, 28-14. No quarterback had ever accomplished such a feat against Notre Dame. The moment was viewed by a Ross-Ade Stadium record crowd of 68,179.

He would accomplish his monument to consistency and belittling pressure by leading Purdue to touchdowns in each quarter. There was nothing new about the way in which he went about the task of sending

185

the Irish away without victory. As he had done in the first two games, he was magnificent on third-down plays.

He faced 19 on this particular breezy afternoon and achieved a first down a dozen times. Purdue's total offense on third-down plays registered an amazing 183 yards.

"Mike was even greater than he was last week against Texas Christian when he threw four touchdown passes," Purdue Coach Jack Mollenkopf said.

In three years against the Irish, Phipps had attempted 78 passes and completed 42 for a .538 percentage. He passed for 645 yards including 213 in his finale. Although he "only" managed four touchdown passes, one in the 28-14 victory, his third and fourth-down record was more than enough to make up for just four TD tosses.

In 1967 he converted six of eight passes in those situations for 166 yards. In 1968 he was five-for-five in third-down passing situations and in his farewell appearance against the Irish he was 12-for-19 for 183 yards.

In the Boilers' 28-21 victory in 1967, Phipps turned four such situations into touchdowns. The result was the same this time.

The Boilers struck first. With the ball on the Irish 37 and faced with a third-and-14, Notre Dame blitzed the inside linebackers. Phipps, who called more than 10 successful audibles, changed the play at the line. Randy Cooper sprinted free for the 37-yard opening touchdown throw.

It was more of the same on the second scoring drive.

Situation: Third-and-13 on the Purdue 34.

Result: Phipps finds Cooper open for a 21-yard gain.

Situation: Third-and-eight at the Notre Dame 43.

Result: Phipps throws in the left flat to speedster Stan Brown (9.6 speed in the 100-yard dash). Brown turns defender Chuck Zloch around before being tackled at the 16.

Situation: Third-and-two at the Irish eight.

Result: Phipps pitches to Cooper and then throws a block to spring Cooper for the first down.

End result: Brown's three-yard burst gives Purdue a 14-0 second-quarter lead.

Theismann, who couldn't get his passing game untracked, led the Irish downfield for their first score, a 10-yard pass to Ed Ziegler.

Notre Dame's momentum carried into the early stages of the second half, forcing the Boilers to punt the first two times they had the ball.

Theismann led Notre Dame to the Purdue 26 where he faced a third-and-one. A five-yard penalty for illegal motion set the Irish back. Theismann tried going to the right side but his pass fell incomplete. With a fourth-and-six at the Purdue 31, Ara sent a play in. Flanker Jim deArrieta was to cross over the middle as Theismann rolled left before throwing.

The play blew up when Purdue's senior left end, Bill McKoy, sacked Theismann for a crucial 17-yard loss. DeArrietta, meanwhile, was open. Instead of driving for the tying score, the Irish found themselves on defense at midfield and still a touchdown behind.

After Phipps took over at the Boilers 48, he connected with Greg Fenner for 13 yards to the Irish 39.

Again it was time for the third-down heroics.

Situation: Third-and-five from the Irish 34.

Result: Fullback John Bullock gets open after Stan Brown pulls the linebacker his way. Bullock takes Phipps' pass to the Irish 15.

Situation: Third-and-14 at the Irish 19.

Result: Phipps finds his primary receiver Fenner covered but spots Brown open for a 16-yard gain.

End result: Phipps uses two quarterback sneaks to give Purdue a 21-7 lead.

At the outset of the fourth quarter, Phipps went 42 yards to tight end Ashley Bell. Brown finished the drive with a two-yard run with 13:39 left.

Theismann and receiver Tom Gatewood did manage to cut the Purdue lead in half with a 20-yard touchdown pass later in the quarter. But by then the story line was complete.

Phipps was 12-for-20, passing for 213 yards. Theismann was 14-for-26 for 153 yards but through the first 54 minutes had recorded just six completions and 55 yards. Purdue outgained the Irish 366-280 and survived 12 penalties that cost them 101 yards. Notre Dame was penalized once for five yards. The score was 28-7 by the time Notre Dame picked up 139 of its 280 total offense yards.

Phipps finished his conquest of the Irish verbally.

"There was never a doubt in my mind," Phipps said. "All we had to do was execute the plays. After looking at the films all week, we felt their team wasn't as strong as last year or the year before that.

"We thought they were kind of weary of coming down here to Lafayette. They don't seem to take the initiative as far as scoring early in the game. We knew momentum would be a big factor, so we wanted to score first. We knew that if we got out in front early, they wouldn't be able to come back. And they didn't."

"Beating Notre Dame three straight years is something I'll probably remember when I'm older and done playing football. But right now, it's just another game, another victory."

"We had to worry about Brown because of his speed," Parseghian said. "When you have to cover a man with his speed you can't blitz the passer much. But Phipps was the big difference. He made the big play on every one of their touchdown drives.

"We'd stop them for two plays and then he'd come up with the key play and keep them moving. He has great poise, a great touch and great

187

leadership. He has had three wonderful games against us."

The victory was not only Phipps' final against the Irish, but it was also Coach Jack Mollenkopf's. Mollenkopf was by far the most successful Purdue coach against the Irish with a 10-4 record. He was also 4-2 against Parseghian-coached teams. Still, the Irish finished fifth in the Associated Press poll and ninth in the United Press International poll while the Boilers were not ranked. Phipps was instrumental in three of the greatest games in the series. The 1967 game pitted a National Championship team versus a Rose Bowl champ and the 1968 game featured a pair of No. 1 poll picked teams.

The victory also spelled the end of the Purdue dominance over the Irish. From 1954 to 1969, the Boilers had an 11-5 record against the Irish. Purdue beat the Irish when they were National Champions and on more than one occasion when the Irish were ranked first in the nation. In that stretch, Notre Dame enjoyed four regular seasons when it lost only one game, twice it was Purdue who beat them. Also in that time, the Irish had four seasons when they only lost twice, Purdue beat them in three of those years. In that 16-year span the Boilers outscored Notre Dame 368-282.

As far as the Irish were concerned, the worst of the rivalry was over. In the next 13 years, they would lose only three.

Besides the incredible Phipps, the Boilers had Stan Brown. (Photo courtesy of Purdue University)

Section VI
1970-1974

The Winding Down
Of An Ara

The era of the great Purdue passing quarterback was fading.

Those who had wrecked havoc upon the Notre Dame secondary and Irish psyche had given way to graduation.

After winning three straight and 11 of 16, Purdue eased back into a secondary position to the once-again powerful Notre Dame teams coached by the great Ara Parseghian.

Purdue had won 12 of the last 20 meetings. For two decades, Purdue not only played Notre Dame even, but actually had the upperhand.

Through the next five years, however, Notre Dame defeated Purdue four times and once again ruled the state of Indiana.

In 1970, Mike Phipps was gone to the National Football League. Notre Dame, behind Joe Theismann and Tom Gatewood, crushed Purdue 48-0, the largest victory and shutout margin of the series.

The following year Purdue regrouped and appeared to be in the process of an upset when, with less than two minutes remaining, Notre Dame took advantage of a blocked punt deep in Purdue territory and nipped the Boilmakers 8-7.

That victory is considered one of the great wins in Notre Dame history.

With Purdue's Otis Armstrong wearing the title as one of the game's greatest college running backs and with Notre Dame quarterback Tom Clements wearing a bigger-than-life question mark, the stage was set for the 1972 encounter.

As usual, the unexpected took place. Clements was uncanny while Armstrong was held at bay. While Notre Dame discovered how successful it could be with Clements at his best, Purdue found out just what it lacked when Otis Armstrong performed like a mere mortal.

In 1973, Notre Dame was rolling toward a National Championship when it met Purdue. The Boilmakers were listed as 24-point underdogs. Yet in front of a large television audience the Boilers grabbed a 7-3 lead, leaving the Irish squirming in their seats.

Purdue couldn't pull off the upset in 1973, but in 1974 they left the Irish with a bad dream they may never forget.

Just moments after watching the National Championship flag raised above Notre Dame Stadium, the Boilermakers went out and scored 21 points in the first eight minutes of the game.

Purdue was a 30-point underdog and Notre Dame had a 13-game unbeaten streak until the Boilermakers stunned Notre Dame with its worst first quarter in history.

Purdue won 31-20, leaving a sour taste in the mouth of Parseghian, who would conclude his Notre Dame coaching career that season. The winning coach was Alex Agase. Agase and Parseghian had built a long relationship through their years together at Northwestern.

The Irish had once again put a little more distance between themselves and Purdue with regard to the overall series record. After 45 games,

Notre Dame held a 26-17-2 edge.

The era of Ara was history. He finished with two National Championships and a 95-17-4 record. Of equal importance was his reputation as a man and a coach. In Notre Dame football lore he ranks with Knute Rockne and Frank Leahy.

It is, indeed, a select group.

1970

Purdue's Reign Ends In 48-0 Disaster

NOTRE DAME, IND.—The biggest pain in the neck for the Irish was now playing in Cleveland. Mike Phipps, the only quarterback to ever defeat Notre Dame three straight seasons, had graduated and turned pro with the Cleveland Browns.

There was no more Phipps and as far as the Irish were concerned there was no more Purdue mastery. After 20 years of what the Irish would classify as near famine, Notre Dame took revenge for all the misery Phipps and his Boilermaker predecessors had laid upon it.

The Irish put together the biggest margin of victory in the series by crushing Purdue 48-0 on a rainy day in Notre Dame Stadium. The shutout was the first for Notre Dame against Purdue since 1957 and the total points were the most scored by the Irish against Purdue since the 49-6 victory in 1946.

The Boilers had come into the game with three straight wins over Notre Dame along with 11 victories in the last 16 meetings. Recently retired Purdue Coach Jack Mollenkoph had posted the best coaching record against the Irish (10-4).

But for every piece of trivia the Boilers brought into Notre Dame Stadium that afternoon, the 59,075 soaked fans knew the one ingredient the Boilers left behind—Mike Phipps.

The opportunity was not lost upon Ara Parseghian either. On the eve of the game the Notre Dame coach told the Irish multitudes that gathered in Stepan Center that the reign of terror would be over in 24 hours.

"Tomorrow," he said, "I promise you, and the team promises you, a victory over Purdue."

Instead of Phipps and Leroy Keyes stealing the show, it was Joe Theismann and Tom Gatewood.

Theismann was superb, completing 17 of 25 passes for 304 yards. Of those 17 receptions, the 6-2 208-pound Gatewood brought down a dozen for 192 yards. Only former teammate Jim Seymour had more against Purdue. Seymour had a record 13 catches in 1966.

Gatewood also accounted for three touchdowns. Theismann adroitly worked Gatewood short and long enough times to totally befuddle the Boilers' linebackers and secondary.

Theismann worked away from Gatewood at the outset then started going to the future All-America.

"We tried to double-team and take Gatewood away from them," first-year Purdue Coach Bob DeMoss said. "That simply failed. They would complete a three-yard pass and Gatewood would turn it into a touchdown or a 15-yard gain."

The route was a simple square-out with Gatewood settling in front of the double coverage of Purdue. No fewer than five times, Theismann connected with Gatewood on crucial third-down situations.

On two of those third-down calls Gatewood scored touchdowns from seven and 19 yards.

"The staff and Joe really prepared me for this game," Gatewood said. "They gave me all Purdue's defenses and told me what to look for. I was ready for eveything I saw. Today, more than any other day, I played smart football, not just football."

While Notre Dame's passing game looked like Purdue's passing games of seasons past, Purdue's resembled Notre Dame's of seasons past.

Chuck Piebes and Gary Danielson combined to complete only seven of 32 passes for a mere 48 yards. Danielson, who came in relief of Piebes, had two of his first three passes intercepted.

The remainder of the statistics served as evidence confirming the severity of the 48-0 defeat. The Irish had 29 first downs, Purdue 11. The Irish rushed for 329 yards, the Boilers 96. The Irish threw for 304 yards, Purdue 48.

And that was just a portion of the story. The Boilers lost six fumbles and three interceptions, setting the Irish up time and time again.

The Irish opened with a drive deep inside Purdue territory. Scott Hempel's 19-yard field goal gave Notre Dame the early momentum.

Following a Purdue fumble and a Purdue interception, the Boilers drove to the Irish 19 before Piebes was stopped by linebacker Tim Kelly on fourth down.

Following a 55-yard bomb to Mark Creaney and a 14-yard toss to Bill

Barz, the Irish closed in on their first touchdown. That was accomplished by Denny Allen who followed the block of guard Larry DiNardo into the end zone. Gatewood had yet to touch the ball.

Another Purdue fumble led to the next Irish touchdown. This time Gatewood touched the ball. The play went 17 yards. With the second quarter still young the Irish had a 17-0 lead.

While Purdue was having its troubles with turnovers, Notre Dame wasn't exactly perfect. The Boilers had one interception that set them up at the Irish 22. Barz lost a fumble, giving the Boilers the ball on the Notre Dame 28, and a fumble following a pass reception by Gatewood gave Purdue possession at the Notre Dame 48.

The Irish errors did nothing to aid Purdue except take the ball out of the red hot hands of Theismann.

Before the debacle was history, Gatewood would score again. Hempel would kick a 37-yard field goal and Larry Parker, on his first varsity run, would put on a 63-yard performance for yet another Irish touchdown.

Trying to put what had happened into persective, Ara said, "This was a great win for us because we've had a long dry spell against Purdue. We got some early breaks and took advantage of them. This forced Purdue to play catch-up football and we know how that feels because we've been in that position before against Purdue.

"We tried not to get our players too keyed up," Ara said. "But I knew they wanted to beat Purdue so badly."

It can be assumed that the Irish felt the same way about the rest of their schedule as well. They rolled up nine straight wins including two more shutouts before losing a 38-28 shootout to Southern Cal. They entered the Cotton Bowl against Texas with a 9-1 record and improved it to 10-1 with a 24-11 victory.

There wouldn't be any National Championship in store for Notre Dame, however. The Irish finished second to Nebraska in the Associated Press poll and fifth in the United Press International ranking. Texas, ironically, was selected as the No. 1 team by UPI.

"Looking back," DeMoss told the Chicago Daily News "all I can remember is that it was just so embarrassing."

Looking forward, it did get better for DeMoss and the Boilers, if only slightly. Purdue finished with a 4-6 record in DeMoss' first season.

Joe Theismann, Notre Dame quarterback.
(Photo courtesy of Notre Dame University)

Joe Theismann scrambles away from Purdue. (Photo courtesy of Notre Dame University)

1971

Irish Block Boilers' Upset Bid

WEST LAFAYETTE, IND.—The Boilermakers were a mere 1:58 from revenge. The Boilermakers were a mere punt away from washing away the horrors of the 48-0 defeat the Irish had shackled on them one season before. Purdue led 7-0 and time appeared to be wasting away on the Irish.

One play past the 58-minute mark, the Boilers were suddenly a mere point away from victory. Just that quick they had been stunned again.

Little did they realize as Walt Patulski and Clarence Ellis bore down on Purdue punter Scott Lougheed that a special place in the hallowed locker room in South Bend would soon carry their team's accomplishment.

The dreary weather and insistent rain hadn't mattered much to the Boilermakers until Lougheed went back to punt the ball out of trouble. Suddenly, the rain meant all the difference in Indiana.

Lougheed was standing two yards deep when center Bob Hoidahl sent the snap hurdling back at him. The ball skidded at the two and bounced in and out of his hands.

"It was like a bar of soap," Purdue Coach Bob DeMoss said.

He scrambled to recover the ball. Just as he went to kick, Ellis came from the blind-side followed by the All-America Patulski. The kick never became airborne. Fred Swendsen fell on the loose ball to cut the lead to 7-6 and cut the heart out of the Boilermakers.

Notre Dame quarterback Pat Steenberge, who until then had completed only six of 25 passes, followed the touchdown with the decisive two-point conversion pass to Mike Creaney, sealing the victory.

"With the clock running out," Notre Dame Coach Ara Parseghian said, "I wondered if we'd ever get a break."

"They only had one sustained drive all day long," DeMoss said. "We made one mistake all day and it cost us."

The mistake belonged to punter Lougheed who failed to take a safety when he realized the kick was doomed following the short snap.

"But I'll take the blame for that," DeMoss said. "I never thought about the safety. I just told him to punt it out of there. It was my fault. I should have told him to fall on the ball if he got in trouble."

Notre Dame All-America end Walt Patulski. (Photos courtesy of Notre Dame University)

The win was Notre Dame's first in its last six visits to West Lafayette and Ross-Ade Stadium. No doubt the crowd of 69,765 that came out and sat under the bruised skies of September 25 figured they were about to witness the continuation of the Irish's West Lafayette losing streak.

Until the fateful blocked punt, the Irish and kicker Bob Thomas had fretted away the best Notre Dame scoring chances.

Thomas attempted two field goals but only one got off the ground. The first attempt failed when the snap was faulty. The second was wide right.

Notre Dame's running game showed signs of sustaining drives a couple times but just couldn't manage the big play to keep the ball.

The passing game of the Irish was also understandably misfiring with the weather. Purdue was having a lot more success moving the ball through the air with short patterns designed more for sustaining the drive than the big play.

Purdue's only touchdown came just before halftime. Boilers' quarterback Gary Danielson brought Purdue out at their own 47 after a Brian Doherty punt. Danielson teamed up with split end Rick Sayers twice for a total of 21 yards to the Irish 21. A third attempt by Danielson to Sayers was barely overthrown inside the Irish 10.

The Danielson to Sayers connection did more than move the ball for Purdue. It also knocked the Irish defense back on its heels.

After Danielson's third try to Sayers landed incomplete, the Boilers were faced with a second down from the Irish 26. Figuring Danielson would revert back to a ground game after three straight passes, the Irish were expecting a run. Danielson figured likewise and faked a draw to his fullback. The Irish defense took the bait.

Danielson, meanwhile, continued his drop and laid a lazy pass out to the left flat where Otis Armstrong made the reception and went in untouched. Purdue had a lead that it thought would stand up.

Lougheed, who would not dodge the last Irish bullet, escaped an earlier shanked punt that could have given the Irish an earlier touchdown. Late in the game, Lougheed sliced a punt to the Purdue 42. Steenberge put together the lone Irish drive of the game, leading them to the Purdue five.

But then it was Steenberge's misplay and fumble that resulted in a Purdue break. Steenberge fumbled on the five and Purdue's quarterback-turned-safety Chuck Piebes recovered.

Unfortunately for the Boilers, they could not move the Irish defense. Lougheed was forced to punt from his own end zone and the disaster ensued.

"It would have had to be one of the wilder finishes in a long time," Parseghian said. "But its the kind of victory you have to get during a season, one you've got to feel a little lucky to get out of."

The 1971 Notre Dame team had its eye on a National Championship after a 9-1 season the year before.

Purdue was forced to regroup. In its opener, Washington and quarterback Sonny Sixkiller held off the Boilers for a 38-35 victory, making the 8-7 loss to the Irish tougher yet to take.

"I'm proud of our defense," DeMoss said. "It was a great football game for them and they didn't deserve to lose. We took two good teams down to the wire and here we are at 0-2.

"Right now we've got some hurt feelings and we'll have to forget them and get ready for Iowa."

The Irish would find their National Championship dream shattered later in the 1971 season. They dropped a 28-14 decision to South Carolina in the sixth game of the season. In the season finale, Louisiana State dropped Notre Dame 28-8.

However, the 8-7 win over Purdue has stood the test of time. In the Notre Dame Stadium locker room there is a stairway section set aside for the crucial Irish wins. Engraved are the victories that have made the Irish and their long successful tradition more than mere legion. There are 42 scores mounted on the wall. One of those scores is Notre Dame 8, Purdue 7.

1972

Ara Cries Wolf, Purdue Cries Uncle

NOTRE DAME, IND.—All during the week preceding the Boilermakers' visit, Notre Dame Coach Ara Parseghian, knowingly or not, had been spreading a discouraging word. He had spent the week publicly doubting the quarterbacking abilities of sophomore Tom Clements. Ara didn't doubt his leadership or his ability to execute. He simply doubted his ability as a passer.

All Clements did was execute the Boilers with his passing.

On the way to a decisive 35-14 drubbing of the Boilers, Clements completed 17 of 24 passes and rolled up 287 yards plus two touchdowns.

By halftime, if Ara wasn't convinced, press box observer and former Purdue Coach Jack Mollenkopf certainly was.

Mollenkopf told Bob Pille of the *Chicago Sun-Times* during the halftime intermission, "I think Ara's been crying wolf about his quarterback. And we haven't spent too much time bothering him either."

Clements had already thrown for 250 yards and the Irish offense had totaled 403 yards.

As Mollenkopf spoke, the Irish had a 21-0 lead even though it was Purdue that caught the first break.

Erik Penick, who would finish the day with 133 yards on just a dozen carries, opened the game by fumbling away the ball to Purdue middle guard Greg Bingham.

The Boilers took over at the Irish 33 and moved to a first down before misfortune fell upon Bill Pedhoretzky. Pedhoretzky fumbled the ball back to the Irish at the 17.

The Irish were on the way to an 83-yard scoring drive which was aided by a roughing-the-kicker call. Faced with a third-and-13 from the Purdue 39, Clements simply found Mike Creaney open at the 20. Creaney took it the remainder of the way.

The Irish coughed up the ball later in the quarter. Once again, Bingham recovered. But once again, Purdue was unable to mount a scoring drive and Notre Dame took over on its own 30 following a punt. One five-yard penalty and six plays later and the Irish had doubled their lead to 14-0.

Clements had again found Creaney open for 30 yards setting up Penick for a 14-yard touchdown run.

Just one play into the second quarter, Clements again proved Parseghian's fears fruitless with a 62-yard scoring pass to Willie Townsend, the longest play from scrimmage of the season for the Irish.

By the time the Irish had surrendered the ball twice in the second half, they held a 35-0 lead. Both touchdowns came on long, well-executed drives.

The first score of the second half came on a one-yard plunge by John Cieszkowski although most of the work was accomplished by Gary Diminick and his 42-yard run.

The final Irish score came on another one-yard dive courtesy of Andy Huff. Again though, the Irish drive consumed 84 yards.

The Boilers countered with a pair of meaningless touchdowns by Skip Peterson and Jack Spellman. Peterson's score came from a yard out and Spellman's on a 24-yard dash. Spellman's run gave him the distinction of outgaining his Boiler running mate, the great Otis Armstrong.

Armstrong, who set Purdue season and career records with 1,361 and 3,315 yards rushing, was held to 45 yards in 11 carries. Armstrong, who was having an All-American season, finished with the Big Ten all-time rushing record.

"Notre Dame has great balance," Purdue Coach Bob DeMoss admitted. "They've got a fast experienced line, good running backs and Clements did a great job at quarterback. We just couldn't stop them."

The win was Notre Dame's third straight over Purdue. It finished with an 8-2 record and set off to the Orange Bowl and a date against Heisman trophy winner Johnny Rodgers and Nebraska. Nebraska rolled to a 40-6 romp over the Irish. Rodgers accounted for four touchdowns with great running and also threw for one touchdown.

Perhaps Ara was feeling a little sheepish about his down-playing Clements before the Purdue game. In the post-game remarks Ara spent a good portion of the time dealing with the play that ended the first half. Or as Ara saw it, the play that shouldn't have ended the first half.

Following a 21-yard screen pass completion to Creaney, the Irish called a time out, trying to bury Purdue deeper before the intermission.

All-America Otis Armstrong rolls on for Purdue. (Photo courtesy of Purdue University)

The sequence was as follows:

Clements threw a pass out of bounds intended for Huff.

Clements connected with Cieszkowski who stepped out of bounds freezing the clock.

Huff was then dropped for a two-yard loss giving the Irish a fourth-down situation with nine seconds left.

Notre Dame players claimed they had tried to call a time-out. Clements, acting quickly, lined the Irish up and promptly threw the ball out of bounds.

Purdue would take over on downs.

The Irish complained to referee Jerry Markbreit. Markbreit, who went on to become one of the National Football League's better officials, called the press box for the play sequence. He then gave Notre Dame possession.

DeMoss, facing the Irish for the final time as the Boilers' coach, complained to Markbreit. Markbreit listened and concurred, giving the Boilers back the ball.

"My players said they requested the time-out," Ara said. "But the officials said they had seen no indication. Anyone on my team can call a time-out and some of them tried to do it.

"I explained to the officials that it was very unlikely that a clever team, advancing the ball while keeping a close watch on the clock would forget to call a time-out with eight seconds remaining."

Right or wrong, Clements was busy on the other side of the locker room telling all who would listen, "I was pleased, too. We showed everyone we could pass. I never had a day like this one."

"Just say," Ara allowed "I'm elated and delighted."

DeMoss wasn't feeling quite the same way. The one-time outstanding quarterback was 0-3 against Notre Dame as a player and finished off his coaching career against Notre Dame the same, 0-3. The Boilers did have their best season under his leadership, finishing with a 6-5 record.

1973

Notre Dame Proves It's Best

WEST LAFAYETTE, IND.—The nerves were beginning to wreck havoc on the psyche of Notre Dame's Art Best. Never mind that the Irish were heading into their ninth National Championship season or that they had opened the season a week earlier with a convincing 44-0 thumping of Northwestern.

Forget all of that. After all, this was West Lafayette and this was Purdue.

There was only one thing Best could think of to settle his emotions. When he was introduced during the pre-game television ceremonies he put his thumb in his mouth and waved good-bye.

"I wanted to calm myself down," he said. "I didn't want to take things so seriously. This ain't death row, you know."

Anyone who doubted his display and its calming influence should just examine the results. On the game's first play, Best went 64 yards to set up a 15-yard field goal by Bob Thomas. The Irish were on the way to a 20-7 victory. Needless to say, Best had put his nerves as well as the Boilers to rest. For the moment anyway.

Purdue's talented answer to Best was former Olympic sprinter Larry Burton. Burton concluded a bizarre 80-yard, seven-play drive with a 53-yard touchdown catch thrown by Bob Bobrowski. The Boilers, unranked and 24-point underdogs, led 7-3 over seventh-ranked Notre Dame.

Both teams exchanged their next possessions via a fumble and an interception. It was a full three series after Burton's touchdown before the Irish were finally able to put together enough of a drive to regain the lead.

Beginning at their 47, the Irish set off on a 53-yard drive made possible by the running of Best and backfield partner, Eric Penick, along with the passing of quarterback Tom Clements.

Best put the Irish back on top with a nine-yard run with 6:48 left in the half. The Irish's running game was turning out an average of 6.5 yards per carry during the drive.

Notre Dame fumbled away their first possession of the second half. Purdue wasn't able to capitalize, however.

Again, it was up to the Irish to sustain a drive. Clements started it with two runs good enough to chew up 26 yards. After Clements connected with Pete Demmerle for 13 yards, Wayne Bullock rambled for a dozen yards and finally for the final one-yard that meant a touchdown giving the Irish a 17-7 lead.

All that remained was for Thomas to kick another field goal, this one from 42 yards out.

Bobrowski completed only 11 of 26 passes for 153 yards and was intercepted twice. His primary target, Burton, missed the second half with a right shoulder sprain.

Clements, meanwhile, had more time and completed nine of 12 passes for 152 yards. He spread out the Purdue secondary exceptionally well by hitting eight different receivers with completions. Meanwhile, Ross Browner, a future two-time All-America end, was making his freshman debut against Purdue a success. He blocked a punt and turned in five solo tackles including one for a 24-yard loss.

"Notre Dame has the same power they've always had," Purdue Coach Alex Agase said. "But they've got speed to go with it in Penick and Best.

"Clements is an established quarterback and he really understands their offense. He is also a good runner. This game gave them the opportunity to use those option plays."

Purdue had its difficulties in the second half. The Boilers managed only 13 yards in the half and four first downs, two of those coming in the final moments.

While Agase was facing the Irish for the first time as the Boilermakers' coach, it was his eighth time overall after going winless in his first seven tries against his former coaching partner at Northwestern, Ara Parseghian.

"We have to keep our heads up," Agase said. "A game can have two winners and today there are two winners. We weren't given a chance before this game and I think we showed them we can be tough."

"Keep playing like this," he told his squad, "and you'll win on the scoreboard, too."

Indeed, the Boilers had played a gutsy game.

On three occasions the Irish had possession of the ball inside the Purdue 30 and on all three occasions the Irish had a first down. On two of the three the Irish moved down inside the 10-yard line. Purdue held

Notre Dame to just three points in those three instances.

"At halftime," linebacker Mark Gefert said, "we encouraged each other. We were down 10-7. We talked tactical and technical. Then Tim Backe and Coach got us emotionally ready."

On one of the three above mentioned occasions, 265-pound tackle Ken Novak stopped Penick at the four, forcing Thomas to kick the first field goal. After Best's 64-yard run, it would have been easy for the Boilers to give in.

Best, who carried 16 times for 125 yards and also scored the decisive touchdown, had Parseghian concerned when he was a high school senior growing up in Columbus, Ohio.

Parseghian was afraid at one time that he'd lost Best to Purdue and feared at another time that Best was headed north to Ann Arbor, Michigan and the Wolverines. Ohio State, however, never had a chance.

"I wanted to get away from Columbus," Best said. "I wanted a good school that combined athletics with academics."

Best never completed his education at Notre Dame. He transferred to Kent State University.

Ara and Alex. (Photo courtesy of Notre Dame University)

While Agase was left looking for the bright spots, Parseghian was praising the Irish's gallant come-from-behind effort.

"This is a young team and it's most difficult to come off a big victory (44-0 over Northwestern) and then win a pressure game. It was also our first road game and the crowd made themselves heard. We just got caught up in a great contest."

The closeness of the game cost the Irish a couple poll positions the next week. After coming into the game ranked seventh nationally, the Irish slipped to eighth in the Associated Press poll and ninth in the United Press International ranking.

The season was still young. Purdue found the same result as 10 other teams that season.

Parseghian's second and final National Championship was topped off with a 24-23 victory over Alabama in the Sugar Bowl.

Bob Thomas, who would one day kick the Chicago Bears into a playoff berth on an icy day in East Rutherford, New Jersey, connected from 19 yards out to send Parseghian's Irish to a victory over the late Paul "Bear" Bryant's Alabama Crimson Tide.

Purdue finished with a 5-6 record but losing to Notre Dame that season was nothing to be ashamed of.

Art Best turns the corner against Purdue. (Photo courtesy of Notre Dame University)

1974

Purdue Ends Another Irish String

NOTRE DAME, IND.—The rains came early and so did the Purdue points. The Boilers had been embarrassed into 30-point underdogs against the defending National Champion Irish who were already 2-0.

The Boilers stood by and watched as the 1973 National Championship flag was hoisted. Then they rolled up their sleeves and went to work.

The nightmare they put the Irish through and a majority of the 59,075 at Notre Dame Stadium lasted only eight minutes but it was long enough and disheartening enough to spin the Irish around so they couldn't get untracked enough to ever erase those first eight minutes. Those minutes were lost forever. And so was the game.

Notre Dame's 13-game winning streak, the longest in the nation, the Irish's 13-game hold over Big Ten teams and the 17-game unbeaten streak the Irish had enjoyed in Notre Dame Stadium all came crashing down.

For the the fourth time in the rivalry, Purdue had washed away a Notre Dame unbeaten streak of at least 12 games. On this occasion the final score was 31-10. In 1967, Purdue ended a 12-game unbeaten streak belonging to Notre Dame. In 1954, it was another 13-game streak the Boilers busted. And of course, in the greatest game of the series for Purdue fans, the Boilers ended Notre Dame's 39-game unbeaten streak in South Bend in 1950.

Whereas, the Boilers built a 21-0 halftime lead in the 1950 game, the latest streak-breaker began to take form even earlier.

In the first eight minutes of the game, Purdue scored 21 points and by the end of the first quarter had built a 24-0 lead. Purdue had written another page in the Notre Dame record book—the worst first quarter ever.

The Irish had nobody to blame but themselves. The three Purdue touchdowns came as a result of a fumble, a punt and an interception. It took Purdue only 11 plays to notch 21 points.

"God, it happened so fast," left end Steve Niehaus said. "I still can't believe it."

On the second play of the game Notre Dame quarterback Tom Clements pitched out to Al Samuels. Samuels bobbled the pitch and Purdue's Rich Oliver recovered on the Notre Dame 32.

Purdue quarterback Mike Terrizzi, playing with a severly sprained shoulder, went immediately to Olympic speedster Larry Burton. Burton, who ran the 200 meters for the United States in the 1972 Munich Olypmic Games, took the ball to the Notre Dame nine. Burton went on to earn All-America honors that season.

"They were double covering me from the start," Burton said. "After that first catch the coverage increased."

After the Boilers advanced to the Notre Dame one, Terrizzi went over for the first score just 3:16 into the game.

On the next possession, the Irish couldn't advance and were forced to punt. Purdue took over near Notre Dame territory. On third-and-six Notre Dame was expecting the pass and overloaded the right side guarding against any plays in Burton's area. The Boilers countered with a running play to the left. Pete Gross burst through the left side and rambled 52 yards for the second touchdown.

According to Purdue Coach Alex Agase the play was supposed to gain only seven or eight yards.

Notre Dame was stunned. But the Boilers weren't finished yet.

On the ensuing possession Clements dropped back to pass, hoping to find Pete Demmerle. He found Purdue's Bob Manella instead. Manella went 21 yards with the tipped pass for the third Purdue touchdown of the quarter.

The last nail in the Irish coffin was delivered by kicker Steve Schmidt. After Terrizzi led the Boilers on another drive to the Irish 31, Schmidt kicked a 47-yard field goal with 2:13 left in the quarter, putting the Irish down 24-0.

The Irish were reeling from the deluge. Slowly Notre Dame began putting its game back together. Four minutes into the second quarter, fullback Wayne Bullock went over from the two, cutting the deficit to 17.

The Irish cut the lead to 10 points in the third quarter when another drive was climaxed by Bullock bulling over from the one.

"I didn't get discouraged," Purdue cornerback and co-captain Fred Cooper said. "I just told the defense, 'don't let them in.' And they never did."

Agase as a Purdue guard, 1943. (Photo courtesy of Purdue University)

In the fourth quarter, Clements had completed a pair of passes to Demmerle and Ron Goodman. It was then that Purdue's Jim Woods snuffed the Irish chances with an interception at the Notre Dame 40.

Mark Vitali, who had replaced Terrizzi at quarterback, went to Burton for 16 yards and then to Paul Beery for 14. Mike Northington took a pitch from Vitali and went the final six yards, giving the Boilers a 31-14 lead.

The Irish would score again when Clements connected with Demmerle for 29 yards. By then the outcome was decided.

The victory was Agase's first over Notre Dame. It also marked Ara Parseghian's last coaching appearance against the Boilers and his former counterpart at Northwestern, Agase.

It had come when the Notre Dame bandwagon was loaded with well-wishers and those with visions of a repeat National Championship season. One newspaper on the day of the game predicted that the match-up would be no contest. It predicted the Boilers didn't stand a chance.

"All week long," cried a joyous Agase, "people asked me and my players, 'Why even bother to show up?' Our players believed. Thank God, they believed.

"I talked to the players during the week and told them the two greatest things in football are winning and respect. We were rated 30-point underdogs and that's disrespect. I don't like it when people say we're no good, but the nice thing is we've got a chance to do something about it.

"I've always said you play the game to see who is best."

Agase considered it his biggest coaching triumph. He claimed it meant more to him than the 1971 upset Northwestern handed Ohio State. ("Only because Ohio State wasn't ranked that year and Notre Dame was ranked No. 2," he said.)

"It's tough to play against guys you like so much and respect," Agase said of Parseghian. The two coached at Northwestern together from 1956-63.

"Ara was tremendous after the game—all class. But I can't tell you how happy I am for our football players. They believed in themselves."

"Let's face it," Parseghian said. "Alex did a helluva job in preparing his kids for this game. We had to abandon our game plan in the first quarter when they scored so rapidly. I guess having a player on the cover of *Sports Illustrated* (quarterback Tom Clements) is the kiss of death."

A kiss of death maybe for one team, but it was like kissing a frog and finding a prince as far as Purdue was concerned.

"I never did like Notre Dame," Manella said. "Everyone in high school loved Notre Dame, but I never did. You know, you dream of something like this, but you never think it will happen."

Ken Novak, a 6-7, 275-pound defensive tackle who would earn All-America honors the following season, was close to tears when he explained, "I am so happy for Coach Agase. His 10th game against Notre Dame and his first win. I'm so happy to be part of one of the greatest upsets in Purdue history."

The Irish took the displeasure of the defeat out on their next seven opponents before losing to Southern Cal in the final game. The Irish did, however, send Parseghian into coaching retirement with a 13-11 victory over Alabama in the Orange Bowl.

The win may have cost the Boilers in intensity. They won only two of their next seven games and finished with a 4-6-1- record.

Section VII
1975-1982

A Devine Rivalry
Still Wrapped
In Heroics

There have been great games in this series played by great players who were assembled into great teams. One need only look to the eight-year span from 1975 through 1982 to see exactly what this series has been all about.

Some of the greatest games have taken place in the last decade. Many have been as thrilling as any college football game anywhere and at anytime.

Consider 1975: Notre Dame's Luther Bradley cuts short a Purdue touchdown drive that could mean victory. His interception in the waning moments turns the tide. The play covers 99 yards.

Consider the heroics of Joe Montana, the fabled Notre Dame quarterback. With two Notre Dame quarterbacks already sidelined in the 1977 game, Montana takes over as Coach Dan Devine's last resort. Purdue is leading 24-14 behind the passing of the gifted quarterback Mark Herrmann. With less than a quarter to play, Montana leads an incredible comeback. Notre Dame wins 31-24. Montana would orchestrate Dan Devine's only National Championship that season.

A year later, a defensive battle ensues and Notre Dame survives, 10-6.

In 1979, it was Herrmann's turn to mastermind a dramatic second-half comeback. Herrmann had never beaten Notre Dame before and it appeared that he was about to go down for the third straight season.

With Purdue trailing 20-7 in the third quarter, Herrmann led Purdue back to a 28-22 victory. He did so with pinpoint passing. One of his receivers was Bart Burrell, Herrmann's best friend.

If Mark didn't already know it he discovered it on that beautiful fall day in West Lafayette: A friend in need certainly found a friend with deed that day.

For Herrmann's sake, the 1979 game should live on forever. For in 1980, in his senior year, the buildup for the Notre Dame-Purdue meeting was awesome. It was a national media event pitting a pair of potential National Champion contenders. Under the direction of Coach Jim Young, the Boilers had grown into a power in the Big Ten.

Herrmann's chance at the grand finale as a senior never came off. He injured his hand a few days before the season opener at South Bend and never played. Scott Campbell filled in admirably, but Notre Dame, not accustomed to sharing the spotlight with any team, let alone Purdue, was too much. Notre Dame beat the Boilers soundly 31-10 to open Dan Devine's final season.

The game left no scar on Campbell's pride. With Herrmann a member of the Denver Broncos in 1981, Scott directed one of the great final drives in the history of the series.

Following the touchdown run of Notre Dame's Phil Carter with 2:57 remaining, Campbell set off on a long drive that ended with a touchdown pass to Steve Bryant. Just 19 seconds remained when Campbell and

Bryant made connections. Purdue still trailed 14-13. Campbell went to Bryant one more time for the two points and a 15-14 victory.

The fans who filled Ross-Ade Stadium, the players and coaches that lined the sidelines were limp when it was over.

The upset nearly occurred again in 1982 when Purdue rallied in the closing minutes of the first half to tie Notre Dame at 14.

Purdue was supposed to be using an inferior team that day. Maybe it was, but it took nearly 60 minutes to prove it.

1975

Bradley Steals Purdue's Thunder

WEST LAFAYETTE, IND.—Frozen in mid-flight, the ball lay lightly in the damp, fall air. The pass launched by Purdue running back Scott Dierking toward quarterback-turned-receiver Craig Nagel, who was standing in the end zone, moved in slow motion.

Nagel watched. He made eye contact with the spiral and reached out quickly, frantically, first for the ball and then for the suddenly streaking Luther Bradley.

Bradley, one of six Notre Dame players suspended a season earlier, raced downfield 99 yards with the ball and also with Purdue's chances of victory. Notre Dame won 17-0.

Bradley's 99-yard touchdown return stands as the longest interception in the series' history as well as Notre Dame and Purdue history.

A crowd of 69,795, the largest crowd to see a football game in the state of Indiana, fell into shock. In a flash, Purdue's chances of upsetting the Irish and ruining Notre Dame Coach Dan Devine's coaching debut against Purdue were dashed.

Purdue Coach Alex Agase called the play the "Miami Special" ever since he had used it at Northwestern to upset Miami 12-7.

Dierking took the handoff from Nagel and began faking a sweep to the right before lofting the pass to the left toward Nagel.

The pass was earmarked for Nagel. The Boilers had stalled on the Notre Dame four-yard line. It was third down. Purdue trailed 3-0 following a 29-yard field goal in the first quarter by Dave Reeve.

While the Irish had wasted more scoring opportunities than Purdue,

Luther Bradley, All-America. (Photo courtesy of Notre Dame University)

Luther Bradley intercepts against Purdue. (Photo courtesy of Notre Dame University)

the Boilers still found themselves in a position to take a 7-3 lead midway through the final quarter.

"It was a great call," Agase said. "And it was the perfect spot for it. But there was a missed assignment."

"I was supposed to cover the tight end, but he blocked (the missed assignment belonged to the tight end)," Bradley explained. "So I stayed right there. It reminded me of the Alabama game my freshman year when they ran the same pattern and scored.

"When I caught the ball, I just thought about the goal line. I was pooped out when I got there. It was a poorly thrown ball, but that's the breaks."

"Bradley wasn't all that far away from me," Nagel said. "I just couldn't reach him when I tried."

"That one mistake (by the tight end)," Agase began. "Just one play did us in. One of our guys didn't carry out an assignment and that's why Bradley was out there."

Bradley wasn't finished yet. After scoring with 11:17 remaining in the game, Bradley came back with another interception, setting the Irish up at the Purdue 21.

Al Hunter, who also missed the 1974 season with Bradley, carried from the one for the final touchdown of the afternoon.

Ironically, Bradley, a product of the Muncie Indiana area, nearly chose Purdue over Notre Dame when he was being recruited.

"My parents wanted me to come to Purdue, especially my mother," Bradley said. "But I felt Notre Dame was the best. Purdue was my second choice."

Outside of a 45-yard field goal attempt late in the first half by Purdue's Steve Schmidt, the Boilers found the Notre Dame defense nearly unmovable.

For example, Purdue had only two first downs in the third quarter, one coming on a penalty.

The win was Notre Dame's second of the season and second within a five-day span. The Irish beat Boston College on September 15. Both games were on the road. Notre Dame managed to outscore its opposition 34-3.

It marked the first time in NCAA history that a team opened on the road with two games in just five days.

"I'm just glad we're going home," Hunter said.

And so were the Boilermakers, who lost their first five games before winning four of their final six.

"Just one play," Agase said over and over again. "Just one play."

1976

To Play Defense Is Devine

NOTRE DAME, IND.—Dan Devine's second season at Notre Dame had started unceremoniously enough the week before when Pittsburgh and Tony Dorsett made life miserable for the Irish in a 31-10 trouncing.

Purdue, a 31-19 winner over Northwestern in its opener, had come into South Bend hoping to duplicate its heriocs of 1974, a 31-20 victory at Notre Dame Stadium.

Devine's game plan was obvious from the outset—the Irish would play this game close to the vest. Caution was the word. Defense, Devine reasoned, could be Notre Dame's saving grace.

"We were determined to stand in the middle of the ring and not back off," Devine said. "We realize that Notre Dame-Purdue games are nose-to-nose alley fights."

Devine's theory and game plan were perfect. For the second straight season the Irish blanked the Boilermakers, 23-0.

Although at the start it appeared as if the Irish might have their hands full.

After taking the opening possession to the Boilers' 36, Al Hunter fumbled a pitch out from quarterback Rick Slager. Purdue's Rick Arrington recovered at the 44.

The Boilers inched into Notre Dame territory before stalling at the 32. From 49 yards out, Purdue's field goal attempt was short.

The Irish came right back, led by Hunter whose 24-yard scamper put the Irish into Purdue territory once again. Freshman Dave Waymer drove 14 yards, helping to set up Dave Reeve's 39-yard field goal with 47 seconds remaining in the first quarter.

Purdue put together another partial drive two possessions later but once again Scott Sovereen's 41-yard field goal attempt was short.

Notre Dame's ability to capitalize wasn't much better. After the Purdue defense forced the Irish to punt, the over-aggressive Boilers were called for roughing the kicker, giving the Irish another chance. On the next play the Boilers were called for pass interference, setting the Irish up at the Purdue 26. Slager then decided to try to cover the remaining distance through the air.

Slager attempted only seven passes the entire afternoon. Chances are he would have been better attempting only six. Paul Beery intercepted for Purdue and brought the ball back to midfield.

The Irish got another break when Purdue punter Dave Eagin attempted a fake punt that caught some of his own teammates by surprise. He couldn't find any receivers open. Luther Bradley sacked him for a 13-yard loss. Notre Dame took control at the Purdue 28.

Hunter started the possession by rushing five yards. Devine then let Notre Dame's hair down slightly.

Slager pitched the ball back to Hunter who threw a wobbly pass to flanker Mark McLane. McLane made the catch and scored the first Notre Dame touchdown.

It was the first completion of the afternoon for Notre Dame and only its third attempt. Nevertheless, McLane's ability to come back and catch the fluttering pass had put the Irish in front 10-0 with 1:51 remaining in the half.

"It was a Joe Kapp-type pass," Hunter said later about his 33-yard touchdown completion. "I don't get the chance very often to pass and I really enjoy it."

McLane was even more elated.

"Ah, Al's a ball hog," the senior co-captain said. "It's about time he let me score. I get about one of those a year."

Purdue had enough time for one more drive before time ran out in the first half. The Boilers went into their hurry-up offense. Its success, coupled with Notre Dame being charged with an interference call, set up Mike Vitali and the Boilers at the Notre Dame 32 with enough time remaining for one play.

Vitali went deep to receiver Reggie Arnold. Arnold made the grab at the one yard line where he was promptly tackled. Just as Arnold got to his feet, the gun sounded ending the half.

"It was a strange game," said Purdue Coach Alex Agase, who was coaching his last game of the series. "We miss the end zone by three feet at the half. And in the end our halfback drops the ball in what should have been a touchdown. It just wasn't meant to be."

The last play of the first half was even more costly to the Irish. They lost free safety Randy Harrison with a fractured forearm.

Purdue opened the second half with a drive that ended at its 45. Eagin's punt went 36 yards but Notre Dame's Ted Burgmeier returned it nearly as far to the Purdue 48.

The Irish advanced to the Boilers' 17 before calling upon Reeve to attempt another field goal. Reeve's attempt was blocked by Cleveland Crosby. Fortunately for the Irish the Boilers were offside and they regained possession. Unfortunately for Reeve he wasn't given the chance at another field goal that afternoon and, therefore, didn't tie Bob Thomas' career field goal record.

The Irish were then faced with a fourth-and-three from the 12 and gambled that Hunter could carry for the first down. He did, along with picking up an additional four yards to the five. Jerome Heavens bulled his way to the one and Slager finished the drive with a one-yard plunge. Reeve's kick made it 17-0.

Burgmeier wasn't finished with the Boilers yet. On the following possession, he picked off Vitali's pass, bringing the ball to midfield.

The Irish went the necessary 49 yards to put the final six points on the board when Hunter plowed over from the two.

A Vagas Ferguson fumble late in the game gave Purdue its last opportunity to break the shutout string the Irish had extended against Purdue to seven quarters.

Vitali, who completed only nine of 32 passes, combined with Arnold for four passes, setting the Boilers up at the Notre Dame seven.

On the first play from the seven, running back Bennie Leverett was jolted by Notre Dame's Joe Restic, the sophomore who replaced the injured Harrison. Leverett fumbled and Restic recovered

The shutout was sealed.

"We failed in some of the strangest ways," Agase said. "We found every way we could not to score."

"Purdue," Notre Dame quarterback Slager said, "came to town with a victory behind them and thinking they'd catch us in the depths after losing to Pitt last week. Purdue didn't realize that this was a game Notre Dame had to have and was ready to take."

"Purdue," Devine said, "happened to hit us on a day when Notre Dame wasn't going to let victory get away."

The Irish used this game as a springboard to win seven of their next nine. After losing to the Trojans of USC on November 27, the Irish concluded the season with a Gator Bowl victory over Penn State.

The Boilers wrapped up the Alex Agase years with a 5-6 record.

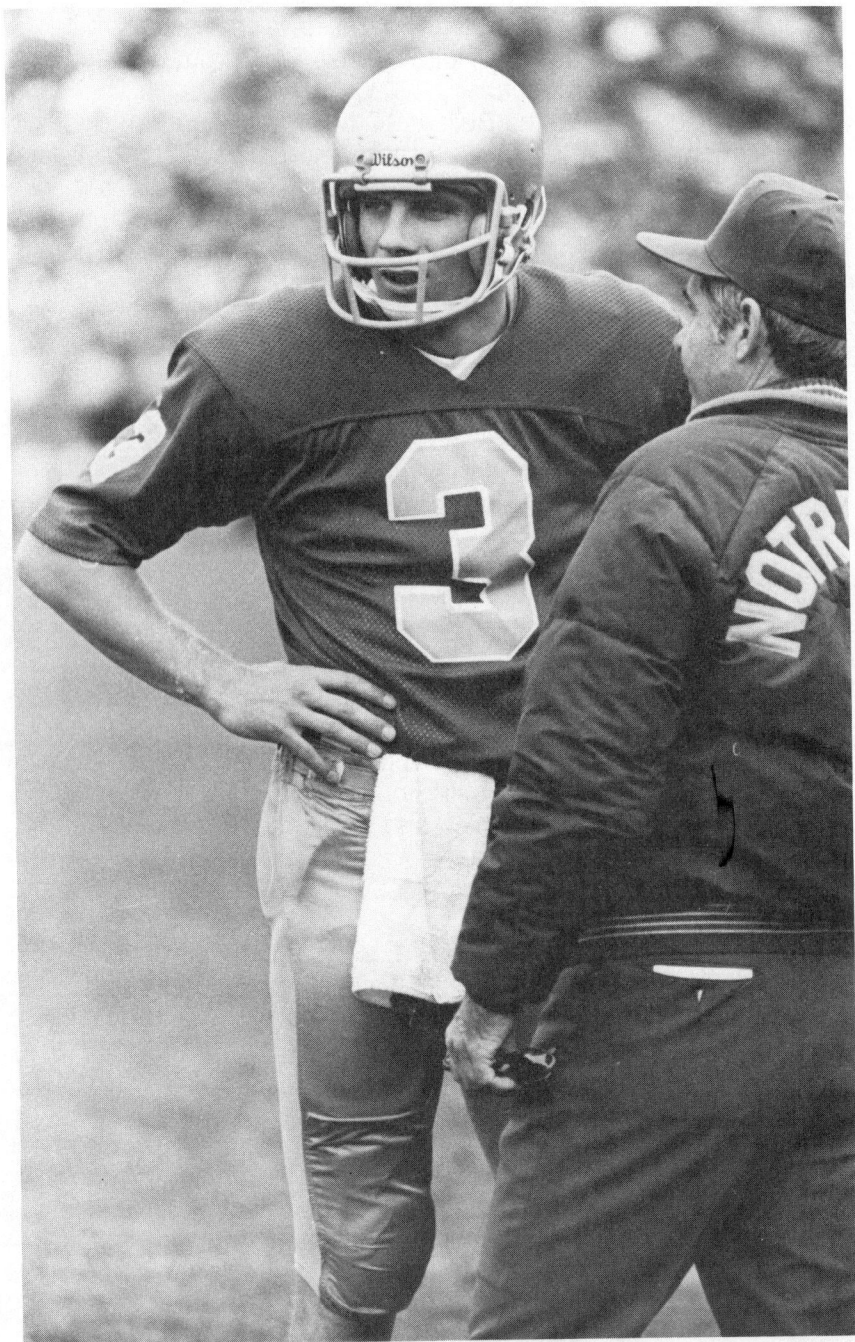

Joe Montana talks over strategy with Dan Devine. (Photo courtesy of Notre Dame University)

1977

Miracle Man Montana
Moves Mountains

WEST LAFAYETTE, IND.—The bulletin board material had been loaded and fired. The freshman quarterback Purdue had persuaded to help write its history was in place. The Irish came forward and waited and waited for the right stage setting. Once all was in order, Notre Dame Coach Dan Devine let out quarterback Joe Montana. And the rest, my friends, is Notre Dame history.

For all that had transpired the week before, it was Montana who broke the shackles off his legs and left the bench early in the fourth quarter. The Irish trailed 24-14.

Before you can appreciate the magnificence and the drama that Montana unfolded in the 31-24 Irish victory and before you could realize the preparation of the Purdue players prior to the game, you had to remember the heat with which Devine was coaching under. The glare of the alumni-pressured spotlight was blinding.

The *Chicago Sun-Times* had reported earlier in the week that the pressure to unseat Devine had grown to near epidemic proportions.

The motto at the Chicago Notre Dame Club was "Get Devine" and they didn't mean it in the biblical sense. More than 40 phone calls were made by members voicing support for the removal of the Notre Dame coach.

"There has never been anything so pervasive," a club official said.

As early as 1975, Devine's first season when the Irish went 8-3, wealthy Notre Dame alumni got together a 'kitty' to try and buy him out, the *Sun-Times* reported.

It didn't help that the week before the Purdue game, Mississippi had upended the Irish 20-13.

Bill Gleason, a columnist for the *Sun-Times*, wrote that Parseghian had an .848 won-loss percentage yet was always blamed for not winning the big one. Frank Leahy had a percentage of .888 and was still blasted because he wasn't Rockne. Rockne himself won .900 percent of his games and still had his detractors. He silenced many by turning to Catholicism.

Prior to the Purdue game, Devine's Irish squads had a record of 17-7 and played one season without six players who were suspended for rules violations. Two of those players were Luther Bradley and Al Hunter. Devine was wrongly blamed for their suspension even though he was never asked about the matter.

If that wasn't enough to get the Irish tempers up, the pre-game quotes by Purdue players John Skibinski and Kevin Motts may have been.

"When you play Notre Dame you are playing the best known team in the country," Skibinski said. "And when you beat Notre Dame, everyone in the nation knows about it."

"I grew up wanting to play against Notre Dame," said sophomore Motts, who grew up in the shadow of the Golden Dome. "It's not a question of gettting ready. I've been doing that for 20 years."

After all the preliminaries it was time to come face-to-face with the game itself.

Mark Herrmann's two-game collegiate resume had already included more than 600 passing yards by the time the Irish walked into Ross-Ade Stadium.

By the time the Boilers' first drive had ended he had added a few more yards. On the 80 yard march, Herrmann threw for 60 yards including the final 10 yards—a pass to Reggie Arnold.

Make no mistake, Herrmann was far from a polished gem in terms of experience. After Scott Sovereen's 25-yard field goal and Herrmann's eight-yard touchdown toss to Arnold, Herrmann overthrew Raymond Smith but not Doug Becker of Notre Dame. Becker scored what appeared to be a touchdown but a clipping penalty brought the ball back.

The delay was only momentary. Rusty Lisch, one of three Irish quarterbacks, threw a six-yard pass to Terry Eurick. The Irish took a 14-10 lead when Lisch and Eurick hooked up for an 18-yard scoring pass.

Herrmann was not to be outdone. He led the Boilers to a pair of touchdowns before halftime, connecting with Smith for 37 yards and Russell Pope for 43. Purdue led 25-14 and Herrmann had shattered the Irish secondary with 270 yards passing.

After a scoreless third quarter, the Irish and Devine appeared to be finished. The best opportunity of the third quarter belonged to Purdue but Sovereen missed a 32-yard field goal.

It was now time for Montana. He had worked his magic two years earlier when he beat North Carolina 21-14 one week and did likewise to Air Force 31-30 a week later.

His task was a mighty one.

"I could see it in their eyes," Skibinski said. "We had them. And then it changed. They got that spark and it was like a whole new game."

"We were at our own 20," Montana told the *Chicago Tribune.* "I was uptight. My opening call was a sprint out pass to Ken MacAfee. That really was the whole ball of wax. My throw was wobbly. MacAfee had to turn and bat it down to keep Purdue from intercepting.

"We came back into the huddle and I said, 'Forget it fellows. I had to get that one out of my system. We'll settle down now."

From then on he completed nine of 13.

It was his first appearance since 1975 after missing the 1976 season with a shoulder injury. On his first series he couldn't lead Notre Dame to a touchdown but he did bring them within range of Dave Reeve's leg. Reeve kicked a 24-yard field goal, pulling Notre Dame within seven points.

"I knew we were on the move," Devine said. "And we had plenty of scoring left so I was perfectly willing to take the three points."

As he had done in the 1975 game against the Boilers, Luther Bradley came up with the crucial interception. He picked off a Herrmann pass and returned it 33 yards, setting Montana up at the Purdue 35.

Montana was rolling now. He threw a sideline pass to Kris Haines and then hit MacAfee down the middle, putting the Irish deep inside Purdue territory. From 13 yards out, he went again to MacAfee for the touchdown. Reeve's extra point tied the score at 24.

"If I hadn't been certain that we still had time to get another touchdown, I would have gambled on winning or losing at that point," Devine said. "But when we chose to tie it up that left all the pressure on them. They knew our defense had started to rush. They knew we were moving."

There was still 10 minutes left when Purdue regained possession, it's two 10-point leads history.

Purdue was forced to punt. Star Purdue punter Dave Eagin shanked the kick 19 yards. Montana and the Irish set up at their 42 with little less than three minutes remaining. Again he went to work through the air.

He threw three times: the first to Haines for 26, then a six-yarder to Dave Mitchell and finally a 16-yarder to MacAfee. The ball was down to the Purdue 10. On first down, Montana went to running back Jerome Heavens. Heavens cut the distance in half. From the five, sophomore Mitchell finished Montana's piece of work with 1:39 to spare.

"It was one of the greatest exhibitions I've ever seen by a team," Devine said. "Sometimes when you back an Irishman into a corner he comes out fighting."

"Notre Dame's defense did a great job in the second half," Purdue Coach Jim Young said. "The things that worked for us in the first half just didn't go in the second half. I can't tell exactly what they did defensively. Nevertheless, it was our inability to move the football that made the difference."

Indeed, the Boilers were shut out in the second half, making themselves a standing target for Montana and the Irish.

"When you come off the bench there is really no time for pressure," Montana said. "Something is going wrong anyway or you won't be coming in."

In his first year as Purdue head coach, Young had witnessed the type of second half that made Notre Dame famous. His Boilers finished with a 5-6 record, but his day to beat Notre Dame would come.

By the time the Irish had defeated Texas 38-10 in the Cotton Bowl they were 10-1. The alumni howling for Devine's scalp had all but ceased. The Irish had seven players who earned All-America honors, including three that were concensus choices—Bradley, Ross Browner and MacAfee. Devine had produced the end result that Rockne, Leahy and Parseghian had done earlier—a National Championship.

Joe Montana rolls out. (Photo courtesy of Notre Dame University)

1978

Purdue's
Not Half As Good
As Notre Dame

NOTRE DAME, IND.—The respect earned by the right arm of Purdue quarterback Mark Herrmann was not taken lightly by Notre Dame. Just the idea of Herrmann and Purdue coming into South Bend was enough to send shivers down the spines of the Irish followers.

After all, the Irish had dropped their first game that season to Missouri and had been handily dispatched by Michigan in their second decision. And now here came Purdue, ranked 20th in the nation with a strong-armed quarterback bent on making Dan Devine's defending National Champions the first team in Notre Dame history to lose the first three games of the season.

It was just a year earlier that Herrmann, then only a freshman, had added his name to the record book by throwing 51 times and completing 24 for 352 yards and three touchdowns.

For some reason, the Boilers decided to pass from using the pass. Herrmann still threw 30 times (completing 15), but most of the tosses went for short yardage. The Boilers gained only 161 yards through the air compared to more than twice as much a year earlier against the Irish.

Purdue did control the ball, but win the game they didn't.

Notre Dame could dent the budding Purdue defense only twice, both times in the third quarter. The Irish, dodging the wrath of their fans and the bullet Herrmann was throwing with their name on it, escaped with a 10-6 victory.

If not for Jerome Heavens' 26-yard run and Joe Unis' first field goal in three years, the Irish may have fallen victim to a Purdue team that could not find its way into the Irish end zone.

It was not Herrmann's arm but Scott Sovereen's foot that gave the Boilers a lead, although limited both in duration and size.

On Purdue's second possession, Herrmann directed a drive that covered 77 yards and 13 plays, ending with Sovereen's 28-yard field goal.

It appeared to be only a matter of time before Herrmann would lead the Boilers to touchdown after touchdown. The fuse was lit. The only question was when would the bomb go off?

On Purdue's next two possessions it drove deep into Irish territory. But instead of building a lead all Purdue could build was frustration.

The first drive ended when Jim Browner jarred the ball loose from Herrmann 28 yards away from the goal line. Browner recovered at the Notre Dame 37.

Still undaunted, Purdue regained possession quickly and set off on another drive. This drive, which ate up most of the middle portion of the second quarter, covered 50 yards and used up 17 plays before fizzling out at the Irish 11. From there the Irish pushed the Boilers nearly out of Sovereen's range. Before Purdue found itself back on its side of the 50-yard line, Sovereen connected for a 47-yard field goal.

Purdue took the 6-0 lead into the locker room. It would be all the points the Boilers would score, but certainly not all the points they would need.

Purdue had run 45 plays compared to a mere two dozen by the Irish. Unfortunately for Purdue, all it had to show for its ball control mastery was six points.

"Sure we were controlling the ball," Purdue Coach Jim Young said. "And sure we were moving it. But it only counts if you move it into the end zone."

Knowing that the game was still within reach and that Purdue had most likely shot its last shot, the Notre Dame defense came on even stronger in the second half. Herrmann was sacked by numerous Irish hits crushing enough that Herrmann missed two series during the third quarter.

Purdue's time was quickly running out. Midway through the third quarter, Notre Dame put together a five-play drive that netted it 46 yards and the eventual winning points. Fullback Jerome Heavens rambled through a hole on the left side for 27 yards and the game's only touchdown. Unis' extra point gave the Irish a 7-6 lead.

Herrmann and Purdue tried to rally quickly. As it turned out, they came on too quickly. On Purdue's next possession, Young called a play that would turn the game and the momentum around.

Young called for a double reverse to be concluded with a Herrmann pass. Mark handed off to fullback Russell Pope. Pope handed off to wide receiver Raymond Smith who in turn lateralled the ball back to Herrmann.

Herrmann let loose with a long pass. Notre Dame's Randy Harrison intercepted the pass and returned it to the Purdue 14. After failing to advance the ball, Notre Dame called on Unis to kick a 27-yard field goal.

"That play," Young allowed, "was the turning point of the game and I called it. We were trying to gain momentum and it was simply the wrong play under the wrong circumstances."

There was still one Purdue drive left and one Notre Dame interception to come.

With 4:35 remaining Herrmann started the Boilers at their 19. Two minutes and 53 seconds later, Herrmann had Purdue at the Irish 37. It was then that Steve Heimkreiter put Herrmann and the Boilers away for good with another interception.

Heimkreiter had caused the Boilers problems all afternoon with his intense tackling. He finished the day with 24 tackles, two shy of the team record set a week earlier by middle linebacker Bob Golic.

All that remained for the Irish and quarterback Joe Montana to complete the mission was to retain ball control.

"Heimkreiter got the ball back for me and then it was my job to keep it," Montana said.

It appeared as if Montana might fail. Faced with a third and five from their 24, Montana called his own number.

"We weren't apt to get five yards from Heavens or from Vagas Ferguson on third down," Montana said. "We hoped Purdue would be thinking pass especially after I started rolling out wide. They did and it left me enough room to turn the corner.

"When I saw daylight and was able to get around the corner for that key first down, I felt I had pulled off my biggest play in a long time."

The defeat did not have a lasting effect on Purdue. The Boilers went on to five straight wins including a come-from-behind victory over Ohio State in which Herrmann was simply superb. The Boilers concluded the season with a tie against Wisconsin, a loss to Michigan and a victory over Indiana in the regular season finale that gave the Boilers possession of the Oaken Bucket Trophy.

After beating the Hoosiers, Purdue went on to the Peach Bowl and a 41-21 victory over Georgia Tech on Christmas Day.

The win over Purdue was Devine's fourth straight and marked the third time the Boilers had failed to score a touchdown against a Notre Dame team coached by Devine. The victory also marked the 591st in Notre Dame history.

"We are on our way," athletic director Ed "Moose" Krause said. "Any time you beat Purdue it's a great one."

Moments later, the Rev. Edmund F. Joyce poked his head into the post-game press conference, caught Devine's attention, and shook his fist victoriously.

"It was really great," Golic said. "After a game like this there's no way we can go back to losing."

He was within two seconds of being absolutely correct.

The Irish were on their way to eight straight victories. The only other Irish defeat came at the hands of Southern Cal in the final two seconds of the regular season.

Undaunted, the Irish went on to the Cotton Bowl against Houston. It was in Dallas that Montana turned in another incredible last second victory. The Irish dropped Houston 35-34 after Joe brought Notre Dame back with a 23-point fourth quarter in a sequence Notre Dame fans believe was the greatest of all the great Irish rallies.

No doubt Purdue fans were relieved it was Houston and not the Boilers who were forced to bear witness to the second Joe Montana miracle.

Devine visits with former All-America performer Paul Hornung. (Photo courtesy of Notre Dame University)

1979

Herrmann Discovers What Friends Are For

WEST LAFAYETTE, IND.—As if time would take the sting and bitterness out ot defeat, he was the last man off the field. Across the way from Notre Dame Coach Dan Devine the celebration was breaking loose.

The pandemonium had been lit by quarterback Mark Herrmann and flanker Bart Burrell. It was they that rescued the Boilers from 13 points down late in the game and tied a 28-22 loss on Devine's Irish.

For Purdue its victory proved as much to the Boilers themselves as it did to the 70,567 fans who filled Ross-Ade Stadium (marking the 22nd straight Purdue-Notre Dame sellout) that the Boilers were indeed worthy of the pre-season billing as a contender.

For Purdue's gifted junior quarterback Herrmann it was proof that he could lead under pressure and that his feet fit the footprints of the great Purdue quarterbacks before him that had stifled the Irish. And for Herrmann's good friend Burrell, it was time to breathe a sigh of relief; after all, Herrmann hadn't forgotten him when the Boilers needed a lift the most.

The burden of Devine's calling left him under the Ross-Ade Stadium stands with a towel over his shoulder, a religious medal around his neck and a pinched look on his face.

The first Herrmann to Burrell pass, good for 28 yards, gave the Boilermakers the break they needed in the third quarter. From that moment the Irish defensive backs knew nothing but confusion.

"We tried everything," Devine said. "They picked up everything we tried."

Herrmann would work with Burrell for three more completions including a six-yarder for the decisive touchdown that brought Purdue back from a 20-7 deficit.

Herrmann to Burrell was something new, yet something old. Back in Carmel, Indiana they teamed up on the seventh-grade team and a friendship began carving itself in stone. The first Herrmann to Burrell pass in grade school turned into the first Herrmann to Burrell touchdown.

The magic continued through high school both in football and basketball. When Carmel High was in the high school basketball state finals it was Burrell that picked up a stray pass and fed Herrmann streaking the opposite way for the title-clinching basket. They were every mother's favorite son. Then came time for high school graduation and an almost inevitable parting of the ways.

"I was interested in playing at Notre Dame," Herrmann said. "But I realized I wouldn't get the chance to play there for a while."

Such dreams were not for Burrell. He accepted a scholarship to play basketball and football at Butler University. Purdue had indicated it would like him to join its program, but only as a walk-on. "I wanted the scholarship. I was ready to play at a smaller school," he said.

Purdue Coach Jim Young had other intentions. He cornered Burrell two weeks before school opened and talked him into attending Purdue.

So Herrmann and Burrell were reunited. They both played a major role during the 1978 season which saw Purdue rise into the Big Ten contending picture. They worked out together all summer. But then along came a surplus of receivers and Burrell's duty suddenly became limited.

"I was getting down," he admitted. "I had only three catches in the first two games (a 41-21 win over Wisconsin and a 31-21 loss to UCLA)," Burrell said. "I decided this week to work harder and make the most of any opportunities I'd get."

That accomplished, he could rest easy while Devine searched for an answer.

"You don't win games by fooling people," he said in reference to the fake field goal Notre Dame turned into its first touchdown and a reverse flanker pass that set up Chuck Male's second field goal giving the Irish a 13-7 advantage at halftime.

Nor do you win by rotating three quarterbacks as Devine did. "We're going to have to settle down and go with one guy next week."

Even then the Purdue victory would be fresh in the minds of all concerned.

The victory was the first for the Boilers over the Irish at home since 1969 and only their second victory in the last nine years.

"This was my last chance to beat these guys," senior linebacker Kevin Motts was saying. Motts was pivotal in the Purdue plans after growing up and attending high school in South Bend.

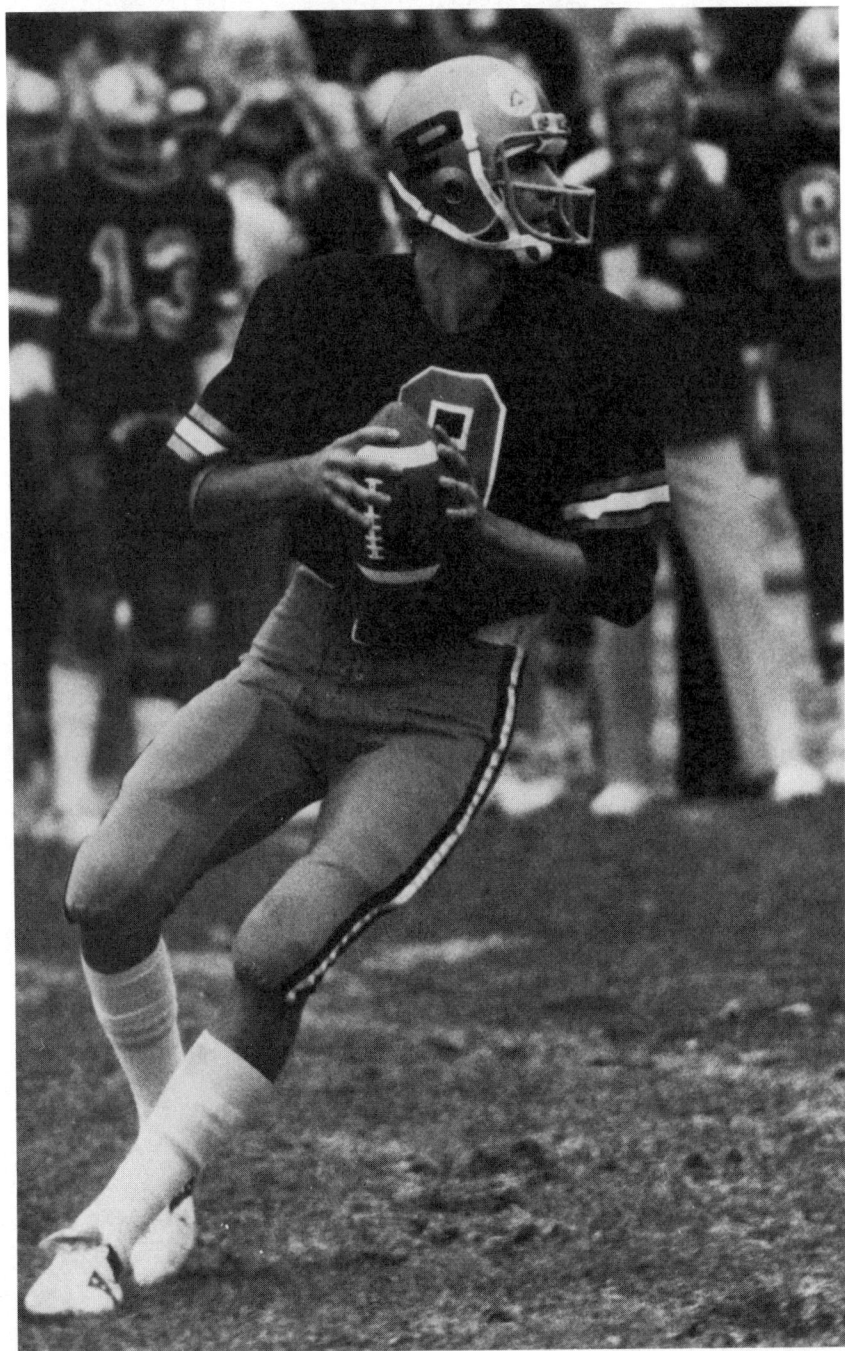

Purdue All-America quarterback Mark Herrmann. (Photo courtesy of Purdue University)

"We had come so close to beating Notre Dame the first two times I played them but we would either run out of gas or lost our poise," Herrmann said.

Neither disaster occurred that day, September 22, 1979. At least not to the Boilermakers.

Injuries hit the Irish hard. In all, 19 of Devine's scholarship players were out for the season.

That coupled with the fact that Devine could not settle on one quarterback helped the Boilermakers. Devine used junior Tim Koegel and Mike Courey to replace the injured Rusty Lisch, who had sprained an ankle the week before in the season's opening victory over Michigan. The fourth-string quarterback and holder Greg Knafelc also saw action as a quarterback.

In fact, it was Knafelc's 17-yard pass off a fake field goal to tight end Dean Masztak that produced the first touchdown.

Herrmann matched the Irish trickery with a 12-play, 78-yard touchdown drive that ended with Herrmann connecting with tight end Dave Young for 15 yards.

The Irish squeezed out a pair of Chuck Male field goals in the second quarter to take a 13-7 halftime lead. Male's second field goal gave him six straight including the four he kicked to beat the Wolverines the week before, 12-10.

Herrmann's friend and receiver Bart Burrell. (Photo courtesy of Purdue University)

Purdue's opening drive of the second half was blunted at the Notre Dame 35 following a 13-yard sack of Herrmann by end John Hankerd. Purdue was forced to punt, but it was the last Boilermaker punt of the afternoon.

The Irish gained a momentary reprieve on the next series when Koegel directed the team 62 yards on just eight plays. Only two of the plays were passes, the second pass and final play of the drive was a four-yarder to tight end Nick Vehr. It was the final moment of glory for the Irish.

Herrmann brought the Boilers out at their own 20. From there he began a perfect drive, mixing fine running of John Macon and Wally Jones with short passes on the flat and a taste of Purdue shotgun.

Herrmann was faced with four third-down situations and found a way to keep the drive going each time. On one third-and-seven play, he hit Burrell with an 11-yard toss.

The drive culminated on another third-down situation. With a third and goal from the one, Jones bolted through the Irish defense for the Boilers' second touchdown.

The crowd of 70,567, the largest to watch a football game in the state of Indiana, was estactic and the Boilers' defense were the main beneficiaries.

On the first play of the Irish's ensuing possession, Koegel had a pair of receivers open yet was sacked for a nine-yard loss. Faced with a third-and-20, Koegel's pass was intercepted by sophomore free safety Marcus McKinnie. McKinnie was finally brought down on the Irish eight.

Herrmann handed off to Jones three times and suddenly the Boilers held a 21-20 advantage.

Purdue's first drive of the fourth quarter produced still more points. Herrmann and the Purdue offense were in gear now. Mark, who would finish among the elite in the Heisman Trophy ballotting, had accomplished miles of accolades. All that he was lacking was a victory over Notre Dame. He could see the moment when he too would defeat the Irish and he wasn't about to let it slip away.

The Boilers took control at their 37. On the following 10-play touchdown drive, Herrmann threw four passes for 41 yards, completing all four.

The last play of the drive was an 11-yard pass to Burrell who had beaten reserve Dick Boushka in the end zone. Boushka had replaced Dave Waymer, who missed the second half with a knee injury.

Herrmann's mastery on the two second quarter scoring drives is evident in the statistics. He completed 8 of 11 passes for 103 yards finishing the game 14-for-20 for 158 yards.

Keeping in part with their never-say-die attitude, the Irish attempted to mount a comeback only to be stopped by another switching in quarterbacks.

After Courey completed a 43-yard pass to flanker Ty Dickerson, Devine pulled Courey and went with Koegel. Koegel was sacked on first down, threw an incomplete pass on second down and was sacked again on third down.

Once again the Irish were thwarted, but once again they were also given another opportunity.

With less than four minutes remaining, Purdue was forced to punt from their own end zone. Punter Joe Linville managed to pick up a poor snap from center and had the good sense to take a safety and not risk the Irish blocking his punt attempt for a touchdown.

Trailing 28-22, the Irish once again had possession only to fail against the Boilers' rigid defense. Ultimately, Purdue regained possession as the clock ran out.

The Boilers' victory was their first over the Irish in West Lafayette since 1969. Macon and Jones gained more yards (86 and 85) than the much-heralded Notre Dame All-America halfback Vagas Ferguson. Ferguson was held to 79 yards.

The Irish, fifth in the nation before the game, had once again fallen victim to Purdue, 17th in the nation. By the end of the season the Boilers were ranked 10th in both polls. It marked the first time since the inception of the polls (1936 for Associated Press and 1950 for United Press International) that Purdue was ranked in the Top Ten and the Irish were not.

1980

Notre Dame
Answers The Hype

NOTRE DAME, IND.— It was Day 307 of the American Hostage ordeal in Iran. George Brett, the Kansas City Royals' hitter supreme, had gone hitless in three trips to the plate the night before dipping below the magic .400 mark for the final time.

Yet for three hours on a picturesque fall day, the thoughts of American collegiate athletes focused in on Notre Dame Stadium and the grandshow— Notre Dame vs. Purdue.

The power behind the American Broadcasting Company (ABC) pushed the game up to September 6, the earliest opener in either school's history. The game kicked off the college football schedule nationwide, drawing not only the national television audience but also 403 press row denizens.

The build-up was enormous, the outcome anticlimatic. The expected showdown was in place. It pitted senior quarterback Mark Herrmann, Purdue's highly-acclaimed "Junk-Defense" against a Notre Dame team that was attempting to find one quarterback after sifting through five candidates and dealing with the promised departure of Coach Dan Devine. The expected heroics never came off.

Herrmann was rendered harmless during the week when he jammed his right thumb on the helmet of a teammate during Tuesday's practice. Herrmann's condition was kept quiet during the week but there was no way he would engineer another victory against Notre Dame. He wouldn't have the chance to give the Boilers a boost in what had been hyped as perhaps the best season in recent Purdue history. No, his chance was finished. It wasn't long before it was apparent that Purdue's chances were also nil.

Herrmann came into his senior season with a mile long of hosannahs. He had passed for 6,734 yards with 530 completions and was considered a very strong candidate for Heisman Trophy honors.

"The way I was throwing in the pre-game made the decisions easy," he said. "I had no zip on the ball."

Purdue's chances were left to freshman Scott Campbell. Suddenly, the quarterback situation of both teams appeared equal.

Mike Courey survived Devine's five-man race to open the season as the Notre Dame quarterback. He completed 11 of 13 passes for 151 yards and a touchdown.

Alas, Campbell was also amazing, completing 17 of 26 for 178 yards. While his performance had been noble, neither he nor Herrmann would have had much of a chance at stopping Notre Dame on its way to a 31-10 victory.

It didn't matter that the Irish offensive line was left in the hands of All-America center John Scully and a host of players who had not started a game before. Truth be told, the Irish were weary of hearing of Herrmann and Purdue. The media machine in its exuberance to build the event had created a monster. The monster proved to be the underdog Irish, not the favored Boilermakers.

Midway through the first quarter, the Irish took a 3-0 lead on a 36-yard field goal by Harry Oliver. Before the end of the quarter, Bob McGarry, making his first and only carry of the season, took an option pitch from Courey for two yards and a touchdown. Before four minutes had elapsed in the second quarter sophomore halfback Phil Carter plunged over from the one, giving the Irish a 17-0 lead.

No doubt ABC and its national viewing audience had to be wondering what kind of ticket ABC was selling and the public viewing.

The Boilers managed to slice into the lead slightly with a 26-yard Rick Anderson field goal. When Notre Dame's Pete Buchanan fumbled away an Irish drive at the Purdue 32, suddenly the Boilers had a chance to change the game's complexion.

After Tim Seneff had recovered the fumble, Campbell, who completed 10 straight passes, took the Boilers to the Notre Dame 45 yard line with less than a minute remaining in the half.

Purdue caught another break when Campbell's tipped pass ended up in the hands of All-America end Dave Young. Young got down to the Irish four.

With only 34 seconds left, Wally Jones bolted over from the four, giving the Boilers renewed hope and only a 17-10 deficit at halftime.

"I thought we needed something to regain the momentum," Devine said. "That second quarter drive helped Purdue because they got the seven points. But it helped us too because that was not the kind of football we wanted to play."

Devine realized at halftime that the Boilers, who had failed to produce even one first down in the first 19 minutes of play, were suddenly a team on the loose.

On the first play of the second half, Devine had Courey go deep to split end Tony Hunter. Courey delivered and Hunter beat cornerback Bob Williams to set the Irish up 19 yards from the Purdue goal line. Six plays later, Courey went back to Hunter for a nine-yard touchdown pass, pushing the Irish margin back to a comfortable 24-10.

"If Purdue had stopped us on the first drive of the third quarter," Courey said. "It would have been a different ball game. It would have been a dog fight."

Courey made the decision final in the fourth quarter with a 14-yard run. Phil Carter, who had replaced senior Jim Stone as the heir apparent to the great Vargas Ferguson, set up the touchdown with a 19-yard run. Carter gained 145 yards in 29 carries.

Carter himself had outgained the Boilers' running attack by 108 yards. The Boilers tried 36 running plays and could net a mere 37 yards. Meanwhile, Campbell was sacked eight times led by Notre Dame's "Big Zs," Mark Zavagnin and All-America end Scott Zettek.

"All we've heard all week long was "Mark Herrmann and Purdue vs. Notre Dame," Zettek said. "Well we are not used to getting second billing around here."

"Mark Herrmann," All-America linebacker Bob Crable was saying, "is just one man. If you think one man can beat Notre Dame you're dead wrong."

Purdue Coach Jim Young had no problem seconding Crable's statement.

"Notre Dame dominated so many areas of the game that a single player couldn't make the difference.

"With our change in quarterback, I had hoped to establish the running game, but Notre Dame took it away from us early."

"It may have been slightly closer if he (Herrmann) had played," Courey said. "But I am happy as hell about it. Not for Mark Herrmann, for me."

"I think playing quarterback at Notre Dame is something special. The wait was worth it."

The Irish took the next weekend off before beating Michigan 29-27 in the final minute. Notre Dame rolled to seven straight wins before tying Georgia Tech 3-3 and beating Alabama 7-0 and the Air Force. It set up a potential National Championship finale. Notre Dame went into the Southern Cal game with a 9-0-1 record.

Notre Dame dropped a 20-6 decision to the Trojans before heading south to the Sugar Bowl and Dan Devine's final game as the Irish coach. It was there they ran into Herschel Walker and the Georgia Bulldogs. Georgia whipped the Irish 17-10 and claimed a National Championship in the process.

Purdue began slowly and was 1-2 after beating Wisconsin and losing to UCLA. Its Rose Bowl visions were intact until November 15 when Michigan knocked off Purdue. By then the Boilers had risen to 7-2, with both defeats coming against non-conference teams. The loss to Michigan was followed by a 24-23 win over Indiana in front of the largest crowd in the state's football history, 71,629 at Ross-Ade Stadium.

In his final Purdue performance, Herrmann led the Boilers to a third straight bowl victory. Herrmann finished his college career with a 28-25 victory over Missouri in the Liberty Bowl.

He was Purdue's career total offense leader with 9,134 yards. He also had 9,946 passing yards, another Purdue record. Yet, his record could have been even better and his spot in Purdue history one notch higher if he had played one more game—the September 6 game vs. Notre Dame.

Dan Devine threw in the towel following the 1980 season. (Photo courtesy of Notre Dame University)

1981

Purdue's Campbell Leaves Irish Crying

WEST LAFAYETTE, IND.—"The (Phil) Carter run," the *Chicago Tribune's* Dave Condon wrote, "as sensational as it was in putting Notre Dame ahead with the clock running down, merely finished setting the stage for a gridiron drama that rivals anything I have ever seen."

Indeed, Carter's 30-yard run with only 2:57 remaining was sensational. It gave Notre Dame a 14-7 edge and put Purdue in a position of near disaster. Unbeknownst to the Irish, they were about to fall victim to a scene they themselves had helped create and master. As Condon, an alumnus and a witness to many Notre Dame miracles in his many years as a top-flight columnist, said, it rivaled anything he had ever seen.

It began when sophomore quarterback Scott Campbell broke the Purdue huddle at his 20-yard line. There were 80 yards in front of him, a tenacious Notre Dame defense inches away and less than three minutes to get the job done. The dramatics that followed were enough to leave Irish eyes crying.

With a steady 20-mile-an-hour wind in his face, Campbell's first play cost him five yards. A gain of 12 and a tailback spurt for two still left the Boilers a yard shy of continuing their drive to destiny. With a four-and-one, Purdue barely made it.

The Boilers moved quickly to their 43-yard line where Campbell was faced with a second-and-10 and a clock that was burning out rapidly.

He dropped back to pass. Open downfield was Steve Bryant. Bryant reached out and caught the pass a yard from the Notre Dame end zone. Suddenly, it was Purdue that was in control of its own destiny. The clock

Purdue quarterback Scott Campbell. (Photo courtesy of Purdue University)

was now its ally.

"I have to be honest," Campbell said later, "I was throwing that pass to Everitt Pickens in the end zone. Bryant just reached up and grabbed it. He came up with a great play."

"The ball was up there," Bryant said. "And either I caught it or nobody did."

On first down, the Notre Dame defense dug in and set Purdue back with a six-yard loss. On second down, Campbell, who threw 12 of his 24 passes during the final drive, threw an incomplete pass. On third down, another pass lay wasted on the Ross-Ade Stadium turf.

It was now fourth-and-seven for the touchdown.

The play would go to Bryant, a flag pass pattern into the corner of the end zone. Campbell dropped back and threw over the outstretched arms of defender Chris Brown. Brown was replacing the injured All-America defender John Krimm. The ball avoided Brown's reach and settled into the hands of Bryant. Purdue trailed 14-13.

With 19 seconds left, Coach Jim Young, who was coaching his final game for the Boilers against the Irish, had another decision to make.

Even with the wind in his face, Rick Anderson probably would not have had too much trouble connecting for the game-tying extra point. But here was a chance to beat Notre Dame.

There was never a doubt. Purdue would live or die with a two-point conversion.

On the sidelines, Young's assistants were yelling their suggestions to the coach in unison.

"I had five plays coming at me at once," Young said.

He went with the same play Dick Dullaghen, the former high school coach of Mark Herrmann, had offered on the preceding play. Purdue would merely change the direction and the side of the field Bryant would run his pattern to.

In mirrored image of the touchdown, Campbell dropped back and lofted a pass over the outstretched hands of Brown and in the cradle-lock of Bryant. Purdue had pulled it off, 15-14.

Notre Dame was about to fall to 0-2 in its first season under Coach Gerry Faust. The Irish had opened the season as the No. 1 team in the nation. Just two weeks later Notre Dame wasn't even the No. 1 team in Indiana.

"I don't think Brown got burned," Faust said. "Both times he was as close to Bryant as he could be. It was just a case of two perfect passes and two perfect catches."

"I just got beat," Brown said. "I wasn't anticipating him trying the same corner route."

"The same play," Faust muttered. "Perfect passes right over our defender's head. They had to be perfect passes."

For Young it was his farewell to the Purdue-Notre Dame rivalries from a coaching standpoint and the vision of his Boilers again playing the role of "Spoilermakers" in pulling off a major upset in miraculous fashion nearly stunned him to tears.

"I asked my players to give everything they had for this game," he said. "They gave that and a little more.

"I sometimes think as a coach you get stuck on having to go for two points in this country. It's wrong to assume that if you're a winner you have to go for two.

"Those kids would have been mighty sad if we hadn't hit those final two points."

There was evidence early on that this game could come down to just such a situation. After a scoreless first quarter, Notre Dame broke through with a one-yard dive by Chris Smith. Smith's touchdown climaxed an 11-play, 71-yard drive that featured a pair of long completions by quarterback Tim Koegel. Koegel connected with Dave Condeni for 21 yards and Mike Boushka for 25.

Purdue didn't tie the game until late in the third quarter when Wally Jones finished an eight-play, 66-yard drive with a one-yard plunge. Campbell's big play of that drive was a 40-yard pass to Cliff Benson.

That is where the game stood until Carter galloped away with what the Irish thought was victory.

"I've won a lot of games at Cincinnati Moeller (high school) like this," Faust said. "But this is a heckuva way for it to come back against me."

"I guess it was just our time to lose one that way," two-time All-America linebacker Bob Crable rationalized.

"I thought Notre Dame was supposed to win games this way, not lose," someone suggested to Faust.

Gerry Faust meets with Devine after replacing Dan in 1981. (Photo courtesy of Notre Dame University)

"That's what I thought, too," he said. "That's what I thought."

Unfortunately for Faust and the Irish, the 1981 season was only slightly better than the first two games. The Irish finished with a 5-6 record, their first below .500 record since 1963, Joe Kuharich's final season as head coach.

Purdue, which hadn't beaten the Irish by one-point since 1963 (7-6), couldn't ride the emotion of the victory for an entire season. In Jim Young's final season as a coach, the Boilers also finished with a 5-6 record.

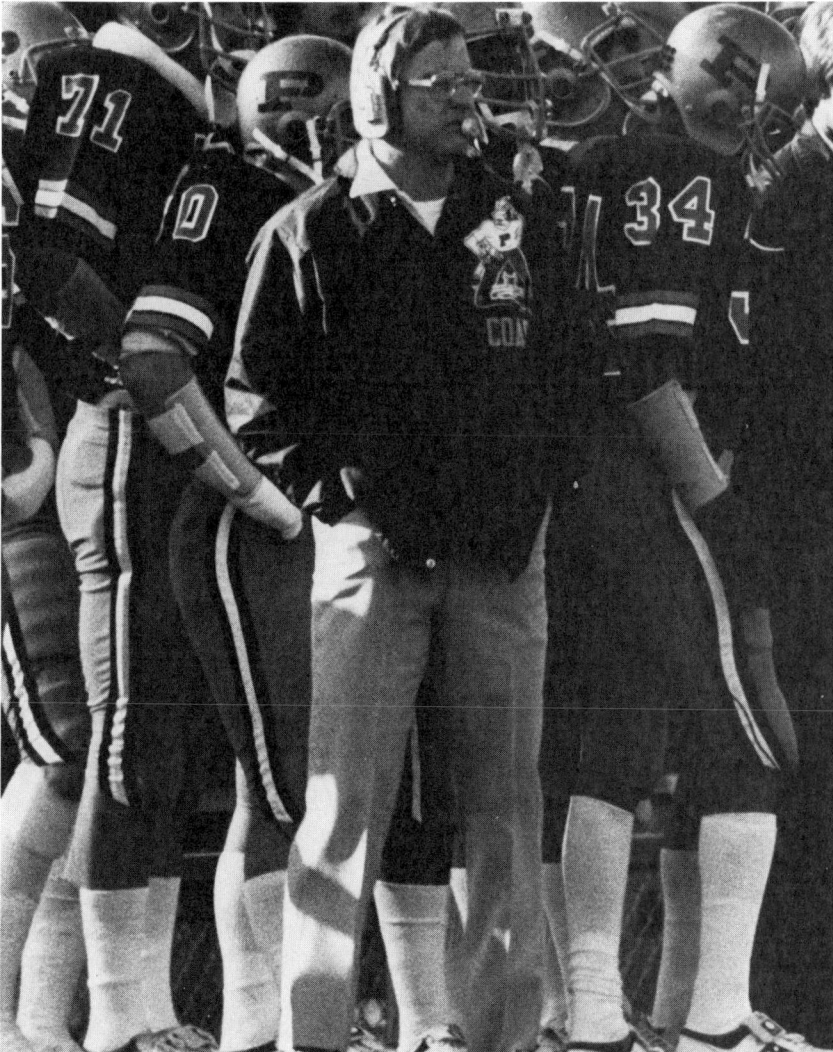

Purdue Coach Jim Young. (Photo by John Turner, courtesy of Purdue University)

1982

Moriarity, Carter Star For Irish

NOTRE DAME, IND.—The naysayers were still prevalent, still saying that Notre Dame under coach Gerry Faust was just a shadow of its former greatness. After a disheartening 5-6 record in Faust's initial season the Irish were put in a position where a loss to Purdue would cast more doubt on the future of Faust and the Irish, Notre Dame's opening game win over Michigan notwithstanding. While the Notre Dame athletic department might have shifted in its seat, yet held its ground, there was no telling what fervor the Irish alumni may have raised.

It was obvious that, as the case usually was, Notre Dame had the most to lose in the 1982 meeting. The Irish would be impressive early in the season but still finished with a mediocre 6-4-1 record.

Dawn broke unannounced on South Bend and the Golden Dome on September 25. A light rain fell most of the morning before fading into a drizzle and then finally fading away.

It was less than a week earlier that Gerry Faust's Irish had dismantled mighty Michigan 23-17 in the first night game ever played at historic Notre Dame Stadium. Yet the days that followed had made the victory seem like years in the past.

"It was a big win last week," Notre Dame defensive line coach Jay Robertson said moments before kickoff. "But it seems like a long time ago right now. Too long ago to mean anything at this point."

The Irish survived but not before Purdue knocked them on their heels. The first half of Notre Dame's 28-14 victory over the Boilermakers could well stand as testimony, a microsection of the rivalry. Notre Dame was coming off the emotional victory over the Wolverines, it was playing in front of its usual throng of 59,075 fans shoehorned into Notre Dame Stadium and it was playing a Purdue team in the midst of a six-game losing streak.

Yet, there was Purdue trailing 14-0 in the first half when Boilers' quarterback Scott Campbell pulled them within another upset with two quick touchdown passes that sent both teams to the locker rooms tied at 14 and sent a mixture of boos and music filtering from the stands.

"Coach Faust was a bit upset," fullback Larry Moriarity said. "He had warned us about Purdue as if we really needed any. He reminded us 100 times this past week that in the second game of the season after Notre Dame opened with a victory, they were beaten 12 times. Ten of those times it was by Purdue."

Moriarty responded with his second straight 100-yard plus game of the season. Moriarty, a 24-year-old senior, had battled back as a teenager from spinal meningitis and at one time was considered too small to participate in sports. A long road of rehabiliation led him to become Faust's strongest player, bench-pressing 470 pounds and squat-lifting 690.

"We had to come after Purdue, both offensively and defensively," he said. "Campbell had completed six straight first down passes in the opening half and was picking the Notre Dame secondary apart at will. Even in defeat he completed 25 of 39 passes for 278 yards and both touchdowns. In three starts against the Irish he had passed for 702 yards (53-for-89) and four touchdowns. On this particular day he bolted past former Purdue quarterbacking great Len Dawson into fourth place on the Boilers' all-time passing yardage chart with 3,523 yards.

The Irish no doubt were also cognizant of Campbell's performances the year before when he beat them in the last minute with a TD pass and two-point conversion.

The Irish elected to receive the opening kickoff and their first possession ended when quarterback/punter Blair Kiel was forced to punt. Kiel, whose parents attended Purdue in the late 1950's, put his parents' alma mater back on its own 10. From there Campbell began working on thwarting the Irish again.

He completed four of six passes during the first possession and moved the Boilers out of danger and into Notre Dame territory at the 38. From there Matt Kinzer was forced to punt. His punt landed in the end zone and the Irish regained possession on their 20.

It took Kiel a dozen plays to go the 80 yards neccessary for the first Irish touchdown. The Irish moved fast, picking up first downs quickly and being forced into third down situations only twice along the way.

Moriarty's 30-yard run on a second-and-seven from the Purdue 42 broke the Boilers momentarily. With a first-and-ten from the Purdue 12 it was only a matter of time before Kiel would direct the Irish in. With the ball on the two, Moriarty blasted through the Purdue defense for the first of his two touchdowns. Mike Johnston kicked the first of his four successful conversions.

Moriarty and Kiel put the Irish up 14-0 early in the second quarter when he completed a 51-yard, eight-play drive with a three-yard run.

It was then that the Irish let up.

"I knew we had been a little complacent in the second quarter," Notre Dame guard Tom Thayer admitted. "We were putting ourselves in a tough spot."

On the series following the second Irish touchdown, Campbell set the Boilers on the road back from his 20. The drive took 10 plays, six of the plays were passes, all complete.

Campbell was masterful in the same way Mark Herrmann had been in the 1979 game and Irish-killer Mike Phipps in the years before. The Notre Dame pass defense, left partially exposed in the waning minutes of its victory over Michigan the week before, was beginning to feel the Boilers pressing on a weak spot.

Campbell connected first with Everitt Pickens for 31 yards, putting the Boilers back in ND territory at the 49. On the drive's second play, Campbell found Joe Linville for 17 more yards. Linville would be the recipient of two more Campbell passes during the drive for gains of 11 and six yards.

Gerry Faust leads the Irish into the 1980s. (Photo courtesy of Notre Dame University)

GOLDEN GLORY

The Irish defense stiffened when the Boilers moved down to the Irish one-yard line. With the Boilers facing a third-and-goal, Jon Autry and Mike Larkin combined to stop 5-9 tailback Mel Gray at the line of scrimmage. Faced with a 4th-and-one from the Notre Dame one, Purdue coach Leon Burtnett had a choice between an almost certain field goal which would have left his team training 14-3 or he could gamble and go for the touchdown facing the possibility of not getting any points if the Irish held again.

Purdue went for the limit. Campbell rolled right and threw across his body to the left, finding fullback Bruce King. Purdue had cut the lead in half.

There was 5:02 left in the half when Notre Dame took over. The Purdue defense, sensing the Irish could be had, tightened and gave its offense the ball back with 3:38 remaining.

Campbell took over at midfield. This time the Purdue strategy was altered slightly. With the Irish fearing the pass, Campbell mixed in the pass with the run beautifully. Purdue moved easily against the Irish until the Boilers had advanced as far as the Notre Dame 28. There the Boilers were faced with a third-and-nine .

249

Campbell found Dave Retherford over the middle for 17 yards and a first down at the Notre Dame 11. Two running plays by Gray put the ball at the Notre Dame four. On third down, Campbell called time out. On the next play, he rolled right and under intense pressure connected with Cliff Benson in the right corner of the end zone. With :50 left in the first half, Tim Clark tied the game with his second conversion.

"When I came into the locker room at halftime," Thayer said. "I saw the score of last year's loss to Purdue on the blackboard. There it was 15-14. That hurt."

"Coach Faust was disappointed in us," Moriarty said. "But he has a way of talking to you that's inspirational and that's what he did at halftime.

"We had to remember that just because we beat Michigan one week and just because we play at Notre Dame doesn't mean we will always win. We still have to play the best we can to win because every other team gets up to play us. Especially Purdue. We finally remembered that in the second half."

Whatever momentum Purdue had generated in the final five minutes of the first half, the Irish began taking apart piece by piece in the second half. The defensive line of Notre Dame began working its way to Campbell quicker. The Irish's offensive line began moving out the Boilers and opening holes big enough to roll the giant Purdue drum through.

Phil Carter, who led both teams with 154 yards rushing, picked up 115 in the second half. His third quarter six-yard touchdown run turned into the game winner. He added the finale with 8:36 left in the game when he bolted up the middle for seven yards.

Moriarty, who had 116 yards against the Wolverines the week before, responded with 106 against the Boilers, 56 coming in the second half. Not only did the Irish snuff out the Boilers' aerial attack but they also burned out the clock with the ground efforts of Moriarty and Carter. Tailback Greg Bell was injured in the second quarter after a 19-yard run that set up Moriarty's second touchdown. Bell suffered a fractured ankle.

Campbell did all he could following the Irish's final touchdown. Midway through the final quarter Campbell completed three passes for 54 yards but had three passes dropped.

"This was by far our best game of the year," Campbell said. "Initially it was a surprise to me that our receivers were getting so open (in the first half). Notre Dame snuffed out the run very well but at least we were having success with the passing game."

"This game," Purdue Coach Leon Burnett said, "boiled down to making or missing the third-down conversions in the second half. They put a lot of pressure on us. In order to beat Notre Dame you've got to put pressure on them by controlling the ball. We couldn't do it. It comes to the point where the offense has to keep your defense off the field for awhile."

Purdue was unsuccessful in all seven of its second-half third-down conversions. The Irish controlled the ball nearly seven minutes longer in the second half than the Boilers.

"Even though we lost," Burnett said, "I feel that we came of age today. It's something to see a young team come in to South Bend and rally after trailing 14-0.

"It's easy when you're trailing and playing Notre Dame in South Bend to pack it in. But we came back and had the momentum at the start of the second half. This Purdue team (which would finish with a disappointing 3-8 record) honestly believed it could come in here and beat Notre Dame."

History shows it has never been any other way.

Leon Burtnett, Purdue Coach. (Photo courtesy of Purdue University)

Section VIII

The Greatest Games

There would be no rivalry without the great games, without those memorable fall afternoons when two teams clash with pride, victory and championships at stake. The Notre Dame-Purdue rivalry has been the stage for many great games. There have also been games that will long be remembered not necessarily because of the closeness of the score but because of the margin of victory. Here is a synopsis of the 12 greatest games and the 10 most memorable in Notre Dame-Purdue history.

The Greatest Games Played Between Notre Dame And Purdue

Notre Dame 6, Purdue 6

November 27, 1902 at Lafayette's Stuart Field. This was considered the first great game matching two great and powerful teams. Purdue fought back from a 6-0 deficit to earn a 6-6 draw in front of the largest crowd in the state's history. Reports indicated that if not for poor weather conditions more than 5,000 fans would have turned out. The game was billed "as the greatest game in the history of Indiana."

Notre Dame 28, Purdue 27

September 25, 1948 at Notre Dame Stadium. Frank Leahy called it the greatest game he'd ever seen. Notre Dame held on for a 28-27 victory and kept its unbeaten streak alive at 18 games. Both teams could almost score at will. There were 14 points scored in the final two minutes. If the two-point conversion had been in existence there is no telling what the outcome may have been.

Purdue 28, Notre Dame 14

October 7, 1950 at Notre Dame Stadium. Purdue's sophomore quarterback Dale Samuels led the Boilers to a 21-0 halftime lead and the victory to end Notre Dame's unbeaten string at 39 games. Samuels threw for two touchdowns and set up two more with long passes. He was the first of the great Purdue quarterbacks who would defeat Notre Dame. The game will live forever in the history of both schools.

Holcomb Old Hand at Irish Stew

Purdue Coach Played Part in Army Victories

Added Speed, Power to Left Turned Tide

Used 5-3-2-1 Defense Throughout Second Half of Early Lead

Misery's Company ∴ By Mullin

NOTRE DAME

DID YOU KETCH A SPANKING, TOO?

4 STRAIGHT

WHIZ KIDS

'We'd Rather Have Pressure On,' Sighs Leahy as String Snaps at 39

Notre Dame 22, Purdue 20

October 7, 1961 at West Lafayette's Ross-Ade Stadium. Notre Dame kicker Joe Perkowski was one of the reasons the Irish were trailing 20-19 early in the fourth quarter. He had missed two field goals and an extra point try. When the game was over he was suddenly the reason Notre Dame had pulled out the victory. His 28-yard field goal with 11:50 remaining gave Notre Dame a victory.

Purdue 7, Notre Dame 6

October 5, 1963 at Ross-Ade Stadium. Purdue quarterback Ron DiGravio led the Boilermakers to a last quarter touchdown drive. Notre Dame had scored the first touchdown on a pass from John Huarte to Jim Kelly. Huarte was bothered by a bad ankle and instead of kicking for the extra point decided to go for the two-point conversion. The conversion failed. Purdue's didn't.

Purdue 25, Notre Dame 21

September 25, 1965 at Ross-Ade Stadium. Purdue was turning the corner into its greatest five-year stretch. Quarterback Bob Griese led a Purdue comeback with the most extraordinary passing performance of the series. He completed 19 of 22 passes for 285 yards. After falling behind 21-18, Griese needed just four plays, 100 seconds and 67 yards to produce the victory in front of 61,921, the largest crowd so far to watch a game in the state of Indiana.

Purdue 28, Notre Dame 21

September 30, 1967 at Ross-Ade Stadium. For the first and only time both teams came into the game as defending champions. The contest matched two great teams coming off two great seasons. The Irish were the defending National Champions and Purdue had won its one and only visit to the Rose Bowl. Purdue had produced another great quarterback—sophomore Mike Phipps. Phipps began a three-year terror of Notre Dame.

Purdue 37, Notre Dame 22

September 28, 1968 at Notre Dame Stadium. One year earlier it had been champion vs. champion. This time both teams were ranked No. 1 in a respective poll. It was the first and only time—and for that matter one of the rare occasions in college football—that the top team in each poll would meet. Phipps again was incredible and he received plenty of help from Leroy Keyes and receiver Bob Dillingham.

Notre Dame 8, Purdue 7

September 25, 1971 at Ross-Ade Stadium. On the stairs leading to the Notre Dame Stadium field, the Notre Dame players pass by gold plaques with the scores of the greatest games in Notre Dame history registered forever. Of the 54 games played between the schools, this game is the only one on the wall. With less than two minutes remaining Purdue punter Scott Lougheed was trying to punt from his end zone. It had been raining all day and the field and ball were slick. Purdue led 7-0 until Walt Patulski and Clarence Ellis crashed into Lougheed, freeing the ball. Fred Swendsen fell on the loose ball and Notre Dame was in business. Notre Dame quarterback Pat Steenberge tossed a two-point conversion to Mike Creaney, sealing the victory.

3D-STRING QB STEALS PURDUE THUNDER

Montana Awakens Irish

By MAX STULTZ
Star Sportswriter

West Lafayette, Ind — Script writers ran for cover in Ross-Ade Stadium Saturday as Notre Dame roared back on the throwing of No. 3 quarterback Joe Montana to snatch a 31-24 decision from Purdue in one of college football's really wild serial duels.

Entering the fray with less than two minutes of third-quarter blasting on the clock and Notre Dame trailing 24-14, the 6-2 junior ran the Boilermakers right through the end zone.

And that wasn't supposed to happen—not that way by that person.

If anybody was going to drop a cluster of bombs, the scenario called for Purdue freshman Mark Herrmann to push the button. But while Herrmann did unload a school record 51 times, three of his heaves winding up as touchdowns, center stage belonged to Montana who might have spent 60 minutes spectating the

debate but for an injury to No. 1 signal-caller Gary Forystek.

PURDUE linebacker Fred Arrington began a chain reaction which brought Montana into the limelight with a tremendous head-on hit late in the first period that sent Forystek to St. Elisabeth's Hospital with head, neck and back injuries.

Notre Dame officials reported Saturday night that Forystek suffered a broken collar bone and was in stable condition in a South Bend hospital.

Thus, when Coach Dan Devine decided starter Rusty Lisch should take a rest with less than 17 minutes left, he was forced to summon Montana and a budding Boilermaker upset was beat.

Nine plays after Purdue's Scott Sovereen missed a 33-yard field goal try, Dave Reeve connected for three on a 24-yarder, closing the gap to 24-17.

Notre Dame had exploded from its 39 with Montana hitting split end Kris Haines twice for 44 and tight end Ken McAfee once for 26 followed by a 4-

Section 2
THE INDIANAPOLIS STAR
SUNDAY, SEPTEMBER 25, 1977

Notre Dame 31, Purdue 24

September 24, 1977 at Ross-Ade Stadium. Anyone who knows Notre Dame football and hears the name Joe Montana must immediately recall this game. The Irish were losing to Purdue and quarterback Mark Herrmann 24-14 in the fourth quarter when Montana suddenly came off the bench and sparked one of the greatest comebacks in the history of college football. Notre Dame rallied for a 31-24 victory. The victory ultimately helped Notre Dame Coach Devine stem the tide of an alumni storm with a National Championship.

Purdue 28, Notre Dame 22

September 22, 1979 at Ross-Ade Stadium. For the 22nd straight game the series was a sellout. More than 70,000 fans watched Mark Herrmann direct the Boilers to a 28-22 victory. Herrmann and Purdue trailed 20-7 in the third quarter before staging a comeback that, while it didn't quite rival Montana's, it did have the flavor that left all involved limp and weary. Herrmann pulled off the upset with the help of his boyhood friend Bart Burrell who caught the deciding touchdown.

Purdue 15, Notre Dame 14

September 26, 1981 at Ross-Ade Stadium. Following in the vein of Samuels, Dawson, Griese, Phipps and Herrmann, Purdue quarterback Scott Campbell led Purdue past the Irish in a classic finish. Those who witnessed the ending are convinced they will never see anything to rival it. Phil Carter scored for Notre Dame with less than three minutes remaining, breaking a 7-7 deadlock. Campbell came back with an 80-yard touchdown drive to pull the Boilers within one point. He connected with Steve Bryant for a touchdown. After some lengthy sideline deliberation, Campbell and Bryant worked the same play to the opposite side of the field for the two-point conversion.

The Most Memorable Games Of The Series

Purdue 28, Notre 22

November 14, 1896 Notre Dame's Cartier Field. Everything in life has a beginning. If not for Alpha Jamison's first touchdown run on the first play of the series there would be nothing else. The first game was memorable for more reasons than Jamison, even though he did score 20 points with four touchdowns in Purdue's first victory. The first game opened something beautiful that has grown and flourished for nearly 90 years. Without game No. 1 and its memorable moments a major portion of true collegiate sports lore would have never come to pass.

Notre Dame 28, Purdue 0

November 6, 1920 at Cartier Field. This was the great George Gipp's final game against Purdue. He became one of the legends of American sports. While his overall contributions to college football are renown, his work against Purdue was equally impressive. The Rockne Era against Purdue was one of the most devastating. Gipp played less than 30 minutes in the 1920 game and contributed an 80-yard run from scrimmage for a touchdown and three extra points.

Notre Dame 20, Purdue 0

October 14, 1922 at Lafayette's Stuart Field. Notre Dame was already established as a national power. For the third straight time Notre Dame shut out Purdue. The Irish had pummelled the Boilers 81-0 during a three-year stretch.

Purdue 19, Notre Dame 0

November 11, 1933 at Notre Dame Stadium. This game is best remembered for two reasons: 1) Purdue shut out Notre Dame for its first victory over the Irish since 1905 and 2) Purdue's Duane Purvis came back from a "leg operation" to lead the Boilers to victory. It was also Purdue's first visit to Notre Dame Stadium and first time in seven games that Rockne wasn't coaching against the Boilers.

Purdue 27, Notre Dame 14

October 2, 1954 at Notre Dame Stadium. Purdue's sophomore quarterback Len Dawson completed only seven passes but four went for touchdowns. Dawson also intercepted a pass and kicked three extra points. The victory was also the first of 11 in 16 years for Purdue over Notre Dame.

Purdue 29, Notre Dame 22

October 25, 1958 at Notre Dame Stadium. Notre Dame trailed 26-7 in the fourth quarter before junior quarterback George Izo led a comeback that brought the Irish within a touchdown at 29-22. It was the running of Bob Jarus that put Purdue out of reach. Jarus scored three of his five career touchdowns against Notre Dame in this game.

Boilermakers Bomb Irish, 51-19

PORTRAIT OF A COACH IN TROUBLE—Trouble is etched deeply on the face of Jos Kaharch, head coach of the University of Notre Dame's Fighting Irish, as he paces the sidelines while watching his team go down in defeat before Purdue University's Boilermakers Saturday in the Notre Dame stadium. The Purdue squad put together a 31-point second quarter for a steady performance to overpower the Irish, 51 to 19.

Purdue 51, Notre Dame 19

October 1, 1960 at Notre Dame Stadium. The crushing defeat of Notre Dame was highlighted by a 31-point scoring spree by the Boilers that took just 10:52 of the second quarter. The 51 points represented the most ever scored by a visiting team at Notre Dame. It marked the third straight time that Purdue had defeated Notre Dame.

Purdue 28, Notre Dame 14

September 28, 1969 at Ross-Ade Stadium. Mike Phipps became the first quarterback in history to defeat the Irish three times. As he had done in 1967 and 1968, Phipps was incredible on third-down situations. Purdue Coach Jack Mollenkopf improved his record against Notre Dame to 10-4, the best of any Purdue coach. It was his last appearance against Notre Dame.

Purdue 31, Notre Dame 10

September 28, 1974 at Notre Dame Stadium. The "Spoilermakers" ended a Notre Dame unbeaten streak for the fourth time by knocking off the Irish. Purdue had ended Notre Dame's unbeaten streaks at 12, 13 and 39 games prior to stopping the Irish at 13 again.

Notre Dame 31, Purdue 10

September 6, 1980 at Notre Dame Stadium. This game was famous more for the pre-game than the game. Notre Dame shook loose from Purdue in the second half for an easy victory. The date marked the earliest either team had opened a season. It was moved up because of national television. All week long the American Broadcasting Company had previewed the game as "Mark Herrmann of Purdue leading the way against Notre Dame." The impact was that Purdue was definitely better than Notre Dame and that Herrmann would put on an exhibition no one would forget. Unfortunately, Herrmann didn't play because of an injured thumb. In the television age, no Purdue-Notre Dame game ever had as much national build-up.

Section IX

The Numbers Game

Complete Notre Dame vs. Purdue Series 1896 through 1982

G	YEAR	DATE	PLACE	WINNER	SCORE	SERIES STANDINGS
1	1896	Nov. 14	Notre Dame	Purdue	28-22	1-0 Purdue
2	1899	Nov. 18	Lafayette	Tie	10-10	1-0-1
3	1901	Nov. 9	Notre Dame	Notre Dame	12-6	1-1-1
4	1902	Nov. 27	Lafayette	Tie	6-6	1-1-2
5	1904	Nov. 24	Lafayette	Purdue	36-0	2-1-2
6	1905	Nov. 24	Lafayette	Purdue	32-0	3-1-2
7	1906	Nov. 3	Lafayette	Notre Dame	2-0	3-2-2
8	1907	Nov. 23	Notre Dame	Notre Dame	17-0	3-3-2
9	1918	Nov. 23	Lafayette	Notre Dame	26-6	3-4-2
10	1919	Nov. 22	Lafayette	Notre Dame	33-13	3-5-2
11	1920	Nov. 6	Notre Dame	Notre Dame	28-0	3-6-2
12	1921	Oct. 15	Lafayette	Notre Dame	33-0	3-7-2
13	1922	Oct. 14	Lafayette	Notre Dame	20-0	3-8-2
14	1923	Nov. 3	Notre Dame	Notre Dame	34-7	3-9-2
15	1933	Nov. 11	Notre Dame	Purdue	19-0	4-9-2
16	1934	Oct. 13	Notre Dame	Notre Dame	18-7	4-10-2
17	1939	Sept. 30	Notre Dame	Notre Dame	3-0	4-11-2
18	1946	Oct. 12	Notre Dame	Notre Dame	49-6	4-12-2
19	1947	Oct. 11	Lafayette	Notre Dame	22-7	4-13-2
20	1948	Sept. 25	Notre Dame	Notre Dame	28-27	4-14-2
21	1949	Oct. 8	Lafayette	Notre Dame	35-12	4-15-2
22	1950	Oct. 7	Notre Dame	Purdue	28-14	5-15-2
23	1951	Oct. 27	Notre Dame	Notre Dame	30-9	5-16-2
24	1952	Oct. 18	Lafayette	Notre Dame	26-14	5-17-2
25	1953	Oct. 3	Lafayette	Notre Dame	37-7	5-18-2
26	1954	Oct. 2	Notre Dame	Purdue	27-14	6-18-2
27	1955	Oct. 22	Lafayette	Notre Dame	22-7	6-19-2
28	1956	Oct. 13	Notre Dame	Purdue	28-14	7-19-2
29	1957	Sept. 28	Lafayette	Notre Dame	12-0	7-20-2
30	1958	Oct. 25	Notre Dame	Purdue	29-22	8-20-2
31	1959	Oct. 3	Lafayette	Purdue	28-7	9-20-2
32	1960	Oct. 1	Notre Dame	Purdue	51-19	10-20-2
33	1961	Oct. 7	Lafayette	Notre Dame	22-20	10-21-2
34	1962	Oct. 6	Notre Dame	Purdue	24-6	11-21-2
35	1963	Oct. 5	Lafayette	Purdue	7-6	12-21-2
36	1964	Oct. 3	Notre Dame	Notre Dame	34-15	12-22-2
37	1965	Sept. 25	Lafayette	Purdue	25-21	13-22-2
38	1966	Sept. 24	Notre Dame	Notre Dame	26-14	13-23-2
39	1967	Sept. 30	Lafayette	Purdue	28-21	14-23-2
40	1968	Sept. 28	Notre Dame	Purdue	37-22	15-23-2
41	1969	Sept. 27	Lafayette	Purdue	28-14	16-23-2
42	1970	Sept. 26	Notre Dame	Notre Dame	48-0	16-24-2
43	1971	Sept. 25	Lafayette	Notre Dame	8-7	16-25-2
44	1972	Sept. 30	Notre Dame	Notre Dame	35-14	16-26-2
45	1973	Sept. 29	Lafayette	Notre Dame	20-7	16-27-2
46	1974	Sept. 28	Notre Dame	Purdue	31-20	17-27-2
47	1975	Sept. 20	Lafayette	Notre Dame	17-0	17-28-2
48	1976	Sept. 18	Notre Dame	Notre Dame	23-0	17-29-2
49	1977	Sept. 24	Lafayette	Notre Dame	31-24	17-30-2
50	1978	Sept. 30	Notre Dame	Notre Dame	10-6	17-31-2
51	1979	Sept. 22	Lafayette	Purdue	28-22	18-31-2
52	1980	Sept. 6	Notre Dame	Notre Dame	31-10	18-32-2
53	1981	Sept. 26	Lafayette	Purdue	15-14	19-32-2
54	1982	Sept. 25	Notre Dame	Notre Dame	28-14	19-33-2

Notre Dame Individual Scoring
1896-1982

(Note: * denotes two-point conversion; # denotes safety)

PLAYER	TD	PAT	FG	TOTAL	YEAR(S) SCORED
Allan, Denny	3	0	0	18	1968, 70
Anderson, Ed	1	0	0	6	1921
Anderson, Heartley	3	0	0	18	1919-21
Andreotti, Pete	1	0	0	6	1964
Azzaro, Joe	0	3	0	3	1967
Barrett, Bill	2	0	0	12	1949, 51
Bahan, Leonard	0	2	0	2	1919
Bergman, Arthur	1	0	0	6	1919
Best, Art	1	0	0	6	1973
Bleier, Rocky	1	0	0	6	1967
Bradley, Luther	1	0	0	6	1975
Brennan, Terry	2	0	0	12	1946-47
Brown, Bob	1	0	0	4	1896
Bullock, Wayne	3	0	0	18	1973-74
Burdick, Henry	1	0	0	6	1907
Bush, Joe	1	0	0	6	1952
Caprara, Joe	0	2	0	2	1950
Carideo, Fred	1	0	0	6	1934
Carter, Phil	4	0	0	24	1980-81-82
Castner, Paul	1	2	2	14	1920-22
Cieszkowski, John	1	0	0	6	1972
Clatt, Corwin	1	0	0	6	1946
Courey, Mike	1	0	0	6	1977
Creaney, Mike	1	2	0	8	1971-72
Crotty, Jim	1	0	0	6	1959
Crowley, Jim	2	0	0	12	1922-23
Dabiero, Angelo	1	0	0	6	1960
Demmerle, Pete	1	0	0	6	1974
Dewan, Darryll	1	0	0	6	1970
Doar, Jim	1	0	0	5	1901
Earley, Fred	0	7	0	7	1946
Eaton, Tom	1	0	0	6	1968
Eddy, Nick	2	0	0	12	1965-66
Enright, Rex	1	0	0	6	1923
Eurick, Terry	2	0	0	12	1977
Gatewood, Tom	4	0	0	24	1969-70
Gay, Bill	1	0	0	6	1949
Gipp, George	3	6	0	24	1918-19-20
Gompers, Bill	1	0	0	6	1946
Grant, Chet	1	0	0	6	1920
Gray, Gerry	1	0	0	6	1961
Guglielmi, Ralph	1	0	0	6	1953
Hanratty, Terry	1	0	0	6	1967
Heavens, Jerome	1	0	0	6	1978
Hempel, Scott	0	9	3	18	1969-70
Hornung, Paul	0	2	0	2	1956
Huff, Andy	1	0	0	6	1972
Hunter, Al	2	0	0	12	1975-76
Hunter, Tony	1	0	0	6	1980
Ivan, Ken	0	5	2	11	1964-65
Johnston, Mike	0	4	0	4	1982

GOLDEN GLORY

PLAYER	TD	PAT	FG	TOTAL	YEAR(S) SCORED
Kegler, Bill	1	0	0	4	1896
Kelleher, John	0	0	1	3	1939
Kelly, Jim	3	0	0	18	1961-62-63
Kirk, Bernie	3	0	0	18	1918-19
Lamonica, Daryle	1	0	0	6	1960
Lattner, Johnny	3	0	0	18	1951-52-53
Layden, Elmer	0	1	0	1	1922
Lemek, Ray	0	0	0	2#	1954
Lewis, Aubrey	1	0	0	6	1955
Lujack, John	1	0	0	6	1947
MacAfee, Ken	1	0	0	6	1977
Maher, Willie	1	0	0	6	1923
Male, Chuck	0	2	2	8	1979
Masztak, Dean	1	0	0	6	1979
Mavraides, Minil	0	8	1	11	1951-52-53
Mayl, Gene	1	0	0	6	1922
McDonald, Angus	0	0	1	5	1899
McDonald, Paul	2	2	0	12	1907
McGarry, Rob	1	0	0	6	1980
McLane, Mike	1	0	0	6	1976
Melinkovich, George	2	0	0	12	1934
Miller, Don	2	0	0	12	1923
Mitchell, Dave	1	0	0	6	1977
Mohardt, John	2	0	0	12	1921
Mohn, Bill	1	0	0	6	1918
Moriarty, Larry	2	0	0	12	1982
Mullen, Jack	1	1	0	6	1896-97
Murphy, John	2	0	0	8	1896
Mutscheller, Jim	2	0	0	12	1950-51
Oliver, Harry	0	6	1	9	1980-81
Oracko, Steve	0	7	2	13	1947-48-49
Page, Alan	1	0	0	6	1964
Panelli, John	2	0	0	12	1946-48
Parker, Larry	1	0	0	6	1970
Petitbon, John	1	0	0	6	1950
Penick, Eric	1	0	0	6	1972
Perkowski, Joe	0	2	1	5	1960-61
Pietrosante, Nick	0	0	0	2*	1958
Raich, Nick	1	0	0	6	1954
Rassas, Nick	1	0	0	6	1964
Reese, Frank	0	1	0	1	1923
Reeve, Dave	0	10	3	19	1977
Reynolds, Frank	2	0	0	12	1956-57
Reynolds, Paul	1	0	0	6	1951
Royer, Dick	1	0	0	6	1956
Ryan, Jim	0	2	0	2	1966
Salmon, Lou (Red)	2	3	0	13	1901-02
Scarpietto, Bob	1	0	0	6	1960
Schaefer, Don	2	2	0	14	1954-55
Schillo, Fred	1	0	0	4	1896
Seymour, Jim	3	0	0	18	1966
Shaw, Lawrence	1	3	0	9	1920-21
Simmons, Floyd	1	0	0	6	1947
Sitko, Emil	5	0	0	30	1948-49
Skoglund, Bob	1	0	0	6	1946
Slager, Rick	1	0	0	6	1976
Smith, Chris	1	0	0	6	1981
Snow, Jack	1	0	0	6	1964
Snow, Paul	1	0	0	6	1967

GOLDEN GLORY

PLAYER	TD	PAT	FG	TOTAL	YEAR(S) SCORED
Snowden, Jim	1	0	0	6	1971
Stickles, Monty	2	2	0	14	1958
Studer, Dean	1	0	0	6	1955
Swendsen, Fred	1	0	0	6	1971
Talaga, Tom	0	2	0	2	1965
Thomas, Bob	0	7	2	13	1972-73
Townsend, Willie	1	0	0	6	1972
Trafton, George	1	0	0	6	1919
Unis, Joe	0	1	1	4	1978
Vehr, Nick	1	0	0	6	1979
Washington, Dick	1	0	0	6	1953
Williams, Bob	2	0	0	12	1957-58
Wolski, Bill	2	0	0	12	1964-65
Worden, Neil	4	0	0	24	1952-53
Ziegler, Ed	1	0	0	6	1969
Zmijewski, Al	1	0	0	6	1948
Zilly, Jack	1	0	0	6	1946

Purdue Individual Scoring
1896-1982

PLAYER	TD	PAT	FG	TOTAL	YEAR(S) SCORED
Adams, Norb	1	0	0	6	1948
Agnew, Robert	1	0	0	6	1948
Allen, Bernie	1	10	1	19	1959-60
Allen, D.M.	4	0	1	21	1904-05
Anderson, Rick	0	2	1	5	1980-81
Armstrong, Otis	1	0	0	6	1971
Arnold, Reggie	1	0	0	6	1982
Bartzell, Bob	1	4**	0	10	1967
Beirne, Jim	2	1*	0	14	1965, 67
Benson, Cliff	1	0	0	6	1982
Brewster, Darryl	1	0	0	6	1951
Brock, Rex	1	0	0	6	1954
Brooks, Dick	1	0	0	6	1959
Brown, Stan	2	0	0	12	1969
Bryant, Steve	1	1*	0	8	1981
Burrell, Bart	1	0	0	6	1979
Burton, Larry	1	0	0	6	1973
Carter, Jim	1	0	0	6	1934
Clark, Tim	0	2	0	2	1982
Conville	1	0	0	5	1905
Cooper, Randy	1	0	0	6	1969
Dawson, Len	0	7	0	7	1954-55-56
DeMoss, Bob	1	0	0	6	1948
DiGravio, Ron	2	0	0	12	1961-62
Dillard, Mel	2	0	0	12	1956
Dillingham, Bob	2	0	0	12	1968
Donaldson, Gene	1	0	0	6	1962
Elwell, Jack	1	0	0	6	1960
Emeis	1	0	0	5	1904
Evans, Roy	0	1	0	1	1953
Farmer, Forest	1	0	0	6	1962
Febel, Fritz	1	0	0	6	1933
Fichtner, Ross	0	2	0	2	1958
Fletcher, Tom	1	0	0	6	1956
Flowers, Bernie	2	0	0	12	1952
Galvin, John	1	0	0	6	1946
Griese, Bob	1	3	0	9	1964-65-66
Gross, Pete	1	0	0	6	1974
Hadrick, Bob	2	1*	0	14	1963-64
Haffmark	1	0	0	5	1905
Haverstock, Art	0	1	0	1	1947
Hecker, Fred	1	0	0	6	1933
Hogan, Gary	0	1	0	1	1963
Huffine, Ken	1	0	0	6	1919
Jamison, Alpha	4	4	0	24	1896
Jarus, Bob	5	0	0	30	1958-59
Jeffery, Harley	1	0	0	6	1948
Jennings, Bill	1	0	0	6	1956
Johnson, Thomas	0	1	0	1	1905
Jones, Jeff	0	1	8	11	1969
Jones, Wally	4	0	0	24	1979-80-81
Kerestes, John	3	0	0	18	1949-50

GOLDEN GLORY

PLAYER	TD	PAT	FG	TOTAL	YEAR(S) SCORED
Kerr, John	2	0	0	12	1953-54
Keyes, Leroy	4	0	0	24	1966-67-68
King, Bruce	1	0	0	6	1982
King, E.P.	1	0	0	5	1905
Knapp, Joseph	1	0	0	5	1901
Krull, Walt	0	6	0	6	1904
Laraway, Jaack	1	0	0	6	1958
Leslie, H.G.	0	1	0	1	1902
Lundy, Lamar	1	0	0	6	1954
Maccioli, Mike	1	0	0	6	1950
Manella, Bob	1	0	0	6	1974
Mayoras, Donn	1	0	0	6	1960
Meeker, John	1	0	0	6	1919
Miller, G.	1	1	0	6	1901-02
Minniear, Randy	1	0	0	6	1965
Moore, Billy	1	0	0	4	1896
Mowrey, J.H.	1	0	0	5	1904
Murakowski, Bill	1	0	0	6	1954
Murphy, Edgar	1	0	0	6	1918
Northington, Mike	1	0	0	6	1974
Ohl, Skip	0	5	4	17	1958, 61-62
Pardonner, Paul	0	1	0	1	1933
Peterson, Skip	1	0	0	6	1972
Phipps, Mike	1	0	0	6	1969
Pope, Russell	1	0	0	6	1977
Prout, Joe	1	0	0	6	1923
Purvis, Duane	1	0	0	6	1933
Reichert, Jim	0	0	1	3	1951
Renie, James	0	1	0	1	1971
Robertson, C.H.	0	0	1	5	1899
Samuels, Dale	0	2	0	2	1952
Schmidt, Neil	1	0	0	6	1950
Schmidt, Steve	0	1	1	4	1974
Seibel, John	0	4	0	4	1979
Smith, Alex	1	0	0	5	1899
Smith, Raymond	1	0	0	6	1977
Sovereen, Scott	0	3	3	12	1977-78
Spellman, Jack	1	0	0	6	1972
Stanwood, C.C.	0	1	0	1	1919
Stinchcomb, Bill	0	3	0	3	1974
Szulborski, Harry	2	0	0	12	1947, 49
Taube, Mel	0	1	0	1	1923
Terrizzi, Mike	1	0	0	6	1974
Teter, Gordon	1	0	0	6	1965
Thomas, H.L.	3	0	0	15	1904
Tiller, James	3	0	0	18	1959-60
Torriello, Dan	0	1	0	1	1934
Trbovich, Rudy	0	3	0	3	1948
Walker, Roy	1	0	0	6	1961
Wiater, Bob	1	0	0	6	1960
Williams, Perry	3	0	0	18	1966-67-68
Yakubowski, Tom	1	0	0	6	1960
Young, Dave	1	0	0	6	1979
Zyzda, Leonard	1	0	0	6	1958

Longest Scoring Plays in Notre Dame-Purdue Series From 50 yards or more

RANK	YARDS	PLAYER/TEAM	TYPE OF PLAY	YEAR
1	99	Luther Bradley-Notre Dame	Interception return	1975
2	96	Nick Eddy-Notre Dame	Kickoff return	1966
3	94	Leroy Keyes-Purdue	Fumble recovery	1966
4	86	Johnny Lattner-Notre Dame	Kickoff return	1953
5	84	Jim Seymour-Notre Dame	Pass from Hanratty	1966
6	80	George Gipp-Notre Dame	Run from scrimmage	1920
7	78	Bob Wiater-Purdue	Run from scrimmage	1960
8	75	John Kerr-Purdue	Pass from Evans	1953
9	74	Jim Tiller-Purdue	Run from scrimmage	1959
10	74	Fred Carideo-Notre Dame	Interception return	1934
11	73	Lamar Lundy-Purdue	Pass from Dawson	1954
12	73	Bill Mohr-Notre Dame	Punt return	1918
13	66	Jim Tiller-Purdue	Punt return	1960
14	65	Joe Prout-Purdue	Run from scrimmage	1923
15	64	Bob Scarpitto-Notre Dame	Run from scrimmage	1960
16	63	Larry Parker-Notre Dame	Run from scrimmage	1920
17	62	Willie Townsend-Notre Dame	Pass from Clements	1972
18	61	Bill Gay-Notre Dame	Interception return	1949
19	60	George Melinkovich-Notre Dame	Run from scrimmage	1934
20	57	Alan Page-Notre Dame	Blocked punt return	1964
21	56	Mike Maccioli-Purdue	Pass from Samuels	1950
22	56	Bill Wolski-Notre Dame	Run from scrimmage	1965
23	53	Larry Burton-Purdue	Pass from Bobrowski	1973
24	52	John Galvin-Purdue	Run from scrimmage	1946
25	52	Pete Gross-Purdue	Run from scrimmage	1974
26	50	Chet Grant-Notre Dame	Pass from Castner	1920
27	50	Duane Purvis-Purdue	Pass from Pardonner	1933

Series Touchdown Passes
Notre Dame

No.	Passer-Receiver	Yards	Year
1.	George Gipp-Bernie Kirk	22	1918
2.	George Gipp-Bernie Kirk	—	1919
3.	Geroge Gipp-Bernie Kirk	—	1919
4.	Paul Castner-Chet Grant	50	1920
5.	Elmer Layden-Paul Castner	15	1922
6.	Harry Stuhldreher-Gene Mayl	20	1923
7.	Harry Stuhldreher-Don Miller	24	1923
8.	Johnny Lujack-Jack Zilly	6	1946
9.	Johnny Lujack-Terry Brennan	19	1946
10.	Johnny Lujack-Terry Brennan	21	1947
11.	Bob Williams-Jim Mutscheller	3	1950
12.	John Mazur-Jim Mutscheller	8	1951
13.	Paul Hornung-Dick Royer	6	1956
14.	Bob Williams-Frank Reynolds	6	1957
15.	George Izo-Monty Stickles	27	1958
16.	George Izo-Monty Stickles	44	1958
17.	George Haffner-Angelo Dabiero	24	1960
18.	Daryle Lamonica-Jim Kelly	7	1961
19.	Dennis Szot-Jim Kelly	17	1962
20.	John Huarte-Jim Kelly	41	1963
21.	John Huarte-Jack Snow	2	1964
22.	John Huarte-Nick Rassas	3	1964
23.	Terry Hanratty-Jim Seymour	84	1966
24.	Terry Hanratty-Jim Seymour	39	1966
25.	Terry Hanratty-Jim Seymour	7	1966
26.	Terry Hanratty-Paul Snow	27	1967
27.	Terry Hanratty-Denny Allan	8	1968
28.	Terry Hanratty-Tom Eaton	13	1968
29.	Joe Theismann-Tom Gatewood	20	1969
30.	Joe Theismann-Ed Ziegler	10	1969
31.	Joe Theismann-Tom Gatewood	17	1970
32.	Joe Theismann-Tom Gatewood	7	1970
33.	Joe Theismann-Tom Gatewood	19	1970
34.	Tom Clements-Mike Creaney	39	1972
35.	Tom Clements-Willie Townsend	62	1972
36.	Tom Clements-Pete Demmerle	29	1974
37.	Al Hunter-Mike McLane	33	1976
38.	Rusty Lisch-Terry Eurick	6	1977
39.	Rusty Lisch-Terry Eurick	18	1977
40.	Joe Montana-Ken MacAfee	13	1977
41.	Tim Koegel-Nick Vehr	4	1979
42.	Greg Knafelc-Dean Masztak	17	1979
43.	Mike Courey-Tony Hunter	9	1980

Purdue

No.	Passer-Receiver	Yards	Year
1.	Paul Pardonner-Duane Purvis	50	1933
2.	Paul Pardonner-Fred Hecker	35	1933
3.	Bob DeMoss-Harry Szulborski	9	1947
4.	Dale Samuels-Neil Schmidt	30	1950
5.	Dale Samuels-Mike Maccioli	56	1950
6.	Dale Samuels-Darrel Brewster	43	1951
7.	Roy Evans-John Kerr	75	1953
8.	Len Dawson-John Kerr	8	1954
9.	Len Dawson-Rex Brock	41	1954
10.	Len Dawson-Lamar Lundy	73	1954
11.	Len Dawson-Bill Murakowski	34	1954
12.	Len Dawson-Leonard Zyzda	13	1955
13.	Ross Fichtner-Dick Brooks	7	1959
14.	Bernie Allen-Jim Tiller	30	1960
15.	Maury Guttman-John Elwell	44	1960
16.	Ron DiGravio-Forest Farmer	27	1962
17.	Ron DiGravio-Bob Hadrick	7	1963
18.	Doug Holcomb-Bob Hadrick	10	1964
19.	Bob Griese-Jim Beirne	28	1965
20.	Bob Griese-Jim Beirne	14	1965
21.	Bob Griese-Randy Minniear	12	1965
22.	Mike Phipps-Bob Bartzell	31	1967
23.	Mike Phipps-Leroy Keyes	11	1967
24.	Mike Phipps-Bob Dillingham	16	1968
25.	Leroy Keyes-Bob Dillingham	17	1968
26.	Mike Phipps-Randy Cooper	37	1969
27.	Gary Danielson-Otis Armstrong	26	1971
28.	Bo Bobrowski-Larry Burton	53	1973
29.	Mark Herrmann-Raymond Smith	37	1977
30.	Mark Herrmann-Reggie Arnold	8	1977
31.	Mark Herrmann-Russell Pope	43	1977
32.	Mark Herrmann-Dave Young	15	1979
33.	Mark Herrmann-Bart Burrell	6	1979
34.	Scott Campbell-Steve Bryant	7	1981
35.	Scott Campbell-Bruce King	1	1982
36.	Scott Campbell-Cliff Benson	4	1982

Ross-Ade Stadium, West Lafayette, Indiana. (Photo courtesy of Purdue University)

Notre Dame vs. Purdue by Site

	W	L	T
at Cartier Field	4	1	0
at Notre Dame Stadium	13	9	0
Totals at Notre Dame	17	10	0
at Stuart Field	5	2	2
at Ross-Ade Stadium	11	7	0
Totals at West Lafayette	16	9	2
Overall totals	33	19	2

Notre Dame Coaches vs. Purdue

COACH	PERIOD	G	W	L	T
1. Frank Hering	1896	1	0	1	0
2. James McWeeney	1899	1	0	0	1
3. Patrick O'Dea	1901	1	1	0	0
4. James Faragher	1902	1	0	0	1
5. Louis Salmon	1904	1	0	1	0
6. Henry McGlew	1905	1	0	1	0
7. Thomas Barry	1906-07	2	2	0	0
8. Knute Rockne	1918-23	6	6	0	0
9. Heartley (Hunk) Anderson	1933	1	0	1	0
10. Elmer Layden	1934,39	2	2	0	0
11. Frank Leahy	1946-53	8	7	1	0
12. Terry Brennan	1954-58	5	2	3	0
13. Joe Kuharich	1959-62	4	1	3	0
14. Hugh Devore	1963	1	0	1	0
15. Ara Parseghian	1964-74	11	6	5	0
16. Dan Devine	1975-80	6	5	1	0
17. Gerry Faust	1981-82	2	1	1	0

Purdue Coaches vs. Notre Dame

COACH	PERIOD	G	W	L	T
1. S.M. Hammond	1896	1	1	0	0
2. Al Jamison	1899	1	0	0	1
3. D.M. Balliet	1901	1	0	1	0
4. C.M. Best	1902	1	0	0	1
5. Oliver Cutts	1904	1	1	0	0
6. A.E. Hernstein	1905	1	1	0	0
7. M.E. Witham	1906	1	0	1	0
8. L.C. Turner	1907	1	0	1	0
9. A.G. Butch Scanlon	1918-20	3	0	3	0
10. W.H. Dietz	1921	1	0	1	0
11. James Phelan	1922-23	2	0	2	0
12. Noble Kizer	1933-34	2	1	1	0
13. A.H. Mal Edwards	1939	1	0	1	0
14. Cecil Isbell	1946	1	0	1	0
15. Stu Holcomb	1947-55	9	2	7	0
16. Jack Mollenkopf	1956-69	14	10	4	0
17. Bob DeMoss	1970-72	3	0	3	0
18. Alex Agase	1973-76	4	1	3	0
19. Jim Young	1977-81	5	2	3	0
20. Leon Burtnett	1982	1	0	1	0

Notre Dame Stadium, Notre Dame, Indiana.

COACH RIVALRIES

Knute Rockne vs. A.G. Butch Scanlon

PERIOD	G	W	L	T
1918-20	3	3	0	0

Frank Leahy vs. Stu Holcomb

PERIOD	G	W	L	T
1947-53	7	6	1	0

Terry Brennan vs. Jack Mollenkopf

PERIOD	G	W	L	T
1956-58	3	1	2	0

Joe Kuharich vs. Jack Mollenkopf

PERIOD	G	W	L	T
1959-62	4	1	3	0

Ara Parseghian vs. Jack Mollenkopf

PERIOD	G	W	L	T
1964-69	6	4	2	0

Ara Parseghian vs. Bob DeMoss

PERIOD	G	W	L	T
1970-72	3	3	0	0

Ara Parseghian vs. Alex Agase

PERIOD	G	W	L	T
1973-74	2	1	1	0

Dan Devine vs. Alex Agase

PERIOD	G	W	L	T
1975-76	2	2	0	0

Dan Devine vs. Jim Young

PERIOD	G	W	L	T
1977-80	4	3	1	0

Series Records

	Yards	Player	School	Year
Rushing, longest play	80	George Gipp	Notre Dame	1920
Most yards rushing, game	142	Mel Dillard	Purdue	1956
Passing, longest play	84	T. Hanratty-J. Seymour	Notre Dame	1966
Most yards passing, game	366	Terry Hanratty	Notre Dame	1967
Most touchdowns passing, game	4	Len Dawson	Purdue	1954
Most pass attempts, game	63	Terry Hanratty	Notre Dame	1967
Most pass completions, game	29	Terry Hanratty	Notre Dame	1967
Passing efficiency, game	.864 (19-22)	Bob Griese	Purdue	1965
Receiving, total yards, game	273	Jim Seymour	Notre Dame	1966
Most receptions, game	13	Jim Seymour	Notre Dame	1966
Most receptions for touchdown, game	3	Tom Gatewood	Notre Dame	1970
		Jim Seymour	Notre Dame	1966
Total offense, player	420	Terry Hanratty	Notre Dame	1967
Total offense, team	633	—	Notre Dame	1970
Longest kick-off return for touchdown	96	Nick Eddy	Notre Dame	1966
Longest punt return for touchdown	73	Bill Mohn	Notre Dame	1918
Longest punt	70	Jack Snow	Notre Dame	1964
Most punts, game	7	Chuck Piebes	Purdue	1971
Longest field goal	47	Scott Sovereen	Purdue	1978
		Steve Schmidt	Purdue	1974
Most interceptions, game	3	Phil Mateja	Purdue	1952
Longest interception return for touchdown	99	Luther Bradley	Notre Dame	1975
Longest fumble recovery for touchdown	94	Leroy Keyes	Purdue	1966
Most points, game (player)	20	Alpha Jamison	Purdue	1896
Most points, game (team)	51	—	Purdue	1960
Most points, shutout (team)	48	—	Notre Dame	1970
Most points, game (both teams)	70	Purdue 51, Notre Dame 19		1960
Most extra points, game	7	Fred Earley	Notre Dame	1946

Section X

References

Newspapers

Chicago *Daily News* 1933, 1939, 1948-49, 1952-55, 1957-58, 1960, 1968-69, 1973, 1977.
Chicago *Sun-Times* 1948, 1956-57, 1960-63, 1965-70, 1972-74, 1976-78, 1980-81.
Chicago *Tribune* 1933-34, 1939, 1946-47, 1950-51, 1954-61, 1963-81.
Indianapolis *Star* 1950, 1960, 1963, 1967, 1977.
Lafayette *Journal/Journal-Courier* 1896, 1899, 1901-02, 1904-07, 1918-23, 1933, 1939.
Notre Dame *Dome* 1921.
Notre Dame *Football Review* 1919, 1921, 1933, 1946, 1948-50, 1962.
Notre Dame *Scholastic* 1896, 1901-02, 1904-07, 1918, 1921, 1923, 1934, 1950-61, 1964-81.
Purdue *Exponent* 1896, 1899, 1901-02, 1904-07, 1919-23, 1933, 1939, 1950, 1967.
South Bend *News-Times* 1918, 1920-23.
South Bend *Tribune* 1946-53, 1957-58, 1960-61, 1966, 1968, 1971, 1976-77.
The *Sporting News* 1950.

Books

Wallace, Francis, *NOTRE DAME FROM ROCKNE TO PARSEGHIAN.* New York, Van Rees Press 1967.
Rappoport, Ken, *WAKE UP THE ECHOES,* Huntsville, Alabama, Strode Publishing, Inc. 1975.

Notre Dame's Al Hunter. (Photo courtesy of Notre Dame University)

Acknowledgements

My team took possession just outside our goal line. When we began our drive to completion we had just slightly less than 100 long and tedious yards to travel.

I began by turning around the right end where my wife Gayle and then-nine-month-old son, Ned Louis III, paved the way for an appreciable gain. Those early summer days locked away in the Notre Dame library built the foundation.

Momentum and ball control were of the essence. The next crucial block that sprung me for additional yardage was thrown by Jethrow Kyles, the fine gentleman who is the curator of the fabulous Notre Dame International Sports and Games Research Collection. It is a room of sports history bound by thousands upon thousands of incredible artifacts. There is no place quite like it.

As already mentioned in the forward, Donald "Chet" Grant, the patriarch of Notre Dame sports history, was the cement that brought the scattered pieces together.

While racing past midfield I encountered the aid of Jim Vruggink, the Sports Information Director of Purdue and Roger O. Valdiserri, the Assistant Athletic Director and Sports Information Director of Notre Dame. Both men's early, middle and late guidance was invaluable. A special thank you is also due Purdue's Amy Foley for her aid in gathering the Purdue pictures and to both universities' photo reproduction centers for their staffs' professional and punctual performances.

A warm thank you is also in order to my mother Dolores and brother

Doug who in the waning days of research rolled up their sleeves and dug in beside me. Their exuberance was refreshing.

With just a few yards remaining there was Herb Juliano, Notre Dame's priceless researcher. Without Herb's assistance the final steps would still be waiting to be run.

I offer deep thanks and appreciation to the staffs of the South Bend Public Library, the Notre Dame and Purdue libraries, the Chicago Public Library and the Indianapolis Public Library. The staffs at each stop were helpful, thoughtful and eager to go the extra yard in my behalf.

The libraries were the source for the endless stream of microfilm that retold the stories of the rivalry through the great newspapers of this era and of eras past. Without the records of history there would have been no place to begin.

With the goal line in sight, I wish to thank all the sports writers who documented the life of the Notre Dame-Purdue rivalry. With respect and honor, I thank Dave Callahan of the *Danville (IL) Commercial-News* and Jon Saraceno of the *Cocoa (FL) Today* for giving the completed work one last look. While the miles between have grown, so have the friendships.

Finally, as I crossed the goal line I noticed to my side my wife Gayle, who had traversed the rugged past year matching my every stride and encouraging my every word.

Peace and thank you all.

About the Author

Ned Colletti has covered college and professional sports for six years. As both a college football and basketball writer and a professional hockey writer, he has traveled the continent to write about sports. His assignments have varied from covering Big Ten football and basketball to the Indianapolis 500 to columns on Jimmy Connors, Renaldo Nehemiah and Wayne Gretzky to World Series, Super Bowl and Stanley Cup champions. His newspaper career began in 1976 with the Press Publications chain in Elmhurst, IL. Just seven months after graduating from Northern Illinois University he was hired as a prep sports writer by the *Chicago Daily News*. In 1978 he joined the sports staff of the *Danville (IL) Commercial-News* and began covering Big Ten football and basketball. After two years in Danville he was hired by the *Philadelphia Journal* to cover the Philadelphia Flyers of the National Hockey League. Upon the closing of the *Journal* in December, 1981, he returned to Chicago to begin a new career in publications and public relations with the Chicago Cubs. He is the co-author of another book, *Cub Fan Mania,* a book that offers a tribute to the Chicago Cubs' baseball fan. Colletti married the former Gayle Benton. Along with their son, Ned Louis III, the Collettis reside in Schiller Park, IL, a suburb of Chicago.